# THE IRISH TIMES
# BOOK
## *of the*
# YEAR
## 2004

EDITED BY
PETER MURTAGH

Gill & Macmillan

Gill & Macmillan Ltd
Hume Avenue
Park West
Dublin 12
with associated companies throughout the world
www.gillmacmillan.ie

© 2004 *The Irish Times*
0 7171 3797 X
Design by Identikit Design Consultants, Dublin
Print origination by Carole Lynch
Index compiled by Helen Litton
Printed by Butler & Tanner, Frome

*The paper used in this book is made from the wood pulp
of managed forests. For every tree felled, at least one tree
is planted, thereby renewing natural resources.*

A catalogue record is available for this book
from the British Library.

1  3  5  4  2

# Contents

# Introduction

At the conclusion of the 12 months that comprised the last *Irish Times Book of the Year*, Iain Duncan Smith was leader of the British Conservative Party. Charlie McCreevy was Minister for Finance and seemed likely to remain so for some time to come. The England rugby team was the best in the world. Few believed Afghanistan was capable of holding a nationwide election in anything resembling peace. Iraq was a bloody mess, and George Bush was president of the United States of America. A year can make such a difference… but not to everything.

There is no such thing as an uneventful year in newspapers and the 12 months from the autumn of 2003 to the end of September 2004 is no different to any other. And yet the period is unique in the events it threw up. A random selection of them is contained within these pages. From life and politics in Ireland, to global events as seen through the eyes of – in the main – Irish journalists, to sport and business, the 12 months herein contains its smattering of villains and heroes.

I hope that the journalism – writing and photography – in this edition entertains, informs and transcends the very limited lifespan of news. Pictures have been selected because of my subjective appreciation of their intrinsic excellence or because they enhance a related piece of writing. The articles have been chosen (also subjectively by me) because I felt they were stimulating, argumentative, informative, witty or, very simply, examples of good writing – the lifeblood of any newspaper. The choices and omissions, right or wrong, are mine alone.

Thanks are due, as always, to my colleagues in *The Irish Times* – to the Editor, Geraldine Kennedy, for her support for the continuation of this book; to my colleague on the foreign desk, Judith Crosbie, who covered my frequent absences from my day-to-day responsibilities; to my colleagues, without whom these pages would be blank; to the photographic department technical staff who help retrieve images for me; and finally, but not least, to my editor at Gill & Macmillan, Deirdre Nolan, who lets me away with murder.

Peter Murtagh
*The Irish Times*
October 2004

# Journalists and Photographers

**Rahul Bedi** is India Correspondent of *The Irish Times*.

**Alan Betson** is a staff photographer with *The Irish Times*.

**Maeve Binchy**, the novelist, is a former *Irish Times* staff journalist.

**Nicholas Birch** is a freelance journalist based in Istanbul.

**Rosita Boland** is a feature writer with *The Irish Times*.

**Mark Brennock** is Chief Political Correspondent of *The Irish Times*.

**Vincent Browne** is a broadcaster and journalist (he edits *The Village* magazine, launched in October) who writes a weekly column for *The Irish Times* Opinion Page.

**Colin Byrne** is a professional caddy who writes a weekly column in *The Irish Times* sports pages.

**Cyril Byrne** is a freelance photographer based in Dublin.

**Donald Clarke** is a freelance film critic.

**Tony Clayton Lea** is a rock journalist.

**Clifford Coonan** is a freelance journalist based in Beijing.

**Carol Coulter** is *The Irish Times'* Legal Affairs Correspondent.

**Paul Cullen** is an *Irish Times* reporter and Development Correspondent who has also specialised in the Flood Tribunal.

**Deaglán de Bréadún** is Foreign Affairs Correspondent of *The Irish Times*.

**Eithne Donnellan** is Health Correspondent of *The Irish Times*.

**Miriam Donohoe** is deputy news editor of *The Irish Times* and a former Beijing correspondent for the paper.

**Keith Duggan** is an *Irish Times* sports journalist who specialises in Gaelic Games and also writes a column in the sports supplement.

**Newton Emerson** is satirist who runs a humorous website, portadownnews.com, and writes a weekly column for *The Irish Times* opinion page.

**Jack Fairweather** is a freelance journalist who reports from Iraq for *The Daily Telegraph* of Britain and *The Irish Times*.

**Brenda Fitzsimons** is a staff photographer with *The Irish Times*.

**Mark Godfrey** is a freelance journalist based in Beijing.

**Peter Hannan** is a freelance caricaturist who illustrates the Saturday Profile in the Weekend Supplement.

**Nuala Haughey** is a former *Irish Times* staff journalist now working freelance in Israel, the Gaza Strip and the West Bank.

**Shane Hegarty** is *The Irish Times'* TV critic and a feature writer with the paper.

**Mark Hennessy** is Political Correspondent of *The Irish Times*.

**Kitty Holland** is an *Irish Times* reporter.

**Bridget Hourican** is a freelance journalist with specialist knowledge of eastern Europe and relations between there and the European Union.

**Joe Humphreys** is an *Irish Times* reporter.

**Tom Humphries** is a sports journalist and also writes a weekly column, LockerRoom, in the Monday sports supplement.

**Róisín Ingle** is an *Irish Times* feature writer and columnist in the Saturday Magazine.

**Matt Kavanagh** is a staff photographer with *The Irish Times*.

**Colm Keena** is a business reporter with *The Irish Times*, specialising in the Moriarty Tribunal.

**Ian Kilroy** is a freelance journalist and feature writer.

**Conor Lally** is an *Irish Times* reporter.

**Eric Luke** is a staff photographer with *The Irish Times*.

**Seán MacConnell** is *The Irish Times* Agriculture Correspondent.

**Dara Mac Dónaill** is a staff photographer with *The Irish Times*.

**Don MacMonagle** is a freelance photographer based in Killarney.

**Lara Marlowe** is *The Irish Times'* Paris Correspondent. She also reports regularly from the Middle East.

**Neil McCormick** is a rock journalist.

**Dan McLaughlin** is a freelance journalist who has reported extensively for *The Irish Times* from Moscow and recently relocated himself to Budapest, Hungary.

**Frank McNally** is an *Irish Times* reporter. He also writes a weekly column, The Last Word, in Saturday's Weekend section.

**Frank Millar** is London Editor of *The Irish Times*.

**Frank Miller** is a staff photographer with *The Irish Times*.

**John Moran** is an *Irish Times* sub-editor and feature writer.

**Gerry Moriarty** is Northern Editor of *The Irish Times*.

**Orna Mulcahy** is Property Editor of *The Irish Times* and she also writes the Irish Lives column in the Saturday Magazine.

**Marie Murray** is a psychologist, specialising in relationships.

**Kevin Myers** writes An Irishman's Diary.

**Breda O'Brien** writes a column for *The Irish Times* Opinion Page.

**Bryan O'Brien** is a staff photographer with *The Irish Times*.

**Carl O'Brien** is a general news reporter with *The Irish Times*.

**Tim O'Brien** is Regional Development Correspondent for *The Irish Times*.

**Conor O'Clery** is North American Editor of *The Irish Times* and is based in New York.

**Fionnula O'Connor** is a Northern Ireland author and journalist. She writes a weekly opinion column for *The Irish Times*.

**Lynne O'Donnell** is a freelance journalist.

**Michael O'Regan** is an *Irish Times* staff reporter working mainly in Leinster House.

**Joe O'Shaughnessy** is a freelance photographer based in Galway.

**Fintan O'Toole** is *The Irish Times'* theatre critic and also writes a column on the paper's Opinion Page.

**Philip Reid** is Golf Correspondent of *The Irish Times*.

**Priscilla Robinson** is a civil servant and freelance writer.

**Wendy Shea** is an illustrator who provides the illustration for the Irish Lives column in the Saturday Magazine.

**Kathy Sheridan** is a feature writer with *The Irish Times*.

**Lorna Siggins** is Western Correspondent of *The Irish Times* and is also the paper's Marine Correspondent.

**Shalini Sinba** is a counsellor on equality and race issues. She has lectured in University College, Dublin, and presented the RTE inter-cultural programme, 'Mono'. She writes occasionally in *The Irish Times* Health Supplement.

**David Sleator** is a staff photographer with *The Irish Times*.

**Denis Staunton** is Europe Correspondent with *The Irish Times* and is based in Brussels.

**Chris Stephen** is a freelance journalist who has written extensively for *The Irish Times* from the Balkans and The Hague (where he covers the war crimes trial of Slobodan Milosevic) and is now based in Moscow.

**Mark Steyn** is a Canadian-born columnist living in New Hampshire. He writes a weekly column for *The Irish Times* and several other publications in America and the UK.

**Gerry Thornley** is *The Irish Times'* Rugby Correspondent.

**Declan Walsh** was until recently an *Irish Times* correspondent based in Nairobi, Kenya, from where he reported on central and southern Africa. He is now based in Islamabad working primarily for *The Guardian* newspaper of London.

**Dominick Walsh** is a freelance photographer based in Kerry.

**Grania Willis** is Equestrian Correspondent of *The Irish Times*.

THURSDAY, 2 OCTOBER 2003

# An Irishman's Diary

*Kevin Myers*

One of the more enjoyable sensations of the past decade or so has been the trumpeted indignation from the Conference of Religious of Ireland at every reduction in income tax. Such pleasure it gave us all, to hear these fine people telling us it was our duty to pay more tax; though of course, for the most part, being registered charities and being immune to – for example – much of the capital gains taxes on the sale of their properties, they no doubt regard tax in a somewhat different light to the rest of us.

Anyway, the years went by, and every time Charlie McCreevy cut taxes, we got the predictable bluster that what was needed was higher taxes to enable the State to give more benefits to the poor. Never mind that the lesson everywhere has been that lower taxes stimulate growth – CORI, apparently, sought an economic policy based on the Four Cardinal Virtues.

Of course, economies no more run on virtue than jet aircraft run on turf. Charlie knew that, which is why the economy grew, soaking up not merely our own unemployment, but causing people to come from all over the world to seek jobs here. But even rampant growth didn't stem CORI's scolding post-budget sermons, which naturally had loud echoes from that ever-vocal constituency, the pious left.

Do you know, it's a funny thing how one's tone changes when the money one is talking about is one's own. For CORI has more recently been putting up a fierce fight to shift the financial consequence of sexual, physical and psychological abuse of children by members of 18 of its affiliate congregations, doing its best to get the State to bear the bulk of the burden. I must say, I can't blame CORI one bit: if I could persuade the State to pay my lawful debts, why, that's what I'd do, and depart chuckling if I succeeded.

Two years ago, the religious orders – with CORI as a lead negotiator – told the Government that they would make one offer in compensation for the terrible deeds done to children by members of religious orders. That offer was £45 million, £20 million in cash, payable over five years, and this would confer a full and binding indemnity by the Government against all outstanding claims. If not accepted, the offer would be withdrawn, and CORI & Co. would exit forthwith from the negotiations. A thoroughly Christian approach indeed.

The blustering arrogance of the approach resembled the manner in which CORI denounced tax-cutting budget after tax-cutting budget. Moreover, CORI *et al.* declared that their offer exceeded 'by a considerable margin' what their exposure was likely to be. In other words, CORI and its associates not merely thought they could

*Michael Adams, aged 8, from Celbridge, Co. Kildare, blowing a kiss to Lír from the Garda Mounted Unit during a rally in Merrion Square Park to highlight Footsteps, Downs Syndrome Honey Days 2003. Photograph: Matt Kavanagh.*

dictate to the State the terms of the settlement, but they also thought they could forecast what the courts would award in hundreds, perhaps thousands of cases, many years down the line.

Two years ago, Charlie McCreevy, who has had the rare pleasure of having his ear regularly chewed off by CORI, was being unusually restrained when he described the offer of the religious orders as 'quite disappointing', especially as it was dependent on a Government-assured indemnity. His estimate was that the costs to the State – i.e. you and me – might run to €500 million. Think again, Charlie. This one could empty the bank: a gaunt Comptroller and Auditor General, John Purcell, sitting whey-faced at his abacus like a widow at her wheel, is counting up to a billion.

Actually, the State should have allowed CORI & Co. to stick to their promise that without unconditional acceptance, they would withdraw their first and final offer. This would then have freed the many hundreds of litigants to sue each order and each school; and then by God, CORI would have known the meaning of pain. Instead, in an utterly cretinous act of financial fecklessness, the then Minister for Education, Dr Michael Woods (oh, what is he a doctor of – political imbecility?) agreed a settlement of €128 million to be paid by the religious orders.

The CORI congregations then proclaimed that they had agreed to make 'a substantial contribution' to the victims of abuse, which would provide them with 'educational support, counselling and financial assistance'. But, funny old thing, the press statement didn't admit the other part of the deal – that they had very single-mindedly secured a full indemnity from the State against all further claims by the victims of religious orders.

So congratulations, CORI! Well done, indeed! Perhaps you might now give night classes on how to wriggle out of paying one's debts, and seminars on how to inveigle the State to indemnify you against legal action by people abused, raped, violated and traumatised by your members and those of other religious orders. The world is your oyster now, and the sky is the limit, so march on over the broad horizons!

Nor did the adeptness of religious congregations cease with the settlement. Just a few months ago, the Department of Education announced that it wouldn't accept some of the land that they were offering in settlement. The land concerned apparently had absolutely no commercial value, because – as CORI *et al.* were just possibly aware – it couldn't be sold on. Nice try.

Don't misunderstand me, CORI. You have – like the rest of us – a duty to defend your self-interests. This you have done. But there's a price to be paid for such defence. It's called prudent silence. So the next time you feel the urge to give us little sermons on economic policy, just give it a miss. Put a sock in it. Stay shtum. Or, as Detective Inspector Regan would have snarled: Shut it. OK?

**SATURDAY, 4 OCTOBER 2003**

# TD 'Will go to Jail' Over Smoking Proposal

*Joe Humphreys*

Independent TD and part-time publican Mr Jackie Healy-Rae has promised to go to jail rather than enforce the proposed smoking ban at his family's bar in Kilgarvan, Co. Kerry.

'I would go to prison, no bother in the world. I'll have to because there is no way I'd turn long-standing friends against me,' he told *The Irish Times*.

Expressing '100 per cent' support for those Kerry publicans threatening to defy the ban, the Kerry South TD said: 'Publicans will have to go to court and defend themselves, and go to jail if needs be. You can't catch these people at the collar – these people who are a part of the family – and throw them out of your pub.'

Mr Healy-Rae said he only worked 'very, very rarely' in the bar, now run by his son, Danny, who last month replaced his father on Kerry County Council. If and when the ban comes in, however, 'there's no way I'll be enforcing it, even if the Minister himself comes in.'

He said there was 'no comparison' between the clientele of a rural pub such as his and the 'big city pubs' that the Minister had in mind.

'We have customers, about five or six customers around 11 or 12 o'clock in the morning; they will walk in and sit down in the little corner where they always sit down. They will get a half a whiskey . . . and they'll sit down and light a cigarette and they'll smoke it away with their drink and maybe after an hour or two they'll talk and chat about what's happening around.

'You can't catch these people and throw them out on the road. The Minister has a way out of this if he puts a proper smoke-free section in pubs. If he makes a regulation that there's no smoking at the counter, that is fine. But he wants it 100 per cent, and he will fail.'

*The smoking ban was introduced without incident on 29 March 2004. Mr Healy-Rea did not go to jail.*

**TUESDAY, 7 OCTOBER 2003**

# Witnesses Tell of Dramatic Pub Raid

*Conor Lally*

A spent shotgun cartridge lying beside a pool of blood outside The Goat pub, in Goatstown, Dublin, yesterday told the story of one of the most dramatic armed raids the city has seen in recent years.

A seat cushion and sheets, both soaked in blood, also lay nearby. In the moments after the

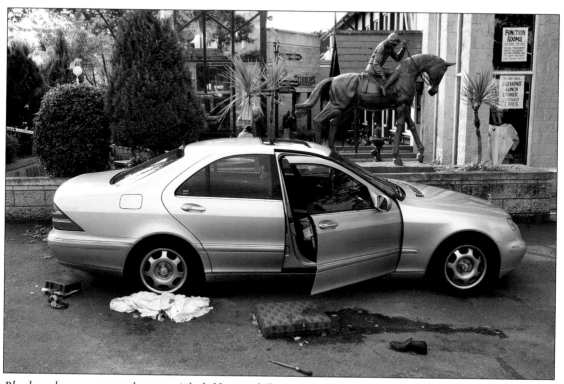

*Blood on the pavement at the scene of the hold-up and shooting at The Goat public house, Goatstown, Co. Dublin. Photograph: Eric Luke.*

popular publican Mr Charlie Chawke was shot just after 12.30 p.m., both had been taken from The Goat by frantic staff and customers and used to try and stem the blood from the victim's leg wound.

Mr Chawke was removing the weekend's takings from The Goat yesterday afternoon when the raiders struck. He had parked his car just out-side the premises, as he always did, and was about to leave the scene when the raiders got out of their red Volkswagen Polo car, ran towards him, and demanded the money.

Mr Chawke's friend, Mr Oliver McDonald, was with the publican when he was shot. He said he feared for his life during the raid. 'They shouted over to Charlie to give the money . . . I shouted to free him and not shoot. He left the money there

for them to take it.' However, the raiders ignored the plea and shot Mr Chawke in the leg.

'There was a lot of blood coming from Charlie's leg. He was in very heavy pain. He was lying across the car and there was blood running down the side of the car,' said Mr McDonald.

Mr James McCoy, the manager of the Black Tie outlet across the road from The Goat, said the raid was over in moments. 'We heard a bang and went to have a look, and we could see there was a man lying on the ground. We saw one of the (raiders) running towards a red car that had been parked there for a while. Just as they sped off a Garda car came along.'

'One of the guards jumped out of the car, hopped over the railings, and talked to the man on

*An Taoiseach Bertie Ahern greets His Highness Shaikh Khalifa Bin Khalifa, the prime minister of Bahrain, as he and his delegation arrive at Government Buildings for a working lunch. Photograph: David Sleator.*

the ground for a second. He then got back into the Garda car and it went after the other car. At that stage a lot of people had come out of the pub. Within no more than a minute there were six or seven Special Branch cars flying up and down the road.' The gardaí chased the raiders as far as Upper Kilmacud Road. At that point the armed pair's lack of local knowledge sealed their fate. They turned into the Stillorgan Heath housing estate only to find it is a warren of cul de sacs.

One of the estate's residents, who preferred not to be named, told *The Irish Times:* 'When they got as far as the bollards at the end of the cul de sac, they could go no further in the car. They jammed on and jumped out. By that stage a Garda car had come flying up the road after them. One of the guys stopped and turned and shot at the Garda car. The two of them then ran into the heath. But at that stage a good few marked and unmarked cars had arrived and there seemed to be gardaí on foot running into the heath from different directions. The guys with the guns ran towards Brewery Road, but they were caught and brought back to their car handcuffed within a few minutes. One of them seemed to be bleeding from his ear.

'The guards sat them on the kerb by the car, put on plastic gloves and searched them. They must have taken away about 10 big paper bags of evidence.'

**FRIDAY, 10 OCTOBER 2003**

# Facing the Legislature Will Be a Reality Check

*Conor O'Clery, in Sacramento*

There is one public forum in California from which Governor-elect Arnold Schwarzenegger is permanently barred. That is the floor of the 80-member house and 40-member senate in Sacramento's historic capitol building.

Here among the century-old desks equipped with laptop computers, liberal Democrats hold sway. In the governor's office, along a corridor from the gold-domed rotunda, the new incumbent may propose and veto bills, but the legislature can dispose of them and kill vetoes with a two-thirds majority. This is the reality that faces the action movie star next month when he moves into the office with its blue carpet bearing the California motto 'Eureka!' (I have found it).

Mr Schwarzenegger wielded a broom at a campaign stop in Sacramento last week as he promised to 'clean house' in the Capitol. That was a 'good visual', he remarked to reporters at his first press conference on Wednesday. But the imagery of Hollywood will count for little when Schwarzenegger encounters the screwed-up reality of governing California, a state where citizens have tied the hands of legislators with legal limits on property taxes, mandated education spending and other ballot initiatives.

The *Terminator* star won populist support for his promise to zap an increase in car tax (from $70 to $210) on his first day, but when he called state senate leader John Burton, he encountered a 'difference of opinion' on what was going to happen. Repeal of the car tax requires Democrats to agree to vote down a 1998 law, according to a capitol official who told me, 'there has never been a happy marriage between a governor and this legislature.'

Scrapping the tax will add $4 billion to a projected $8 billion fiscal overrun, meaning draconian cuts in services. 'I told him, "Man, it's going to be a tough road,"' said Burton, a seasoned Democratic partisan. 'He said, "Anything worth doing is tough; it's not going to be easy."'

Everything depended on what Schwarzenegger wanted to do, the senate leader told the *Sacramento Bee*. 'If he wants to take money from the aged, blind and disabled . . . poor women and children, I don't think so – not while I'm around. Once you take that oath of office, unless you're a total whack-a-do, reality sets in and you find out campaign rhetoric can't solve the problem.'

Schwarzenegger could get lucky if a tech recovery provides a revenue surge and if he succeeds in getting Burton and other Democrats – who hold a 60 per cent majority in both houses – to co-operate on his plans for cutting services and making California more business-friendly.

With his strong personality and overwhelming celebrity appeal Schwarzenegger at least gets attention. When he telephoned Democratic Senator Diane Feinstein yesterday she hastily broke off a press briefing to take his call. World leaders, from the first President Bush to Nelson Mandela, made congratulatory calls throughout Wednesday to Schwarzenegger, whose fame as an Austrian now matches that of Mozart, Strauss and Sigmund Freud.

When President Bush called, the governor-elect told him he would be asking for 'a lot of favours' to help the finances of California, which gets back just 77 cents of every dollar it sends to Washington. Senator Edward Kennedy also rang to wish his Republican nephew-in-law well. 'The Kennedy family has its own big-tent policy,' said the leader of America's most famous Democratic dynasty. One of the enduring images of the campaign was Kennedy's sister, Eunice Kennedy Shriver, mother of Schwarzenegger's wife Maria and founder of the Special Olympics, enveloped in the huge embrace of the actor at a final campaign rally. This provided a 'good visual' for hesitant Democratic voters. It didn't work in San Francisco, however, where 80 per cent of voters rejected the recall. At Democratic Party headquarters in California's liberal

*Arnold Schwarzenegger is swarmed by the media after he voted in Pacific Palisades, California. Photograph: AP/Joe Cavaretta.*

*Lightning over Dublin. Photograph: Marc O'Sullivan.*

redoubt, Mary Jung, who headed the city's 'No Recall' campaign, pulled the plug on the TV set as Schwarzenegger declared victory. 'We should secede,' she fumed; 'we're totally surrounded by idiots.'

However, Schwarzenegger got more votes state-wide than the No campaign – 3.75 million to 3.56 million – giving him an important legitimacy as he tries to substitute style with substance in his crucial first budget at the end of the year. Legislators in Sacramento also have to take into account that frustrated voters could unseat them if they are seen to be obstructive. In the wake of California's political earthquake, Schwarzenegger is meanwhile adjusting to new realities – such as the unaccustomed silence that greeted him when he walked into his first news conference after the election. 'Don't get excited with the applause,' he quipped to the reporters.

He made one more promise there that will not be hard to keep, and may be welcomed by some film critics. There will be no more movies, said the actor, who came from Austria 35 years ago, and was wakened on Wednesday morning by his daughter Katherine with the words, 'Mr Governor, your coffee is ready.'

**FRIDAY, 17 OCTOBER 2003**

# SDLP is Simply Not at the Races

*Opinion: Fionnula O'Connor*

Once there was a plan that the two governments would pull together to help the SDLP against the rise of Sinn Féin. For a long time, it was just about the only plan. Anglo-Irishry, some unionists called it darkly, seeing correctly that they had been found wanting as agents of progress and the SDLP was to be rewarded for John Hume's vision. For a number of reasons the plan combusted,

*Minister for the Environment, Heritage and Local Government Martin Cullen photographed putting on his apron at the launch of 'The Race Against Waste' campaign at the Irish Film Centre, Eustace Street, Dublin, on 15 October. Photograph: Brenda Fitzsimons.*

not least because the Hume vision came to pass and republicans inherited its lustre.

This week David Trimble and Gerry Adams came out of Downing Street and adjourned to the Northern Ireland Office for further talks. Not long ago, the very idea of that combination of talkers would have been major news. Now, as indeed for months past, Ulster Unionism and Sinn Féin are busy negotiating the next step, the SDLP is not at the match and no one is surprised. To complete the effect, the negotiators clearly have the blessing of Tony Blair, Bertie Ahern, and US envoy Richard Haass.

Will there be a deal? If so, and down the road after an election, will that deal produce a new executive? These are imponderables, ponder though many do. It is hard to imagine how Mr Trimble can come out the other side of the polls with fewer than five anti-agreementeers in his Assembly party. Five

would be enough to tip the balance conclusively against a vote for Mr Trimble as First Minister and Martin McGuinness as Deputy First.

Hold on, you say. Are there not whispers about lowering the vote threshold? And Sinn Féin the second biggest party? Mr McGuinness, not Mr Durkan, as Deputy First? When did that become a sure thing? Nothing is certain in elections.

The SDLP to date has been only narrowly outpolled by Sinn Féin. They still have more seats in local government. But times are a-changing, almost as we watch. Looking like a winner is electoral magic. The sight of the republican leadership strolling out of 10 Downing Street within minutes of Ulster Unionists is worth votes. The absence of Mr Durkan means fewer votes for the SDLP. Perception looks on course to become reality.

The SDLP leader's increasingly hurt and angry tones are not electoral magic. Unproved it may be, but with each successive moment that Sinn Féin is taken to be the party with whom Mr Trimble must deal, so it settles more comfortably into the role of leading nationalist party. Well might Mr Durkan complain: what's a man to do?

He had a rum choice to make and fell awkwardly between the two unpleasant options. Band with us to exclude Sinn Féin, said Mr Trimble. Stick by Sinn Féin, said the voice of electoral wisdom, or you're a goner. Mr Durkan turned his back on Mr Trimble, very properly citing inclusion as the fundamental precept of the Belfast Agreement, but as proofs or apparent proofs of republican wrongdoing began to accumulate, he couldn't defend Sinn Féin. Now the SDLP is a goner anyhow, at least in being seen to count as the senior nationalist representative. Virtue is its own

reward, but goodness may not comfort those the voters reject.

Anti-agreement critics scold that this was inevitable once Sinn Féin was allowed to box above its weight, using the IRA for leverage. True enough, the SDLP has no arms to decommission, nothing to barter with Mr Trimble or Mr Blair. Seen in close-up through several elections, however, the contest between the two nationalist parties is more complicated than that.

Republicans' appetite for politics is what distinguishes them first on the ground – the sight of young Sinn Féiners with clipboards registering their way through constituencies, beating the bushes for new, tired or disillusioned voters. In organisational drive and skill republicans most resemble the DUP. Next comes an Ulster Unionist

*People taking part in the demonstration against refuse charges, organised by the Dublin Council of Trade Unions, outside Mountjoy Prison. Photograph: Eric Luke.*

*Gerry Stembridge (left) with Neil Jordan (centre) and Roddy Doyle in Dublin to highlight their concerns over the possible ending of tax incentives for the film industry. Photograph: Frank Miller.*

Party more coherent on the ground than at senior level, though with much less youthful support than the other two. The SDLP's effort is only patchily visible to other interested parties, at a much lower rate than necessary to hold its vote, never mind increase it.

How can Mark Durkan reverse the judgment of both governments that it is Gerry Adams they should deal with on behalf of nationalists, not him? Can't be done, but his party needs saving. He could beat his colleagues out to beat the bushes, for a start, and stop sounding like a loser.

Harsh words for a decent man who leads a decent party, but then politics is a harsh trade. The SDLP leader is right to feel aggrieved, and right that Dublin and London have both let him down, if only in presentation. The trouble is that except once for the record, there are no votes in saying so.

**TUESDAY, 21 OCTOBER 2003**

# Tearing Down Past in Rush to Modernise

*Letter from Beijing: Mark Godfrey*

I returned again recently to my old neighbourhood in Fengtai district, on Beijing's western outskirts. When I first came to the city I lived near the ancient Marco Polo bridge, crossed by the famous explorer on his entrance to the Chinese capital.

Down by the Chinese-Japanese War Memorial gardens the city tapers off into stretches of pretty tile-roofed cottages built along narrow alleyways. The skyscrapers of the inner city have barely reached this hard-scrabble part of town. Locals here live in quadrangular red and grey-bricked bungalows, the small houses being typical of Beijing.

A bus ride along the Jingshi freeway, westward toward Hebei province, reveals a neighbourhood in deconstruction. Sundays are particularly busy, little blue Futian trucks moving household possessions as armies of men in their seven-day suit jackets scramble over roof rafters with pickaxes and sledges, setting about the walls of the three-roomed brick cottages. Helpers below pile up bricks and scavenge for salvageable metal.

In a year this neighbourhood will have been changed utterly. High-rise blocks are planned for the area. Peddlers are already handing out brochures for the scheme down the road at the busy bus junction of Luliquiao. The *dalou* or high-rises are pictured beneath an impossibly blue sky, the trees and grass optimistically plentiful and a verdant green. The apartment blocks when finished will rise to 30 storeys.

Many Beijingers are glad to see the back of the city's traditional housing. While looking quaint and pretty, *hutong*s are often cold and damp in the depth of Beijing's cold winter. Most have no toilet, residents sharing dank and fetid smelling public toilets.

Standing in the courtyard of a *hutong*, the city's imperial courtyard housing, or walking the alleyways that wind through the houses, one could only be in old Beijing, the city of Maoist fervour and legendary community spirit. Most prized among city historians and architectural heritage buffs, *hutong*s are ancient city alleys composed of a series of courtyard homes. Many were built around the Forbidden City during the Yuan, Ming, and Qing dynasties, and are considered unique to the Beijing landscape.

The uniqueness of the buildings isn't lost on many who live there. Grey-uniformed security guards outside Beijing's municipal complaints office had an unusually busy time this summer when former residents of *hutong*s came out to vent their anger.

One protester's placard was unambiguous: 'Because of the Olympics Games, the government ordered my house to be demolished and my right to exist was taken from me.' Carrying a loudspeaker, an old man urged fellow protesters to come to the office every day until justice was done. Hundreds of disgruntled Beijingers took their placards to the streets in sporadic protests this summer after being pushed out of their homes to make way for government-backed real estate developments.

Owners of a typically-sized three-room *hutong* will be paid 110,000 yuan (€11,400) to move out. Demonstrators claimed that those who dared to stay put had their houses torn down.

Filmed discreetly by police, the protesters were largely elderly people whose old-style bungalow housing was levelled to make way for new apartment blocks. City bosses have claimed that the new developments are intended to beautify the city, but protesters' placards claimed the schemes are purely for profit.

Last week I visited a new housing development in Dongzhimen, a north-eastern city neighbourhood. Retaining the names of the 500-year-old *hutong*s which only a few months ago stood here, the six-storey apartment blocks were snug and comfortable inside and brightly painted on the exterior. But they were as anonymous and universal as any mediocre apartment development in any of the world's cities.

Beijing's shortage of affordable housing is constantly aggravated by the incoming *waidiren*, out-of-towners moving to the capital in search of work. However, demolition and compensation quarrels are not confined to cities.

A Chinese farmer attempted to burn himself early one morning in Tiananmen Square in protest at the government moving him and his family off their land to make way for a new road. The compensation he was offered was below the market value, claimed 45-year-old Zhu from East China's Anhui Province who poured petrol over himself after making the long train trip to Beijing with his wife.

Not far from Tiananmen Square, Shichahai Lake on Beijing's north-western side is part of an artificially-created system of waterways and lakes stretching from the legendary Forbidden City and dating back to the Yuan imperial dynasty of the thirteenth century. Surrounded by palaces, temples and *hutong*s, and lit by red lanterns, night-time dinner boats pass from here on and under the Yinding bridge towards Houhai lake.

Houhai is Beijing's latest mistake. Guests on the boats make a wish while lighting candles are carried along the water on paper boats. Meanwhile, on the banks charming old houses are being gutted and turned into gaudy western-style bars hung with fairy lights. Cars now clog ancient bridges and alleyways designed for handcarts and bicycles.

City officials grabbed at the stable door after the horse had bolted when they announced this summer that 200 of the city's *siheyuan* or traditional courtyards will be protected, years after thousands of such buildings began to face the developers' bulldozers to make way for bars, nightclubs, supermarkets and unremarkable high-rises.

China's new breed of fast-buck builders rarely allow aesthetics or morals to get in the way of a new block of apartments. A family of three was tied up and their house torn down by a gang of 'heavies' hired by a developer in Beijing's north-westerly Haidian district in August this year. The family had refused to move as the developer had offered them too little compensation.

In an interesting twist to the tale, several Beijing real estate agents are doing a roaring trade selling and leasing renovated *hutong*s to foreigners. The old houses, fitted with a kitchen and bathroom, have proven particularly popular with business people who like to entertain in the *hutong*'s courtyard.

'The city government has had little or no vision to preserve the old city,' laments US businessman and architectural conservationist Laurence Brahm, who has purchased several *hutong*s. Brahm recently participated in a TV discussion on the preservation of the *hutong*s with a senior government architect.

The government official suggested during the programme that all of Beijing's old architecture should be replaced by modern developments. Only the Forbidden City, the Temple of Heaven and some lesser temples deserved sparing. The architect also claimed it was impossible to restore old brick and wood structures. 'That's pure idiocy!' said Brahm, himself the veteran of several successful *hutong* renovations.

As Beijing's forest of cranes gets thicker every day, there's no sign of any leashing of the developers' bulldozers. Beijing is all the while readying itself for the 2008 Olympics Games. By that time, alas, there may not be much of the original Beijing left.

**WEDNESDAY, 22 OCTOBER 2003**

# They All Stepped In, But Some Stepped Out Again

*Frank McNally, in Belfast*

In retrospect, it was like staging *Riverdance* without a rehearsal. It didn't matter that you had everybody else lined up in a row. All the talk of careful choreography was just asking for trouble in a production whose two main stars lead with different feet.

For most of the day, in fact, events had proceeded with a stately grace that suggested dancing of the ballroom variety. Veteran instructor Tony Blair led the couples on to the floor with the announcement of elections, and probably gave his pupils some last-minute reminders: 'First, place the hand of history on your partner's shoulder . . .'

Then Gerry Adams and P. O'Neill did their thing; Gen. de Chastelain cut in and swept P. O'Neill off into a corner; and David Trimble glided on to perform his two-step with the general, who in turn was supposed to hand him back to Mr Adams.

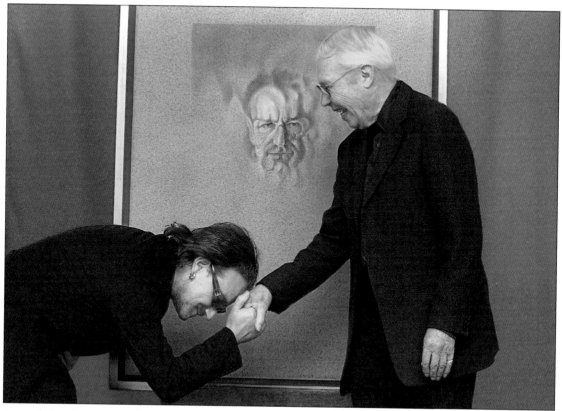

*Bono (left) and artist Louis le Broquy at the unveiling of his portrait of the rock singer at the National Gallery in Dublin to mark the re-opening of the National Portrait Collection on 20 October. Photograph: Dara Mac Dónaill.*

Instead, suddenly, the UUP leader fled the dancefloor, clutching his dignity. It was unclear whether the hand of history had gone somewhere it shouldn't, or whether Mr Adams had just stood on his toes. But either way, Bertie Ahern and Tony Blair, who'd booked each other for the last waltz, were outstanding.

Rather than a sequence of peace moves, we now had a sequence of crisis press conferences. The grave-faced Mr Trimble declared the process 'on hold'. An equally grave-faced Mr Adams said the first he knew of the UUP's difficulties was from the radio.

A party that knows the value of dress rehearsals, Sinn Féin is famous for taking its collective tie off on occasions, as if to say: 'Our work is done.' A measure of the crisis last night was that they did not resort to evening wear for a hastily convened conference on the Falls Road. From which, still in working suits, they headed for Hillsborough for emergency talks with the prime ministers.

Even before the process unravelled, West Belfast was sceptical. Typical of the mood on the Shankill yesterday was Mary Greer, who questioned Gen. de Chastelain's credentials: 'How do we know he's telling the truth?' And little as she trusted the general, she trusted Trimble even less: 'Too much power and too much money.'

Over on the Falls there was more confidence, although it didn't extend to the UUP leader. Waiting for a No. 13 bus, Ann Donnelly expressed optimism on the prospects of a deal: 'But to be honest, after the election, it's Adams and Paisley who'll have to work together.'

Mr Paisley was unusually quiet last night. Maybe the man with the booming voice decided not to compete with *Concorde* which visited Belfast yesterday. It flew out just before tea-time, and it was hard to tell the sonic blast from the bang with which so much preparation came unstuck.

**WEDNESDAY, 22 OCTOBER 2003**

# Bitter Times for Beleaguered Darjeeling

*Rahul Bedi, in Darjeeling*

The dilapidated state of the once majestic Darjeeling Planters' Club mirrors the decline in the fortunes of what helped pioneering Scotsmen set it up 135 years ago in the shadow of the Himalayas in north-east India – the region's world-famous tea. Like the rundown club (Mallory and Irvine stayed here shortly before leaving for their ill-fated Everest 1924 expedition) with its feeble attempts at colonial gentility, peeling walls and a once regal library withering away under dust and neglect, Darjeeling's delicately flavoured tea too faces a crisis.

It is being squeezed by low productivity that has dropped by over 11 million lbs to around 20 million lbs a year, mounting labour expenses, up by 62 per cent, and production costs that are out-stripping returns.

The collapse of its main market, the former Soviet Union, which bought nearly 50 per cent of Darjeeling's aromatic leaf tea, a steady drop in domestic consumption and a halt to increasing exports to Iraq due to the current unrest have all further imperiled the subtle Himalayan brew.

Extortion and killings by insurgent groups in tea plantations in neighbouring Assam state, another major tea region, have added to producers' expenses, which include security costs, medical care, housing, electricity, education and food rations for the work-force, all mandated by a 1951 law.

Consequently, 2.2 lbs of tea costs today around $1.62 (€1.40) to produce but sells for around $1 (€0.85). A majority of Darjeeling's 78 tea gardens, mostly located at a height of around 5,000 feet, sold their harvest last year for around half of what it cost to make.

'Fierce competition from tea-growers in Kenya, Sri Lanka and neighbouring Nepal, soil erosion, environmental degradation, indiscriminate use of chemical fertilisers and tough legislation have landed Darjeeling tea in this serious predicament,' Sanjeev Seth, head of the Darjeeling Planters' Association, said.

He said tea requires a special biodiversity that has been destroyed. If this continued, all that would remain would be a collection of motley 'bought-tea leaf' factories, supported by small growers with no commitment to either product quality or labour welfare, he added.

The region's woefully inadequate natural forest cover, plundered by politically connected 'timber mafias', has exacerbated the slide in Darjeeling's 175-year tea industry by accelerating soil erosion in the rain-soaked hills at heights averaging 5,000 feet. Deforestation has also resulted in reduced rainfall patterns in what was one of the world's wettest regions and landslides that threaten to engulf tea estates.

To add to the planters' woes across Bengal state, nearly 75 per cent of all tea bushes are over 80 years old, many either diseased or beyond their productivity period and badly in need of being replaced. But most plantation owners – many of them rapacious traders with little or no experience of growing tea – are desperate for quick profits and opt for chemicals and other short-term means to enhance fertility rather than wait seven years for new bushes to become productive.

And though a handful of plantations have recently turned to organic gardening – 22 of 78 gardens in Darjeeling – and are attempting to rejuvenate the forest cover, the restoration process will take decades.

*Professor Michael Porter speaking on business strategy during his briefing in the new IMI conference centre in Dublin. Photograph: Frank Miller.*

Of Darjeeling's 78 estates – covering 17,000 hectares and employing around 90,000 people – seven have so far closed or operate erratically. In the neighbouring Dooars and Terai plains that produce a substantial proportion of India's 1.75 billion lbs of tea annually, another 20 have been abandoned.

Over the past two years, tens of thousands of tea-workers have been laid off in Bengal and Assam and in southern India's Nilgiri Hills, where the crisis is far worse. Following the closure of the Kathalguri tea estate in Jalpaiguri, 110 miles south-east of Darjeeling, around 8,000 workers were rendered jobless last year and since then at least nine have reportedly died of starvation.

Prabir Bhattacharya, of the Indian Tea Association, said additional gardens were likely to close this winter after plucking stopped in December, further increasing joblessness in a sector that employs over one million people, second only in its importance for the country to Indian Rail.

'The prognosis for the tea industry is grim,' said J.S. Tarayal, who manages the estate producing the famous Lopchu brand of Darjeeling tea. For the moment there seems to be little sign of light at the end of the tunnel, he added. The only hope for the industry is to recapture the Russian market and move into the US, where tea is increasingly being seen as a health drink.

Impractical legislation to realise the full value of Darjeeling teas has also contributed to the problem. Selling Darjeeling teas blended with inferior brands as Pure Darjeeling abroad led to India instituting protectionist measures like the certified trade mark. This followed revelations that though only 19.8 million lbs of Darjeeling tea were produced in 2000 over 880 million lbs were sold globally.

Under certified trade mark regulations, only Darjeeling's gardens were recognised as *bona fide* producers of its leaf tea. But these measures ran into trouble when international tea cartels refused to open up their stocks for inspection by the Indian Tea Board, as CTM rules required them to.

'Many major European buyers were not ready to tolerate this and began promoting alternative teas from Nepal and high grade Ceylon teas that are close in flavour to Darjeeling tea and marketed them as such,' a planter said.

With declining profits, standards of living on tea estates have undergone radical change. 'It's no longer a way of life. It's become a job,' Mr Harsh Kumar, a planter for 30 years said.

The number of servants the *burra sahib*s (plantation managers) were allocated, for instance, had reduced by a third from around 30 per household, while entertainment, fuel and soft furnishing allowances had been drastically cut. Even the legendary Moog and Barua cooks from further east, who jealously guarded their vast culinary repertoire, had disappeared.

'Gardens are no longer run by managers but by accountants who know nothing about ground realities,' one deprived *burra sahib* said. Club life that centred on tennis, football and golf, the bar and parties, and was the core of tea life until the early 1990s, has almost been obliterated.

'Clubs are a sad shadow of what they once were,' S. Mohankrishnan lamented, adding that driving 40 miles for dinner at one of them was routine some years ago, but no longer. Many plantation managers said the good days in tea were over and socialising no longer formed the mainstay of the *sahib*'s life, having been supplanted by cable television, home movies and the Internet. Besides, the majority of new recruits into tea estates were from backgrounds vastly different from their predecessors and more concerned about getting ahead professionally than being social, club- or sports-minded.

'The old breed of planters, like the British and the Indians who emulated them, played hard and worked hard,' Vijay Parmar said. The new ones are too busy adjusting to changed times.

**MONDAY, 27 OCTOBER 2003**

# The Sting in Sudan's Tale of Vanishing Penises

## *Opinion: Mark Steyn*

I haven't really followed Sudanese current events closely since, oh, Gen. Kitchener's victory over the Mahdi at the Battle of Omdurman in 1898. But a recent story from that benighted land happened to catch my eye.

Last month mass hysteria apparently swept the capital city, Khartoum, after reports that foreigners were shaking hands with Sudanese men and causing their penises to disappear. One victim, a fabric merchant, told his story to the London Arabic newspaper *Al-Quds Al-Arabi*. A man from West Africa came into the shop and 'shook the store owner's hand powerfully until the owner felt his penis melt into his body'.

I know the feeling. The same thing happened to me after shaking hands with Hillary Clinton. Anyway, as *Al-Quds* reported, 'The store owner became hysterical, and was taken to the hospital.' The country's 'Chief Criminal Attorney-General' Yasser Ahmad Muhammad told the Sudanese daily *Al-Rai Al-A'am* that 'the rumour broke out when one merchant went to another merchant to buy some Karkady [a Sudanese beverage]. Suddenly, the seller felt his penis shrivelling'.

The invaluable Middle East Media Research Institute, in its exhaustive coverage, noted that the penises of Khartoum were vulnerable not merely to handshaking. 'Another victim, who refused to give his name, said that while he was at the market, a man approached him, gave him a comb, and asked him to comb his hair. When he did so, within seconds, he said, he felt a strange sensation and discovered that he had lost his penis.'

Tales of the vanishing penises ran rampant round the city, spread by cellphones and text messages. Sudan's Health Minister Ahmad Bilal Othman said that the epidemic was 'scientifically groundless', and that it was 'sorcery, magic, or an emotional problem'.

The Attorney-General Salah Abu Zayed declared that all complaints about the missing penises would be brought before a special investigative committee, though doctors had determined that the first plaintiff was 'perfectly healthy'. The evidence wouldn't stand up in court. Or rather … oh, never mind.

By now you're probably saying, 'Oh, come on, Steyn, this Sudanese penis thing is all very well, but you're supposed to be a columnist. There's some big geopolitical argument behind all this tittering at shrivelling manhoods, isn't there?' Absolutely.

For one thing, a week after the Malaysian Prime Minister told an Islamic summit that their 'enemies' the Jews control the world and got a standing ovation from 56 fellow Muslim leaders, it's useful to be reminded that the International Jewish Conspiracy is comparatively one of the less loopy conspiracies in the Islamic world. That said, they'll probably figure out a way to pin the disappearing penises on some or other agent of Zionism. After all, according to reports in Middle East newspapers, Israel laces Arab chewing-gum with secret hormones to make Muslim men hot for Jewish babes who turn out to be Mossad agents.

Come to think of it, remember those stories in *The National Enquirer* after 9/11 about Osama bin Laden being, ah, somewhat under-endowed in the trouser department? He spent much of the 90s in Sudan. Who's to say some Zionist didn't sneak up and shake his hand while he was on a shopping trip to Khartoum? It is, in that sense, the perfect emblematic tale of Islamic victimhood: the foreigners have made us impotent! It doesn't matter that the foreigners didn't do anything except shake hands. It doesn't matter whether you are, in fact, impotent. You feel impotent, just as – so we're told

– millions of Muslims from Algerian Islamists to the Bali bombers feel 'humiliated' by the Palestinian situation. Whether or not there is a rational basis for their sense of humiliation is irrelevant.

One of the things I'd feel humiliated about if I lived in the Arab world is that almost all the forms of expression of my anti-Westernism are themselves Western in origin. Pan-Arabism was old-school nineteenth-century nationalism of the type that eventually unified the various German and Italian statelets. Nasserism was transplanted European socialism, Baathism a local anachronistic variant on 'tween-wars Fascist movements. The Arabs even swiped Jew hatred from the Europeans: though there was certainly friction between Jew and Muslim before the twentieth century, it took the Europeans to package a disorganised, freelance dislike of Jews into a big-time ideology with the Protocols of the Elders of Zion, *Mein Kampf* and all the rest. Even Islamic fundamentalism, though ostensibly a rare example of a home-grown toxin, has, as a practical matter, more in common with European revolutionary movements than with traditional expressions of Islam – an essentially political project piggybacking on an ancient religion to create the ideology of choice for the world's troublemakers.

There's something rather sad about a culture that has to import even its pathologies. The telling detail of the vanishing penis hysteria is that it was spread by text-messaging. You can own a cellphone yet still believe that foreigners are able, with a mere handshake, to cause your penis to melt away.

Aside from its doubts in its collective manhood, Sudan is no laughing matter. Two million people have been slaughtered there in the last decade. The Christian minority is vanishing a lot faster than that fabric merchant's wedding tackle. Osama certainly found the country fertile ground for his ideology: Sudanese mujahideen have been captured as far afield as Algeria, Bosnia, Chechnya and Afghanistan. An economic basket-case with a 27 per cent literacy rate has managed to find enough spare cash to export revolutionary Islam to many other countries. And they've got half-a-billion dollars' worth of state-of-the-art Chinese weaponry from Iran.

A handshake-fearing guy with a cellphone is one thing; what happens when the handshake-fearers have cellphones and a suitcase nuke? It's at the intersection of apparently indestructible ancient ignorance and cheap, widely available Western technology that the dark imponderables of the future lie. In 1898, after Kitchener slaughtered the dervishes at Omdurman, Hilaire Belloc wrote a characteristically pithy summation of an advanced society's built-in advantage: 'Whatever happens/ We have got/The Maxim gun/And they have not.'

But the dervishes have cellphones now. Those and some dimestore boxcutters and a couple of ATM cards were all they needed to pull off 9/11. And there are plenty of people out there willing to help them get the cheap knock-offs of the twenty-first century's Maxim gun.

THURSDAY, 6 NOVEMBER 2003

# IDS Uses Last Hurrah to Remind Blair to Watch His Back

*Frank Millar, in London*

On the face of the plotters, only smiles. They had come to watch Iain Duncan Smith's last joust with Tony Blair at Prime Minister's Questions – a necessary and important parliamentary 'event' before the resumption of business as usual.

Sitting immediately beside the departing Tory leader was Michael Howard, the man who hopes at noon today to make good his undisputed claim to the Tory crown. As he waited for Mr Speaker Martin to call the House to order, the great man

had no further to look to know where treachery lay. Indeed if Mr Blair was still in doubt, Mr Duncan Smith would not depart the chamber without giving him fair notice.

For if Mr Howard has 'something of the night about him', IDS – as he reminded the prime minister yesterday – has developed something of 'a sixth sense' about leadership bids. All thought of himself and care for his position now gone, the demob-happy Duncan Smith was only too happy to bestow the wisdom and sage advice of the older-but-wiser statesman. And so, with a passing reference to Chancellor Gordon Brown, who is back from paternity leave, IDS gravely warned the prime minister to tread very, very carefully.

Mr Duncan Smith had won few (if any) rave reviews for these Wednesday sallies. But for sheer *chutzpah*, his last would almost certainly be described as a bravura performance.

Not that there had been much hint of it when he first rose to the despatch box. The welcoming (if ironic) 'hear, hears' were conspicuously louder on the Labour side. Some of the suspected Tory assassins sitting behind Mr Duncan Smith thought this a suitable moment to inspect the Gothic splendour of the Commons' ceiling.

IDS's choice for his first three questions – Iraq – was in any event a signal to MPs to be on best behaviour rather than an invitation to wave their order papers in partisan display of approval. And it fell to Mr Blair and the Liberal Democrat leader Charles Kennedy to offer their personal good wishes to the man who hopes to clinch an alternative career as a writer with today's launch of his new novel, *The Devil's Tune*.

Still, Mr Duncan Smith was determined nothing would spoil his party. To that ironic welcome from the Labour benches, IDS told them it was too late and that they would have needed to have registered their vote by last Wednesday.

He provoked Labour laughter, and invited Tory discomfort, when – in devil-may-care-mode – he looked quizzically over his shoulder to the

*Modern art met medieval architecture as Brazilian artist Ivana Panizzi unveiled The Reredos Project, a sculptural installation using bottles, in the Chapel of Trinity College, Dublin. Photograph: Bryan O'Brien.*

backbenchers who had deposed him as Mr Blair expressed confidence that the whole House wished him well for the future.

Then, finally, one last time, he did his duty by his party, prompting the cheers which would cover its embarrassment as he attacked Labour on the one issue on which he had always been, in that well-worn Thatcherite phrase, 'one of us'. IDS had done his sums and calculated he had asked Mr Blair the same question 18 times over the previous two years. As he wryly observed, 'a fat lot of use it's done me.'

Still, he would give it one more try. With this week's announcement of three more on the issue of devolution for the English regions, Mr Duncan Smith said Labour had allowed 37 referendums since coming to power. If they could have one to decide whether to have a monkey for mayor in

Hartlepool, why not another on the much more important question of a president of Europe?

Mr Blair assured him the 19th time of asking wouldn't do him much good either, again insisting there would be no referendum on the proposed new EU constitution because it did not fundamentally alter Britain's constitutional relationship with Europe.

Undeterred, IDS pointed to Mr Brown's demand in *The Daily Telegraph* – 'of all papers' – for categorical assurances that the constitution would not lead to fiscal federalism. They laughed again as he confided that sixth sense for leadership bids and advised Mr Blair to 'watch very carefully'.

Then, after one last refrain of the soundbite he had made his own – 'nobody believes a word the prime minister ever says any more' – IDS was gone. And Chancellor Brown smiled on.

# John Major's 'Brass Neck' in Face-off with Gaybo

*Deaglán de Bréadún*

I f you shake your family tree you never know what you will find. John Major thinks his grandmother was almost certainly Irish. Nothing remarkable in that, but he says her name was 'Sarah Mara or Sarah O'Mara'. We know someone else in modern politics called Mara, don't we? Could Major be related to the man who introduced the concept of *Uno Duce, Una Voce* to the Irish vocabulary, Charles Haughey's faithful spokesman and advisor, P.J. Mara?

Gay Byrne was interviewing John Major at the National Concert Hall in Dublin at the weekend. It's part of a series called *Face-To-Face*, featuring different public figures. The political 'anoraks' and *cognoscenti* paid from €40 to €80 to attend. Gaybo didn't explore the possibility that 'P.J.' might have a blood relationship with a British prime minister as well as a political relationship with an Irish one. But he did ask the question that was on everybody's mind.

Even his critics would concede that Mr Major is polite and civil, almost to a fault. His background

*Tony Marsh of France is tackled by Ireland's Brian O'Driscoll during their Rugby World Cup quarter final in Melbourne, Australia. Photograph: AP/Ross Land.*

*Gay Byrne (right) and John Major in Dublin before the second in the series of Face-To-Face inter-views in the National Concert Hall. Photograph: Alan Betson.*

is in banking and he is just the type of person who could refuse you an overdraft while making you feel he had done you the biggest favour of your life. But as the ex-PM burbled on in his usual amiable fashion, the unspoken tension in the audience grew and grew. Would Gay ask him about his much-publicised extra-marital relationship with a colleague, or would he 'Currie' favour, so to speak, by refraining from any mention of it?

The Old Master didn't let us down. Major had just finished reminiscing about life in the House of Commons when Gaybo paused and then simply said: 'Edwina!' Quick as a flash came the reply: 'I have said what I had to say about that before, and I don't intend to say any more than that.'

Major even got a round of applause. Gaybo said: 'Do you get away with this?' Major hit back: 'I just have.' Muttering about brass necks, Gay moved on.

We never quite got to understand how Major made the transition from near-Dickensian squalor, as the son of a retired trapeze artist and failed businessman, to high office as Prime Minister of the United Kingdom. But he kept us regaled with well-polished anecdotes.

He clearly had a soft spot for Boris Yeltsin. One time, he asked the Russian leader to tell him 'in one word' how things were in Russia. Yeltsin replied: 'Good!' Feeling he might need more information, Major asked him to summarise the situation in two words this time and Yeltsin answered: 'Not good!' On another occasion, at a meeting in the Kremlin, Yeltsin asked Major if he would like a 'coffee' but when the mugs were brought to the table they were filled with neat vodka.

George Bush snr was 'one of the loveliest men in the world', but there were a few little digs as well as some compliments for Bill Clinton. When the pair of them were about to address an audience, Major would ask himself, 'Are they going to like what I'm about to say?' But Clinton would be wondering: 'What can I say that they are going to like?'

Or so Major says. There was a certain amount of false modesty ('I have a fairly average brain') as well as some heavy-duty name-dropping. The squarest man in the world watched cricket with Mick Jagger: what did they talk about? He seems to have mixed feelings about the woman he refers to as 'Margaret' and the rest of us know as Maggie.

But there was unadulterated praise for Albert Reynolds, who was present in the audience with his wife, Kathleen. 'Albert's a very special person,' Major said. Despite the fact that they had 'some of the most spectacular rows I have ever had with anyone', Major predicted they would still be best buddies when they were 'zipping around on Zimmer frames'.

**WEDNESDAY, 19 NOVEMBER 2003**

# New Victims Emerge from Horrors of Brutal War

*Declan Walsh, in Goma, Congo*

A pungent odour wafts through the room. Hands folded on her lap, Rosette, a 23-year-old with twists of black hair, waits patiently. The operation was the next day, she says. Surgery should get rid of the smell.

Rosette was waiting for doctors to rebuild her vagina. Two years earlier, a gang of armed men destroyed it. They stormed her village in eastern Congo, killing six men, including her husband. Then they raped the women. For four days Rosette lay there, battered and unable to budge. When help came, her rescuers followed a swarm of flies buzzing overhead.

Rosette suffers from vaginal fistula, a medical condition which has virtually disappeared in the developed world. It persists in some African countries where there is poor childbirth. In eastern Congo, however, a flood of new victims is emerging, marking the horrors of a barbaric conflict. Aid

*President McAleese meeting the Pope in Rome. Photograph: Arturo Mari.*

workers call it the war against women. Normally resulting from childbirth complications, fistula in Congo is the product of particularly violent rape. Severe internal injuries cause immense pain and debilitating incontinence. Social ostracisation often follows.

Dozens await operations at a clinic in the eastern capital, Goma. Many have had objects – sticks, fingers, gun barrels – thrust inside them. Some have been shot in the vagina. One teenager has had her eyes poked out. For those treating them, the cruelty is incomprehensible. 'It numbs you. How can human beings do that to each other? They must be possessed,' said Lyn Lusi of Doctors on Call for Service (DOCS), the US-funded charity running the clinic.

Along with the plunder of diamonds, gold and coltan, savage sexual violence has emerged as one of the defining characteristics of the five-year Congo war. In the vast eastern forests, gunmen – rebels, local militia, armed refugees from Rwanda – rape with abandon. Sometimes the aim is to subjugate an entire community. Other times, it seems, they do it just because they can. 'They want to show power and strength, that they can do whatever they want to,' says hospital worker Fred Kahunde.

In just six month this year, the DOCS clinic in Goma treated 1,000 women, 83 of whom required fistula operations. An older hospital to the south in Bukavu has healed hundreds more. The attacks in turn fuel the spread of HIV/AIDS – 12 per cent of

*David Trimble (right) is confronted by an angry man on Shankill Road in Belfast during an election walkabout with local Unionist candidate Chris McGimpsey (centre). Photograph: PA/Paul Faith.*

women tested positive, many of whom had not been sexually active.

Patients wait in two large white tents donated by UNICEF, and eat rations from the World Food Programme. Last week, Mwasi (18) stumbled through the flapping door. Her eyes had been beaten to a pulp. The gunmen also damaged her hearing, so doctors shouted questions into her ear. Now she replies in a low whisper, nervously fingering the zip on her jacket. Tears continuously stream down one cheek. Staff are unsure whether it is a medical reaction or just sadness. 'They killed

my parents, then they beat us to show them where the food was,' she says. Her assailants were with the Interahamwe, the Hutu militia which fled Rwanda after leading the 1994 genocide, she says.

Aid workers say all armed groups – including the main rebel group, RCD-Goma, the Mayi Mayi militia – are guilty. 'They are all as bad as each other,' says Dr Abuka Longombe, a Congolese surgeon who carries out many of the operations.

The big, burly man reached into his drawer and pulled out a photo. It showed a woman whose lips were cut from her face. For a moment he was lost for words. 'My youngest patient was five, the eldest was 73. How can you do this to a grandma?' he asks, throwing his hands open. 'I don't have an explanation, but one thing is sure: their goal was to destroy.'

Dr Longombe has seen the worst of the Congo war. Last year he narrowly escaped the slaughter at Nyankunde, in north-eastern Ituri province, when Lendu fighters killed more than 1,000 people from the rival Hema tribe. In the hospital where he was director, the militia hacked at least 40 patients to death in their beds. 'Some were just after surgery, so they were still in traction. It was impossible to escape,' he recalled.

Nyankunde was among the worst atrocities of the five-year war; some of the dead appeared to have been cannibalised. He believes a war crimes tribunal is necessary to end the culture of impunity. Hopes for justice, though, are thin. Congo's judicial system is crumbling and rebel armies rarely discipline their soldiers. The RCD-Goma commander in North Kivu province, Brig-Gen. Laurent Nkunda, denied his men committed mass rape. 'Yes there has been some rape,' he shrugged, 'but where there is war, there is abuse. War is not a recommendation.'

A few days later, the UN under-secretary for Humanitarian Affairs, Jan Egeland, was visiting Goma. He said: 'I have told the leaders the international community will hold people accountable for war crimes.'

For now, though, the outside world is concentrating on cementing the fragile peace between President Joseph Kabila and his former rebel enemies. A transitional government is sitting in the capital, Kinshasa, but in the east, fighting has slowed but not stopped and looting, murder and rape continue.

After her operation, Rosette recovered on a narrow bed in the white tent. Beside her, about 40 other women waited for their operations. Amid the talk of peace, their battle for survival continues.

*Names of victims have been changed.*

# Not a Hint of Emotion From the Man Who Once Ruled the Roost

*Paul Cullen*

One hand gripping a book of Percy Shelley's poems, the other an umbrella for support, George Redmond remained impassive and expressionless as the guilty verdict in his case was

*Former Assistant Dublin City and County Manager George Redmond leaving court following his conviction for corruption. Photograph: Bryan O'Brien.*

*Bronagh McConville, a granddaughter of IRA murder victim Jean McConville, releasing a dove as a symbol of peace in the Holy Trinity cemetery, Lisburn, on 1 November, in a final graveside gesture watched by family members. Photograph: Matt Kavanagh.*

read out. The 79-year-old pensioner's face betrayed no hint of emotion and his trademark golden tan masked any trace of a pallor. Two deep breaths were the only noticeable reaction from the first senior public servant in the history of the State to be convicted of corruption.

Across the crowded courtroom, however, the strain of the moment was written on the faces of the jurors. Six men and six women, most of them less than half the age of the defendant, had taken six hours and 42 minutes since the previous day to deliver the guilty verdict by a 10-2 majority.

While Redmond's solicitor Anthony Harris bowed his head, detectives from the Criminal Assets Bureau congratulated each other on the success of their investigations. Four years ago, they had arrested Redmond on his return from a tour of the Isle of Man's banks and now they had secured a

difficult but historic conviction based on legislation drawn up in Victorian times.

There was, in the quiet interlude that preceded the discussion on sentencing, a sense of how much times have changed.

In the 1980s, when Redmond ruled the roost as *de facto* county manager in Dublin, Michael White was a Workers Party activist railing against the establishment. Yesterday, Judge Michael White, horsehair wig in place, sat stage-centre in the seat of justice while Redmond, the man who once ran Co. Dublin, awaited his fate on a bench to the right of the court. After a brief adjournment, the judge set to his task, only for a garda to tell him that Redmond was 'in the loo, my lord'. Another adjournment followed before Redmond, in a blue jacket and tie and grey trousers, re-entered the court.

As he fitted the earpiece he has been using to amplify the proceedings, the lawyers discussed his fate. It took until after lunchtime for the previously unthinkable to happen, when the judge placed the corrupt official in custody, pending sentencing in a month's time.

And with that, Redmond was led away to prison, looking for all the world like Shelley's once vain Ozymandias, 'whose frown/And wrinkled lip, and sneer of cold command' were now reduced to 'that colossal Wreck'.

**FRIDAY, 21 NOVEMBER 2003**

# The City Streets 'Were Crimson with Blood'

*Nicholas Birch, in Istanbul*

Just before 11 o'clock yesterday morning Ayse Kaya was shopping with her mother in preparation for next week's Seker Bayram, which marks the end of the holy month of Ramadan.

'We were looking for presents for my two children,' she said, white-faced and holding tightly onto her mother's arm. 'And then the bomb

*The courtyard of the British consulate in Istanbul after the bomb attack. Photograph: Hurriyet newspaper.*

struck. I've never seen such horror. The streets were crimson with blood. There were dead and wounded people lying all over the place.'

Around the British consulate, barely 70 metres away from one of Istanbul's busiest shopping streets, the devastation was appalling. All that remains of the two consular buildings that surrounded the heavily guarded main entrance of the compound is a three-metre-high pile of grey rubble and twisted metal. Thirty metres of the consulate's red brick wall has disappeared. The rest sags out over the pavement.

'The force of the explosion threw everybody to the ground,' said Celal Korkunc, who has worked as a security official at the consulate for 10 months. 'We were half buried in rubble. When the salvage crews pulled us out, I saw that nothing was

left of the $1^{1}/_{2}$-ton security gate that led into the compound. It had been blown away.'

Ansel Mullins, an American working in offices 50 metres away, was at the scene within minutes. 'The closer you got to the main entrance of the consulate, the worse the damage was,' he said. 'On the corner there were two cars, both totally burned. One had been flipped over. I saw a man lying between them in the street. A minute later, two men came out of a nearby shop and covered him with a piece of blue tarpaulin. I guess he was dead.'

Within 15 minutes of the blasts, Turkish security forces cordoned off a huge triangle surrounding the consulate. Traffic on the wide road that runs directly behind was stopped, causing massive congestion in central Istanbul.

As crowds gathered to watch the salvage efforts

*An Iraqi girl looks up at an American soldier from Charlie Company, 1st Battalion, 22nd Regiment (1-22) of the 4th Infantry Division while he patrols the streets of Tikrit, Iraq. Photograph: EPA/Stefan Zaklin.*

from afar, one enterprising street seller was hawking hand-held radios at $2 a piece. Barber Celal Gurbuz was offering free haircuts. 'I've just come back from taking one of my customers to hospital,' he said, gesturing to the shattered remains of his shop window. 'I need to be doing something to take my mind off things.'

Over in Levent, the scenes outside the headquarters of HSBC Bank were no better. 'This looks as though it was bigger than the bomb attacks this weekend,' said rescue worker Tarhan Bulan, standing in the broad avenue that runs in front of the 20-storey building.

The bank's white marble casing was blown off by the blast, and a huge fountain of water from its fire extinguisher system spurted out on to the plaza in front. The skyscraper 150 metres away on the other side of Buyukdere Avenue lost all its windows.

Six hundred people are thought to have been in the HSBC building when the explosion happened. Although many may have been saved because they were at a meeting at the back of the building, some may have died, said Tarhan Bulan. 'I saw between six and 10 bodies,' he said. 'Most were in front of the bank, but there were several inside the lobby.'

Beyhan Saltan was in her office on the first floor when the blast occurred. 'The roof partially collapsed and the fire extinguisher system went on,' she said. 'It looked like a scene from hell, and everybody was panicking.'

'The whole building swayed, like in an earth-quake,' said Ozgur Sahin, two floors above. 'There was thick smoke and an overpowering smell of ammonia, and it was almost impossible to breathe.'

Nobody knows for sure what bombs were used or where they were planted. Frequent eye-witness references to the smell of ammonia suggest they could have been similar to Saturday's bombs, which were made from a mixture of ammonium sulphate, nitrate and compressed fuel.

Eyewitnesses in Levent reported seeing a green van slowing at the traffic lights in front of the bank before exploding. Near the consulate, shopkeeper Hakan Ozan was convinced he saw the bomber.

'I saw a white van, going fast, cross Istiklal street and go into the narrow lane that leads up to the consulate,' he said. 'Ten seconds later, there was a huge explosion. The sun was blocked out by a cloud of yellowish smoke.'

In the market just next to the consulate, the white tarpaulin covering stalls was ripped off. Strands hung down onto the floor covered with splinters of glass and goods upended by the force of the blast. A couple of hopeful fishmongers contin-ued to tip cold water over their morning's catch.

Visibly angry, Bulent Arikan, an elderly shop-keeper, picked up shards of glass that had covered stacks of honey pots and spices. 'God damn the people who planted the bombs,' he said. 'What have any of us done to deserve this?'

**MONDAY, 24 NOVEMBER 2003**

# Perfect 10 has World at his Feet

*Gerry Thornley, in Sydney*

Up on the first floor of the manic Manly Pacific Hotel, a media scrum of 100 or more had congregated in a room ill-prepared for the stampede toward one man which was suddenly taking place. To be honest, it was all a little unseemly.

But what's a journalist to do? The world's most famous sportsman, for this week anyhow, was in the room. Everybody wants a little piece of Jonny Wilkinson, though, as ever, he seemed as unfazed as he was when lining up last Saturday's momen-tous drop goal.

Twenty seconds from the end of the last minute of a 100-minute epic, 20 seconds left of the 3,860 minutes (or thereabouts) of a tournament that began six long weeks ago with the first of 48 matches. You could hardly have scripted it. With that Wilkinson had propelled English rugby and himself into stratospheric sporting celebrity.

You sensed his life had changed irrevocably. He was last off the pitch, after the sequence of

*Liam Keane of Limerick walks a free man from the Four Courts in Dublin after the Director of Public Prosecutions entered a nolle prosequi in his trial for the murder of Eric Leamy. Photograph: Courtpix.*

*England's Jonny Wilkinson lines up a penalty kick during their Rugby World Cup semi-final match against France at Sydney's Olympic stadium. Wilkinson kicked England to a 24-7 victory to win a place in the final against Australia. Photograph: Reuters/Mike Hutchings.*

post-match TV interviews he had given behind the backdrops that had been erected in the in-goal area where his drop goal had sailed between the posts.

It explained why there were still thousands of only white-clad supporters left in the ground. They had been drained by the most extraordinary Rugby World Cup final yet, hours of entertainment and atmosphere that had the skin tingling without interruption; oblivious to the teeming rain. They just wanted a glimpse, a pictorial memory, of the 24-year-old from Frimley in Surrey, on this day of all days. He waved once, a little sheepishly, then a second time, and finally as he walked down the players' tunnel he applauded them.

According to one of the men who knows him best, his mentor and coach at Newcastle, Rob Andrew, 'he would have seen it as just his role in that final play'. Indeed, he can be quite a robotic individual, and his game is a manifestation of that. He will never be a Carlos Spencer or a Steve Larkham. Virtually everything he does has been honed over endless hours on the training ground.

But yesterday he revealed a more human side than one can ever recall. Asked what was going through his mind as he addressed his fifth drop-goal attempt of the night, Wilkinson admitted: 'I was thinking "I hope this isn't zero from four." I had more time on that one and once I hit it I wasn't sure but I looked up and saw it was going between the posts.'

Asked how he felt in the moments when he eventually had time to himself for reflection afterwards, he said: 'I tried to get a sense of calmness after the madness at the end, to put the eight long, hard weeks in perspective and what it all meant. To try not to waste it, to try and embrace it. These feelings are not something I'm going to forget but they don't last necessarily. I can't go on thinking about this, because soon I'll be back playing again.'

And then, you sense, he'll be at his most harmonious with the world around him. Yet, yesterday he was also impressively relaxed, and even unusually humorous. Asked when he would

resume practising again, he said: 'Not today,' a little self-deprecatingly, and added: 'Not tomorrow either. I've packed the boots for the flight, but once I get back I'll get on with it, but the first few sessions might be slightly relaxed.'

Perhaps with a World Cup winners' medal to go with a Grand Slam, he can indeed start to relax a little. 'I'm trying to find a balance,' he conceded. 'I've always put a lot of pressure on myself to perform, but I'm trying to enjoy it more as well.'

Good. It would be a shame if his emotions were just of perfection. It was nice to see the mask come down at the full-time whistle, as he spread his arms, beamed, jumped up and down, and appeared unsure of what to do next before he and Will Greenwood embraced. Real elation.

But there'll probably always be an innate restlessness about him. 'I'm grateful to be here so I can't afford to have any regrets. I'm going to go at it for a long time. I want to try and win things. I want to be part of a fantastic team. And if it brings that little bit of attention that's maybe a bit much then that's something I'm going to have to learn to deal with better. I couldn't live with that feeling of regret if I don't make the most of what I've got now.'

Even now, he spoke of getting to know Newcastle's game plan, settling in with the Newcastle players again. 'I owe a lot to Newcastle,' he explained. The notion that a World Cup medal might sate this extraordinarily driven individual is faintly ridiculous.

'I have many goals written down on paper and some of them I've been able to tick off. I'll always be able to say that and I'll always be grateful to people who've helped me do it. I've got many other goals to keep me going and one of them is to improve my general play. I've had games in this World Cup when I think "yes, we've won" but deep down you should have done things a bit better.

'I want to be able to find a way of doing those things better, for personal development, but also for going back to Newcastle and winning things

*The Aurora Borealis, as seen from Strandhill, Co. Sligo. Photograph: James Connolly.*

there. It's a great motivator and I've got lots to work on.'

It's clear he has a huge support network that he feeds off. His parents, his coaches, his team-mates, some of whom he wanted to be photographed with immediately, like Will Greenwood and Matt Dawson, who are always on either side of him in dressing-rooms, the 'hugely supportive' Paul Grayson and Mike Catt.

With increased fame will come countless commercial opportunities, which will require careful selection, not least as he won't want them to interfere with his devotion to practice and self-improvement.

He's been the centre of attention for much of the last two months, and he spoke of coming down to the team breakfast room, of sitting away from where the newspapers were stacked, and then having to move if a teammate sat down at the same table with a paper.

'It's a hard life avoiding it because that sort of thing comes with the job. At times you think "when will this stop?" and that's when you draw on energy from your teammates. That's when you sit down and realise it's not everything. It's a massive part of my life right now, and I want it to be massive, but at the end of the day I've got my family to go back to and it's a great life to go back to.'

And what will his impact be on the game? His example is as much one of diligence and the concept of practice making near perfect, as one of innate flair. But that's no bad thing. He is a fine role model in many ways. Actually, Eddie Jones, the Australian coach, perhaps put it best. 'There are probably kids out there in the Northern Hemisphere buying Adidas boots and practising their field goals, and probably a lot of them aren't going to sit down and have Christmas dinner with their parents. They're going to be out there practising.'

# Race is on to Save Apes from Extinction

*Declan Walsh, in Mubi, Congo*

The baby chimp squirmed in the corner of a mud-walled house, deep inside Congo's eastern forests. Eyes wide with fear, he desperately gripped a red blanket. Banana skins littered the ground. Overhead stood the poachers who killed his mother.

'I brought him here because you white men pay money for them,' said an aggressive man in a dirty T-shirt. The asking price was $2,000, he said. With a little bargaining, we could probably have got him for $20.

To parade his merchandise, he tried to scoop up the terrified chimp. It screeched deafeningly and he dropped it on its head. Did the poacher know that chimpanzees were headed for extinction? 'Yes, yes,' he said impatiently. 'Now how much are you going to pay?'

At the crisis meeting to save the world's great apes, which opened in Paris yesterday, experts told how mankind's closest living relatives have been pushed to the brink of extinction due to a combination of habitat destruction, poverty and unforgiving wars.

Great apes share more than 96 per cent of their DNA with humans; for chimpanzees the proportion is as high as 98 per cent. But every species –

*A baby chimpanzee held by poachers in Mubi village in eastern Congo rests by the foot of one of its captors. Photograph: Declan Walsh.*

*Photograph: Declan Walsh.*

including gorillas, orang-utans, chimpanzees and bonobos – is heading for annihilation within 50 years, according to the World Conservation Union.

'If there is a doomsday clock ticking, then it's at one minute to midnight,' said Mr Doug Cress of the Secretariat of Pan-African Sanctuaries. The Paris meeting brings together scientists, activists and officials from 23 African and Asian countries to revive the Great Apes Survival Project (Grasp), a UN initiative set up two years ago but which has had little impact.

The enormity of the task is clear in Kahuzi-Biega National Park in eastern Congo. Kahuzi-Biega is home to the Grauer gorillas, a rare sub-species also known as silverbacks. The last time it was safe to count, in 1996, there was an estimated 8,000. Now there are probably less than 1,000, of which only 120 are accounted for.

War and poverty has decimated the population. During the Congo's five-year war, which is now winding down, warlords and their gunmen seized control of vast swathes of park to mine coltan, a precious mineral used to manufacture mobile phones and other electronics. The miners cleared the forest, depriving the gorillas of their habitat. The soldiers shot them for food. The hunt for bushmeat, particularly in a country where 17 million people need food aid, also fuelled the slaughter.

'The Bantu women come to the forest to collect firewood for charcoal. The pigmy people come for honey and mushrooms. And they set traps in areas where gorillas live.' A photo gallery of 50 silverback gorillas hangs on the wall of the park headquarters. 'Every one of these is dead,' said ranger John Karekwa.

Mazaruka, one of the oldest gorillas, is lucky to be alive. Years ago his right hand was chopped off in an antelope trap. Rejected by most of his group last spring, the lonely male now wanders the park with one female and three-year-old Chubaka.

During the war, the beleaguered rangers controlled only 15 per cent of the 6,000-acre park. With the return of some stability, the park is slowly opening up. Now rangers say that poverty must be tackled to protect the remaining silverbacks. A local charity, the Pole Foundation, has started the work, employing dozens of ex-poachers as part of an ambitious re-education programme.

Pygmy trappers are being trained to chisel gorilla ornaments from wood instead of killing the real thing. Right now they are rushing to fill an order of 900 from the US. Sewing projects allow Bantu women to make money without entering the forest.

The race to save the great apes is on. If we lose even one single species of great ape, according to UNESCO, which is hosting the Paris meeting, 'we destroy part of the bridge to our own origins and part of our humanity.'

**FRIDAY, 28 NOVEMBER 2003**

# Combine harvester of Sinn Féin's election machine sweeps ahead in search of seats

*Frank McNally, in Belfast*

Like cross-dressing, cross-community voting is a minority taste in Northern Ireland.

But the extent to which the electorate was prepared to experiment on Wednesday might yet decide whether the Belfast Agreement can be saved when the last seats are filled.

As it was last night, the benefits of an open-minded approach to fashion were obvious. Sinn Féin, traditionally the more macho of the nationalist parties, discovered its feminine side years ago and has been borrowing the SDLP's clothes ever since.

Sadly for the latter party, the stuff looks better on the leaner, republican figure, and the Shinners were yesterday confirmed as Northern nationalism's preferred model. Similarly, on the unionist side, the DUP has been cleaning out David Trimble's wardrobe of late. The combination of traditional, below-the-ankle Paisleyism, with a tendency to show just enough leg to nationalism to make things interesting, has also proved popular.

The big issue last night was whether, amidst all the sartorial confusion, the UUP and SDLP would break the final taboo and swap their cast-off preferences to preserve David Trimble's precarious position as the leader of unionism.

One thing was obvious. The gang of four was tightening its grip on Northern politics, and everybody else was nowhere. There were no individual count announcements in Belfast's King's Hall, with election officials emerging from the count centre periodically to write the figures on a wall-mounted billboard.

And for the smaller parties the writing on the wall was grim. Not that they had any seats there to begin with, but West Belfast summed up their fate. The Alliance Party managed all of 75 votes, as the combine harvester of Sinn Féin's election machine swept ahead in search of five of the six seats. The SDLP's Joe Hendron – once the local MP – couldn't finish in the top half-dozen yesterday. But when the republicans' vote management fell just short, it was – typically – the DUP that slipped through the gap.

This was proportional representation, but not as we know it in the Republic. There were no

*David Trimble at Ulster Unionist Party headquarters in Belfast after paint was thrown at it. Photograph: PA/Paul Faith.*

*Gerry Adams (left) of Sinn Féin with Nigel Dodds of the Democratic Unionist Party during a radio interview after their respective parties emerged victorious in Northern Ireland's Assembly elections. Photograph: Dara Mac Dónaill.*

tallying operations. The media were not admitted to the counts, only to a draughty annexe, where those lucky enough to have seats hung on to them as grimly as any candidates.

There were no counts, officially, only 'stages', and percentage transfers saw the DUP pick up 0.09 of a preference from Sinn Féin's Gerry Kelly. However confused Irish journalists were, it was nothing to the bewilderment of some British ones, as they stared at the wall in blind incomprehension.

Raucous DUP cheers from the count centre last night greeted the election of another woman, when Diane Dodds – wife of Nigel – took the final seat in West Belfast.

This confirmed another trend in Northern politics: the DUP husband-and-wife team (Iris and Peter Robinson blazed the trail). And maybe it also edged closer the possibility of another marriage: a shotgun version between Paisleyism and Sinn Féin.

---

**MONDAY, 1 DECEMBER 2003**

# Forging Canada in Smithfield of Our Souls

*LockerRoom: Tom Humphries*

The kids got the gift of some ice time on Saturday night so we bundled off into Smithfield, strapped blades to their feet and pushed them away across the brilliant white floor. They came back of course, but still.

It was all a surprise. We lived in Chicago for a while back in the once upon a time when we were younger and the city there provided a great big ice-skating rink on State Street in the winter. It being free and we being stingy we pushed the kids off onto the rink plenty of times and sat drinking coffees and watching them narrowly avoid having their flailing limbs severed by lardassed Chicagoans attempting camp figure-of-eight manoeuvres. Fun.

That was Chicago though, where the waterways freeze over most winters and people have a chance to skate. Such things are part of the culture there. In Smithfield we expected to see the winter version of Guernica. Bodies everywhere, a great debris of limbs being pushed around the puddled ice, which would be pink from the mass bloodshed.

Instead all the Paddies and Patricias were skating like they grew up in Saskatchewan. There were young fellas who must never have seen ice except in supermarket fridge-freezers and they were whizzing around pulling sharp turns in front of young ones who responded with graceful pirouettes of indifference. All good fun till somebody loses an eye, we muttered bitterly. You have to hate young people.

Myself, I refrained from skating. Several reasons. Being elderly and infirm there was the fear of falling hard. Worse, the fear of falling hard and creating an embarrassing fissure either in my head or in the ice, the latter of which might require the rink to be closed for repairs as people gave me the hard stare.

Then there were the bad memories. Back in the seventies, while dating a grand young woman from Raheny, I was dragged – not once, mind, but twice – to the premium entertainment novelty of those times, the Rollerdisco in Sardis in Portmarnock. Southsiders who knew only the sophisticated pleasures of the Bective dance may wish to avert their eyes at this point.

The Rollerdisco was everything you didn't want in a night out if you were gangly and prone to finding your legs wrapped around each other like twined pipe-cleaners. It was also everything you didn't want if you were a boy subject to the desires of adolescence. There were no lurches, just those periods you spent clinging to the shoulders of your giggling partner as you attempted to stop the floor coming up to meet your face. The Rollerdisco deprived you of your winklepicker shoes and got the seat of your white trousers dirty. The Rollerdisco deprived you of everything you

*Royal National Lifeboat Institution lifeboats from Howth, Dún Laoghaire and Skerries pass the Bailey Lighthouse off Howth, Co. Dublin, to mark 200 years of lifeboats in Dublin Bay. Photograph: Eric Luke.*

needed as a young man with bad intentions. It deprived you of your health, your dignity and the free use of your hands.

It was a period when being a male at a disco you were obliged at some stage to remove your jacket and twirl it over your head, thus making yourself look like a centaur – half helicopter, half Elvis. You twirled and you also twitched your body in approximate time to the music. This was what we called nigh' fevah, nigh' fevaaaaah. Yes, we had a way to do it.

Nigh' fevaaaah manoeuvres could be mastered with practice. Rollerskating just couldn't. We had no way to do it.

The chief diversion of the grand young woman from Raheny was to prise my fingers from the perimeter wall, or her shoulders, and face me towards the other end of the rink. Then she'd lean

into the small of my back and push me off like a bobsled.

I had an idea that if I fell, some callous rollerskater would remove my fingers while skating by, so I kept my limbs and hands tucked in tight like an alpine skier. Even when I tumbled over I went down rigid, like a Baghdad statue.

Eventually it got to the stage where my date could shove me the length of the rink and until somebody hit me a passing glance or I skated over a cigarette butt I could sail through Sardis with the elegance of a shopping trolley being blown around a supermarket carpark. Occasionally people would skate along beside me pretending to brush the floor in front of me, as in the sport of curling. Not really. Things weren't that droll in Sardis in the seventies.

I think myself and the Raheny woman broke up after our second visit to Sardis. A relationship has no future when one partner has all the testos-terone and none of the dignity.

It struck me on Saturday night though that the world has changed. All those prissy little prohibitionists who scutter about the place warning us about drinking and smoking have never done a damn thing to provide us with any other form of winter entertainment. In my day it was drinking, smoking and shifting that you did on weekend nights and 200 years on it's the same prescription for getting through youth. Some blurred years and then a mortgage.

That's why seeing Irish people ice-skating on a Saturday night was such a thorough shock. At last a new way to bump into the other sex. The young fellas looked as suave as Cary Grant.

If we keep using the aerosol sprays and if the earth holds to its part of the deal on the global warming thing, we should soon be having very cold winters and tropical summers. Our entire sporting culture will be adapted; we'll skate on the Liffey and surf off Dollymount.

And we'll get better sports books too. With few exceptions, books about the GAA never actually capture its cultural importance. The books are all about who slapped who and who left the club when their family was insulted and who is a bigger fecker than you'd think. Meanwhile, there is a great, living canon of fine books to be had about ice hockey and ice skating and the broad pastimes of slipping and sliding.

In fact my theory has been that with this climate-prompted shift in our behaviour patterns we will get a big improvement in the general standard of our literature as a whole. No more books about dark, drink-soaked depressives standing on the edges of dark, forbiddingly moonlit lakes on dark rainy nights before they walk into a dark drowning

*Chinese students from the English Language Institute in Dublin, including (left to right) Hong Qu, Xue Wang, Li Wei Wei and Eli Zhang Hua, outside the Civic Offices following the official launch of the city's first Chinatown Festival to mark the Chinese New Year, the Year of the Monkey. Photograph: Matt Kavanagh.*

*Maura Mallon, a catering volunteer at the Royal Dublin Society, holds the hand of her daughter Brona, a Special Olympics Athlete and also a catering volunteer at the RDS, at the unveiling by the Taoiseach of a special commemorative sculpture in the grounds of Dublin Castle incorporating the names of all 30,000 volunteers who worked at the Special Olympics World Games last June. Photograph: Bryan O'Brien.*

depth in order to escape the memories/the family/ RTÉ's new reality show where you win a house in Mullingar.

The lake will be frozen and fringed with fairy lights and there'll be people roasting chestnuts on the bank and there'll be a carousel and nearby men will be fishing for mullet through holes in the Tolka and there'll be some winter hurling to be played with an orange *sliotar* on the crisp snow tomorrow and there'll be some spotty genius just skating around in circles all night thinking of what happy nothings he's going to write when he gets in close to the warm glow of the laptop. He'd be like the 03 team in the Sindo except that he'd wear warm clothes.

That thought sort of sobered me up. So I came home on Saturday night and got stuck into Ken

Dryden, the bard of ice hockey. 'Somewhere in our souls,' he said, 'is a spiritual Canada. Most probably its bedrock is of snow and ice, winter and the land. And if we were to penetrate it a little deeper, chances are we would find a game.'

And then I thought that, yes, somewhere in *our* souls too is a spiritual Canada or a damp version of the same. So yesterday I headed out to see some winter hurling. And I found it on a bedrock of mud and grass. It was so good that I decided never to bother with deodorising sprays ever again. Suits us being tight-lipped and damp.

Bah, forget the frozen lakes and the rinks, let the 03s and the Cary Grants suffer in rollerdiscos and winklepickers like their parents and their parents' parents before them. I'm telling you, unless you begrudge them their bloody youth they won't thank you later.

THURSDAY, 4 DECEMBER 2003

# Charlie's Local Election Express Pulling In at All Stations

*Budget Sketch: Frank McNally*

Like railway station announcers, Charlie McCreevy is frequently indecipherable. But he came over loud and clear yesterday as he trumpeted the delayed departure of the Government decentralisation scheme, stopping at Newbridge, Portarlington, Thurles, Mitchelstown, and 49 other towns, en route to next year's local elections. Passengers for Killarney – and the Department of Arts, Sport and Tourism – should change at Mallow.

Government backbenchers cheered the announcement and jumped on board. But the opposition was sceptical, and decided to wait for the next one, or maybe get a bus. Mr McCreevy's train had no timetable, they'd noticed, and with an allocation of only €20 million, it looked a bit low on fuel too. In autumn 2004, with the elections out of the way, the scheme might be delayed indefinitely by leaves on the line.

Nevertheless, as Mr McCreevy established an implementation committee to 'drive' the project, the opposition looked a bit forlorn standing on their (anti-Government) platform. Details of implementation might be vague, but the breadth of the plan – eight full Government departments, ministers and all – was every bit as radical as the Minister claimed. And the mere fact that names had finally been matched to places was designed to capture imaginations, as well as votes.

Particular talking points were the transfer of the Foreign Affairs development agency to Limerick (a bit harsh) and the planned move of

*Brother Richard (left) and Fr Liam, Cistercian Monks from Mount Saint Joseph's Abbey in Roscrea, Co. Tipperary, in the St Stephen's Green Shopping Centre, Dublin, to publicise the monks' first album – a collection of hymns in Latin, English and Old Irish in celebration of their life at the monastery. Photograph: Bryan O'Brien.*

50 Revenue officials to Limerick West, the constituency of Michael Collins. But there were plenty of others. And no sooner had the Minister sat down than there was a mass decentralisation of Government TDs, many of them rushing outside to shout the good news ('I'm on the train!') into mobile phones.

In an emptying chamber, Fine Gael's Richard Bruton acknowledged Mr McCreevy had 'pulled a rabbit out of a hat'; while Labour's Joan Burton suggested that this particular rabbit had made so many previous appearances at Government events, the Minister didn't even have to pull it. Both agreed that the plan could run out of steam the far side of June, and that the real story of the Budget was the continued erosion of incomes by stealth taxes and the Minister's failure to widen tax bands.

But with Mr McCreevy well insulated by the late tax windfalls, there was little controversial in this, the seventh 'chapter' of his self-styled fiscal epic. The social welfare increases were decent, the lobby to save film tax relief was satisfied, and even farmers refused to be angry last night. The closest he got to controversy was in announcing the phasing out of the 'Dublin mindset' from Government policy, which at first sounded like bad news for the Taoiseach, but turned out to be just another predicted effect of decentralisation.

In fact, if it hadn't been for this one big idea, chapter seven would have been his dullest yet. And the failure of the subsequent debate to take off was summed up when Ms Burton complained at one point: 'This is Christmas pantomime stuff.' To which the Greens' Paul Gogarty replied: 'Oh no it isn't!'

**FRIDAY, 5 DECEMBER 2003**

# China Takes to the Miss World Stage

*Clifford Coonan, in Sanya, China*

Miss Ireland, Rosanna Davison, wears a turquoise one-piece swimsuit cut away at the waist. She shakes her long blond hair during a poolside photo session at a tropical holiday resort on the Chinese island of Hainan.

As winner of the Miss Beach Beauty contest, the 19-year-old UCD sociology student is now a favourite to win China's first officially sanctioned beauty pageant in 54 years – and become Ireland's first Miss World. She was the first of 106 contestants to go through to tomorrow's final in Sanya city.

'It is great to be chosen from a lovely group of girls like this,' says Ms Davison, daughter of

pop-song writer and performer Chris de Burgh. She is keeping a low profile until the big day, accompanied by her father and boyfriend.

It's the kind of comment you'd expect from a beauty queen – but this is a country where until very recently beauty contests were considered bourgeois and disreputable, a hangover from pre-communist days when rich and powerful men attended pageants to choose a concubine. Just last year, Chinese officials closed down the first Miss China contest. The winner flew secretly to Puerto Rica for the Miss Universe finals – and came second runner-up. Back home, officials took notice.

A year later, China is in a pageant frenzy. As well as regular contests it has held a Miss Village Beautiful contest and a Most Beautiful Camel contest (the criteria: upright humps, lush hair and a mild temper). There was even a Miss Ugly contest in Shanghai, with the winner given thousands of euro to pay for plastic surgery.

Ireland may never have won Miss World, but Irish women are playing a significant role in this year's competition. As well as favourite Davison, TV personality and Dubliner Amanda Byram is co-hosting the evening. The former Ireland AM and Big Breakfast star, who now lives in Los Angeles, jumped at the offer.

'I literally went – I'm there! Immediately! There's just something about it that went click. I enjoy gigs I can have fun on, I don't like to think about things too much,' she said, settling in to a teak-wood chair at the Sheraton Sanya hotel.

A consumer boom in the world's most populous nation is feeding into a more relaxed attitude towards pageants, with officials hoping to make money from advertising and sponsorship as China surges ahead economically.

But in a sign that disapproving attitudes linger, the Communist Party mouthpiece newspaper, *The People's Daily*, insisted Miss World was not just an ordinary beauty pageant. 'Miss World is in the middle of moving away from being the kind of

*Miss Ireland, Rosanna Davison (centre), after being named Miss World Beach Beauty, together with runner-up Miss Switzerland, Bianca Nicole Sissing (right), and second runner-up Miss Bolivia, Helen Aponte Saucedo, in Sanya on China's tropical island of Hainan. Photograph: Reuters/Miss World Organisation.*

traditional beauty pageant that turns women into decorative objects,' it said recently. 'Miss World is increasingly becoming a link in our patriotic education and a forum for co-operation between countries,' the paper enthused.

In China there are fashion show catwalks in shopping malls and in front of department stores countrywide, while billboards advertising beauty products and fashion brands are everywhere – a far cry from the days when the only models celebrated publicly were workers and farmers.

But the Communist Party remains in charge, keeping a tight control on the media and tolerating no public dissent that might threaten China's image

abroad. After last year's debacle in Nigeria, when bloody rioting forced the contest to decamp to London at the last minute, organisers are clearly happy to have a secure environment for their contest.

'I was the driving force behind holding the contest in China. I love China,' says Miss World chief executive Julia Morley. Miss World is in talks with officials in Sanya city to return next year.

Local authorities on Hainan, an island province of white sandy beaches, sweeping bays and palm trees, paid €4.8 million for the licence to hold the event, and a further €3 million to upgrade roads and bridges. Work on a new theatre for the

*Kim O'Neill from The Teresian School in Donnybrook, Co. Dublin, keeping a close eye on the project she and classmates Abigail Cornwell and Aoife Quinn entered in the Esat/BT Young Scientist & Technology Exhibition. Photograph: Eric Luke.*

finals began in August. Yesterday, workmen were putting the finishing touches to it.

Aware of the contest's failing critical popularity, Ms Morley is determined to give it a more acceptable face. 'Beauty with a purpose' is the new slogan, and the main beneficiary is charity. Proceeds of a six-city, three-week tour of China by the Miss World road show will go to the China Charity Foundation.

Miss China, Guan Qi (21), insists there is more to Miss World than just commercial and political considerations. 'Holding Miss World in China is a great opportunity to show China's openness to the world,' says Ms Guan.

In an internet questionnaire on one of China's most popular websites, Sina.com, around 75 per cent of those surveyed approved of holding the competition in the country. Organisers expect Miss

World to attract a global TV audience of 2.5 billion viewers. It's proven a big hit with Chinese people – 50,000 people turned out in the city of Xian to get a glimpse.

*(Rosanna Davison went on to win the competition)*

**FRIDAY, 5 DECEMBER 2003**

# A Funny Way to Fight a War

*Shane Hegarty*

It was meant to spark a battle of the chat shows, but Eamon Dunphy's effort is bad enough to make the 'Late Late' look good.

It is three months to the day since 'The Dunphy Show's' début, and its host still cuts an awkward figure on stage at the Helix theatre, from

*Stephanie Barrett, aged 3, from the Little Angels Choir of St Joseph's Nursery School of Maryland, Dublin, dressing for her performance to mark the official opening of the Irish Farmers Association live crib outside the Mansion House, Dublin. Photograph: Matt Kavanagh.*

where his programme is broadcast. When he stands away from his desk, Eamon Dunphy's body looks unruly, as if his legs have taken fright and are straining for a return to cover. He introduces musical acts with a peculiar diffidence. He reads from the cue cards with the uncertain rhythm of a man squinting at an optician's wall chart. It was the same that opening night in September, but at least Dunphy could then take comfort in the knowledge that the kinks would be smoothed out in time.

They haven't been, and just as Dunphy should be looking forward to a well-earned Christmas holiday − he reportedly recorded tonight's show last weekend, to help get his holiday season off to an early start − the programme's impending five-week break is instead being construed as something more sinister: the beginning of the end, the first

cracks in the hull of TV3's flagship show. Almost 200,000 people are watching Dunphy every week. But 150,000 are watching Judge Judy every day.

There is a sense that 'The Dunphy Show' is not learning its lessons. A man once famed for his unpredictability fronts a programme that has developed a worrying monotony. Dunphy has overindulged in journalists, politicians and sports stars: the sort of people, in other words, he feels conformable talking to rather than those we necessarily want to hear.

At the beginning, for instance, that Peter Mandelson, Alastair Campbell and Robin Cook arrived in quick succession showed an enthusiasm for the machinations of the British Labour Party that will have been shared by few in the audience. Dunphy also has a wearisome habit of bringing almost every conversation around to the war in Iraq. When it's with Mandelson you can accept it. When it's with Chris Eubank it's time to turn over.

He remains an inconsistent interviewer, sometimes getting more than you would expect from his subject, sometimes getting nowhere at all. Even with sports stars he is unreliable. Robbie Keane, he explained, had been one of the guests he had been most keen on talking to, yet it was an interview of unremitting blandness. That he interviewed Roy Keane, whose autobiography he ghosted, represented only Dunphy's ultimate indulgence.

Outside of his specialist topics the guest list becomes shallow. Eubank, Keith Duffy, Peter Stringfellow and Jordan. This is increasingly the

*Dawn at Newgrange, Co. Meath, on 21 December. Photograph: Alan Betson.*

guest list of a Northern Ireland chat show. 'The Late Late Show' has the luxury of RTÉ's schedule from which to pluck guests. It can call on Hector Ó hEochagáin or raise Duncan Stewart from his hospital bed. Along with its more regular musical interludes, it at least gives the programme a comparative effervescence and a changing texture that Dunphy's lacks.

In fact, Dunphy's most bothersome achievement is to have made Pat Kenny look good. Kenny can explain a competition. He can introduce a guest. He can read from an autocue. He can stand up straight on national television. 'The Late Late Show', though, is the same programme with the same problems as it was pre-Dunphy. Nor has Kenny been upgraded. There are constant reminders of his weaknesses. He remains one of television's greatest straight men. His interview with Eddie Izzard last month was a classic of mortification, an interview during which Kenny attempted to match the comedian's pace only to be dragged along mercilessly.

Izzard is now as famous for his transvestism as he is for his comedy. 'The royal family,' began Kenny. 'Do you fancy any of them?' On Izzard's success in America: 'Did the success of Mrs Doubtfire help you?' You wanted to climb into the television and, on behalf of all of Ireland, dissociate yourself from the questions.

On other occasions, though, he has displayed notable composure. The only people to mention Dunphy on 'The Late Late Show' have been its guests, and Kenny has largely ignored the bait. 'The Dunphy Show', meanwhile, acts like the little guy trying to pick a fight with the ex-champ. Its Gay Byrne puppet sketches are a triumph of witlessness. It has mistaken spite for satire, and the result is a drain on the show's dignity and a constant reminder of an institution it has yet to erode. The show cannot forge its own personality while it continues to refer to that of another.

That, ultimately, is at the core of The Dunphy Show's problem. In both format and time slot it

*A gallop on Ballyheigue strand, Co. Kerry. Photograph: Dominick Walsh.*

chose to take on 'The Late Late Show' at its own game, but it may have found that its eyes were bigger than its stomach. Perhaps it was financial need, or maybe a mix of opportunism and bravado, that led it to decide to do that, but in doing so it gave itself no time to develop. It might have been wiser to launch on another night over a shorter time slot, to have played to both TV3's experience and Dunphy's strengths in a format that concentrated on itself rather than on what was happening across the dial.

Dunphy is right when he asserts that competition is good, but there are ways of being competitive without playing chicken with your opponent.

*(The following day, TV3 dropped 'The Dunphy Show')*

SATURDAY, 6 DECEMBER 2003

# Hector the Great

*Róisín Ingle*

Hector Grey didn't like the word cheap. The vast selection of light hardware, ornaments and souvenirs imported from the Far East and sold in his shop in Liffey Street, Dublin were not cheap, which he thought implied a certain tackiness. They were, more accurately, inexpensive. Even today, if you suggest to his son Alex that Hector Grey's was the original pound shop, he will tell you it was never a pound shop. We were the original bargain store, he corrects, as Hector looks down proudly from a large photograph on the wall of his office above the shop.

Of course his real name wasn't Hector, but that's what half of Dublin called him anyway. His real name was Alex Scott. He got the name of the shop from Hector Grey, a jockey in Australia. Alex, or Hector, wasn't from Dublin either. He travelled from Scotland to this country to investigate why the Irish were all emigrating. He married an Irish girl, but she didn't take to Glasgow life so they moved back to Dublin and he started selling things from a tray on Henry Street.

Then he started importing toys from Japan. Hector was one of the first to travel to Japan after the war. He had a tiny shop on Middle Abbey Street, across from the old Adelphi Cinema, selling toys and souvenirs. Souvenirs were the only item that had to have the country of origin stamped on them. But some English people didn't like the tag Made In Japan and wanted the souvenirs to be made in Ireland. Canny Hector got around this by printing *An tSeapáin tír a dhéanta* on the back of the ashtrays and the porcelain figurines, so the fussy English customers were none the wiser.

But it was toys and stocking fillers that made Hector Grey famous. My family used to get all our Christmas presents there. For £5 you would be able to buy for your brothers and sisters, and still have enough left over for marbles. It was like a treasure trove. It still is.

On a busy Thursday evening last week, I made one of my regular visits to the shop. There are clothes organisers for €4.50 or 24 colouring pencils for €2.50. Giant chalk sticks are competitively priced at €1.35 while a packet of eight kazoos is only €2.50. (We always got a kazoo in our stocking. It was the only other constant apart from a tangerine and chocolate coins.)

You can buy a pocket-sized travel brush with built-in shoehorn and a multi-purpose, spring-loaded holder for tea towels and still have change from a fiver. Mousetraps sit beside Sisal play mice for cats. And, of course, there are miles of tinsel and hundreds of tree ornaments all over the shop.

Hector Grey also stocks a range of religious paraphernalia. There are 3D Christmas cards featuring Jesus and Mary which have to be seen to be believed. And they are flying out of the shop, apparently. Alex says people his age, in their late 60s and 70s, are buying them. The cards are even more popular than the Jesus address books, which are inspired examples of the Christian collectables that sit easily alongside oil paints on the shelves at Hector Grey's.

This year our family are doing Kris Kindle for the first time, so we only have to buy one of our siblings a present, instead of all eight. This decision was driven by economic factors, but I'm thinking now that I could get something useful for all of them in Hector Grey's without breaking the bank. I mean, everyone needs cotton buds and at Hector Grey's a packet of 1,000 sells for €2.25, which, incidentally, would also buy you 100 incense sticks.

The shop is as much a part of Dublin folklore as the Ha'penny Bridge. Hector used to call it the metal bridge, and even at 81 he could be seen selling stuff out of boxes there before going up to The Oval for a few glasses of whiskey. That's what he did on the day he died in the 1980s, before he went home and fell asleep in his longjohns. It was a nice way to go, says Alex.

Alex has been working in Hector Grey's for exactly 50 years. He keeps telling his wife Sally that he will stop, but she doesn't believe him. She says, if you are giving it up, then why do you keep walking out the door every morning? As a young man he won a scholarship to Trinity College to study history, but his father told him that history wouldn't put meat on the table and that was that.

Alex doesn't know how long more he will be working, but he reckons his younger brother Robert will keep the business going for as long as he is able. After that the future of Hector Grey's is unsure. Alex's children are doctors and lawyers and dentists and computer programmers. None of Hector Grey's grandchildren has any interest in taking on the shop. We should treasure this gem

*Children from the Krishi rice market in Dhaka, Bangladesh. Photograph: Brenda Fitzsimons.*

while it's still around to sell cheap (sorry Hector) Jesus address books and Sacred Heart candles. Alex says they drew the line at religious ashtrays.

**TUESDAY, 9 DECEMBER 2003**

# No Food, No Pay, But a Glimmer of Hope

*Rosita Boland, in Dhaka*

The smell emanating from Dhaka's covered Krishi rice market is over-poweringly strong. The odour is not the usual Asian market smells of decaying rubbish, pollution and human waste but that of jute. The air is dense with fibres from thousands of rice-filled jute sacks. The sacks are stacked to the roof, making the dim interior even dimmer. Loose rice crunches underfoot on the filthy floor.

For a minute or two the place looks like a huge, anonymous warehouse; then I see that the market is carefully divided into alcoves, each presided over by its male owner. Each alcove has a home-made scales, one of the low wooden structures that serve both as bench and bed in Asia, and a few personal items, such as tin dishes, flasks and trays.

At the far end of the market, in the darkest corner of all, is a ramshackle stairway blocked by junk. We have to squeeze past and wait for our eyes to adjust before ascending the dank stairs to the rooftop. I don't yet know why we've been brought here by Plan, the international child-focused development aid organisation, on this first of four days visiting some of its Bangladesh-based projects. Then the door swings open.

On the flat roof of the market are some 60 children between eight and 13 years old. They are sitting in rows on strips of carpet in two groups,

*Children from the Krishi rice market in Dhaka, Bangladesh. Photographs: Brenda Fitzsimons.*

boys and girls, in the shade of sheds on the roof, which give some protection from the searing heat of the city. Neat little stacks of books, copies and pencils stand in front of each child, and blackboards are propped against the shed walls.

The stacks seem the only orderliness in the chaos of the urban landscape – the stumps of half-finished breeze-block buildings that are nonetheless occupied, the broken roads, the sea of rubbish that flows along the streets, the electricity wires that coil dangerously and randomly everywhere. Even by Asian standards Dhaka is a grim city, terrifyingly overpopulated – up to 15 million people in an area no bigger than Dublin – with a correspondingly disastrous infrastructure and slums nobody can enumerate.

Many of the boys on the roof smile and jostle each other. When the teacher's eye is temporarily off them, they scamper further down the roof to pet a tethered monkey. There is some vestige of mischief, of play, about the boys, but most of the girls fold their hands into their dresses and look solemn. They smile for the camera, then their smiles fade, as if they are not used to smiling much. All of them look about four years younger than they are: recent surveys have shown that Bangladeshi children are so malnourished that they are smaller and thinner than their counterparts of 50 years ago.

They work in the rice market from 6 a.m. to 6 p.m., seven days a week. They arrive at first light, to make tea for the men and to fetch their breakfasts. The rice market is owned and run exclusively by men, all of whom have homes elsewhere. The children run errands all day and keep the place tidy by sweeping up the rice that gets spilled when being weighed and bagged. The boys lift the sacks and carry them from place to place.

They are not paid for their work, but they are given any leftover food that the men they work for don't finish. They also get to keep and bring home whatever rice they have gleaned by sweeping it from the filthy floor. Most of the girls have at least

one parent they go home to, but the boys work and live full time in the rice market, sleeping on the floor, where rats run freely. The boys' families are in villages far from Dhaka or in slums where conditions are so bad that living in the market is preferable.

For two years, Plan, in association with Dhaka's Assistance for Slum Dwellers (ASD), has been running a school on the roof for these children. For two hours a day, from 3 p.m. until 5 p.m., they are allowed time off by 'their owners', as Shaida Begum, the programme manager, unconsciously describes them. The children are taught numbers, Bangla and some simple English. They also sing, play music and do art, activities they have requested. This two hours a day of learning is the only playtime they'll ever have. The teachers are provided by ASD and paid for and overseen by Plan, which also pays for the books and materials.

'I like singing,' says Ruma, who is nine, shyly, formally standing up. 'I want to learn how to read and write.' She has no known family name; her father is dead. She has three sisters, one elder and two younger. She picks up the bundle of twigs each child has, then squats to show us how she sweeps up the rice. Containers to hold the rice are precious, closely guarded by each child. Ruma's is a dirty old Red Cow powdered-milk can that she brings out from its hiding place behind the blackboard and returns, carefully, after her demonstration.

'I came from a village,' says Monir Hossen, a stick-thin, big-eyed 12-year-old boy who has been living in the rice market for two years. 'My family lived in a slum in Dhaka, but now they have gone back to the village. I stayed here because my family are too poor to keep me.' He grins widely. Clearly excited to be picked from the rest of the boys to talk to us, Monir is eager to please, and he answers my questions, but he looks at me in amazement when I ask if he gets scared at night, sleeping in the rice market. 'No!' he laughs. There is no self-pity or sadness in his voice as he tells his story; Monir is 12 in years but much, much older in experience.

There is a more subtle agenda to the children's schooling: the teachers, who report back to Plan, also act as unofficial supervisors and counsellors; the children are encouraged to confide in them. 'The girls are sometimes asked to massage their employers,' says Muzammal Hoque of ASD. 'Their employers get excited and …'

Sexual abuse by the men who run the market is unhappily common, although it has become less frequent with the schooling, as the children now have someone to report the abuse to. Sometimes, when a Plan contact or teacher speaks out, the children's owners are embarrassed into leaving them alone for a while. But there is no official system to take action in cases of abuse. I find myself unable to stop wondering if this is why the girls don't smile.

When the children turn 14 – the age when one is considered an adult in Bangladesh – they must leave the market. The boys go to work elsewhere; the luckier girls are married off. The Plan people discreetly point out one child. Little Shanaj, her shining hair tied in peach ribbons, was taken off the street as an abandoned baby and is being raised by an 'aunt'. Shanaj does not know it yet, but when she leaves the rice market she will be sent to work as a prostitute.

There are no easy answers to Bangladesh's problems. With 120 million people, it is the world's most densely populated country. It is also one of the poorest. Neither Plan nor any other aid organisation can yet provide solutions for the thousands of children who face similar futures to that of Shanaj: Dhaka alone has 225,000 abandoned children. But aid must start somewhere. The two hours of schooling a day that Plan provides in such basic circumstances offers a small

*Five-year-old Seamus Woods from Baltimore in the USA runs towards his Granny, Mary Woods from Tallaght, Co. Dublin, after arriving at Dublin Airport to spend Christmas with her. Photograph: Bryan O'Brien.*

but vitally important project: if these children did not have it, they would have nothing at all to enliven and enrich their long, hard days.

Sadeka Akhter is standing under mango trees in her lovely village of Dhalodia, near Gazipur, an hour north of Dhaka. Chickens run about under-foot, bamboo rustles nearby and the lush rice paddies we walk through to get here are shoulder high, due for harvest in three weeks.

The 13-year-old is holding a well-thumbed blue notebook, which she usually keeps propped up beside plates and glasses on a shelf in her house. It is Sadeka's savings book. In 2001, Plan gave money to this village and 23 others in the area for a micro-finance project, to be administered like a credit union. Anybody over 15 can take out a loan to buy equipment for work or for personal use. They have to pay it back within a year, at 4 per cent interest.

Under-15s are encouraged to save the few taka that come their way. In Sadeka's village, 76 of its 400 children now have savings books. 'My mother gave me 50 taka to start off,' Sadeka explains. The first entry in her book is for June 26th, 2001; she has since saved 378 taka (€5.40).

There are four children in her family: an older sister and a younger sister and brother. Her father, like many other Bangladeshi men, is labouring in Saudi Arabia. He hasn't been home in two years, but he sends money back, and Sadeka's mother gives her a few taka from time to time. She doesn't want to say so in front of her male translator, but later I'm told she uses some of her savings to buy sanitary towels. She is saving for her eventual marriage and hopes to reach 2,000 taka (€28.50), a sum that no longer seems as unattainable as it once did.

In the far north of Bangladesh, around Saidpur, close to the Indian and Nepalese borders, Plan runs several other projects. One is a community market-gardening project, which children are also involved in. The village of Balapara, with 735 households, is a pilot project that has been running for three years

in conjunction with the Rural Improvement Foundation, a local non-governmental organisation (NGO). It has proved so successful that it is to be repeated in eight other local villages.

Flooded so often, the soil in Bangladesh is exceptionally fertile, as so much of it is pure silt — sandy and loamy. The area round Balapara was traditionally used for growing tobacco, which is a good cash crop but exhausts the soil. Few vegetables were grown. Plan put up money for saplings – trees help reduce soil erosion – and seeds; the NGO provided training for each family to plant and maintain a market garden.

Sumantho Bula, a 17-year-old, has been help-ing his mother garden since the project started. For two years, in their perfectly kept plot beside their mud house, they grew only vegetables; now they also have 40 lemon trees, as well as beans, aubergines, tamarind, spinach, melons and cauli-flower. Sumantho's father is dead, now he and his mother work full time in the garden. 'One of my jobs is to get the compost,' he says. This is water hyacinth, found in local rivers but used as compost only since the beginning of the project. He carries it home on his back. The other form of compost is dung.

Sumantho has two younger brothers, and he is teaching them what he knows. Their jobs are watering and making sure the village animals are kept at bay, both by chasing them out and by regularly checking the fencing round the plot. He also knows how to raise beds and transplant seedlings, when produce is ready for harvest and exactly how much everything fetches at the local market, as he is the one who does the selling.

As is usual in Bangladeshi families, he doesn't get to keep any money himself; it all goes to his mother. 'Lemons are one taka, two for a big one. Each of our trees gives about 100 lemons; one harvest.'

He presents me with a huge lemon, straight off the tree, and it has the freshest, zingiest citrus tang I've ever inhaled. From depending almost exclusively on a rice- and potato-based diet three years ago, this family, like the 734 others in the village, is now impressively self-sufficient. They keep what vegetables and fruit they need for themselves and sell the excess in the market beside their house. His own favourite produce from the garden is red spinach.

So does Sumantho do any cooking? When he hears this translated, he howls with laughter, as does the male translator. 'No, no,' he squeals, 'cooking is women's work!' No matter where you are in the world, it seems, some things remain constant.

**MONDAY, 15 DECEMBER 2003**

# Bremer has the Pleasure of Relating the News

*Jack Fairweather, in Baghdad*

When Ambassador Paul Bremer entered the conference hall to a round of applause, people had already guessed what was coming. But Bremer's words – 'Ladies and Gentleman. We've got him' – nonetheless brought the house down. He stood before the room, packed with Iraqi and Western media and civilian administrators, flanked by the senior commander of Coalition forces in Iraq, General Sanchez, and Iraqi governing Council president Adnan Pachachi.

Roars rose up from Iraqi journalists, US officials, and a phalanx of soldiers, who had come to witness a moment of history. One Iraqi journalist began shouting 'Long live Iraq, death to Saddam.' Several Iraqis wept silently as Bremer continued.

'For decades hundreds of thousands have suffered at the hands of this cruel man. For decades Saddam Hussein divided citizens against each other. For decades he threatened and attacked their neighbours. Those days are over forever.'

Saddam's arrest will come as a personal victory for the man President Bush hand-picked to turn around the fortunes of the country. Iraq was teetering on the brink of chaos when Bremer, a former head of US State Department's counter-terrorism office, moved into the confines of Saddam's press conference.

Although the security situation has deteriorated, the progress that has been made in rebuilding Iraq's infrastructure is seen as being a result of his leadership.

'Now it is time to look to the future, to your future of hope, to the future of reconciliation. Iraq's future has never been more full of hope,' Bremer said. Bremer showed little emotion and was keen to hand the centre of attention to his Iraqi counterpart, Adnan Pachachi.

But there was little disguising his happiness when he described not getting a wink of sleep all night. Privately, the thought that he had finally caught the man he has accused of being at the centre of anti-coalition attacks had made Bremer 'as pleased as punch', according to one Coalition Provisional Authority official.

One journalist asked what was the progression of phone calls made after he heard the news of Saddam's arrest. Bremer smiled wryly. 'The minute-by-minute account will have to come out at a later date.' There were jokes among the press corps of a summer bestseller. 'This is the first good news he had to announce since he's got here,' said another official. 'He deserves it.'

As General Sanchez stepped forward to describe the details of the operation and a video put up on giant screens in the auditorium relayed images of Saddam's hideout, the ambassador stepped demurely backwards.

The moment of theatre had already passed, although pictures of the unkempt-looking Saddam still raised gasps from the auditorium.

There was time left for a few final questions. 'Does this mean we can all go home now?' asked the Italian journalist. There were smiles all around from the triumvirate. 'Not to my knowledge,' said General Sanchez with a nod and a grin from Bremer.

*Lieutenant General Ricardo Sanchez, commander of U.S. forces in Iraq (centre), with Paul Bremer, top US administrator in Iraq (right), and Governing Council President Adnan Pachachi (second from left), shows images of Saddam Hussein in custody during a news conference in Baghdad. Photograph: AP/Dusan Vranic.*

On the streets of the city, the first rumours of capture were greeted by a volley of speculative gunfire at lunchtime. The confirmation brought a moment of shocked silence as the face of the dictator flashed on television screens in electronics stores where many had gathered.

'I don't believe it,' shouted Khalid Mahmud, at one store as the news broke, but his brother was already dashing outside with an AK47 to fire jubilant rounds in the air.

As evening fell the party had moved out onto the street. The electricity was out, but for once no one seemed to care now the news was released. Wasam Adain, 23, a music shop owner, was just shutting up shop to find members of his band. 'Thank you, Bush. I shall be playing my trumpet until the dawn,' he said. A band began knocking out a beat on an empty jerry can.

On Baghdad's main commercial street another band had already begun playing: tribal drums and wailing horn. 'Saddam has gone the way of other tyrants,' the revellers sang, as they apparently made up the verses on the spot.

American soldiers also celebrated. Helicopters buzzed overhead, while soldiers 'high-fived' on the ground. 'This is what I would call a morale booster,' said one American soldier.

**TUESDAY, 16 DECEMBER 2003**

# Questioners Find Saddam Unrepentant, Defiant and Utterly Beaten

*Jack Fairweather, in Baghdad*

Saddam Hussein had just woken up from a nap. The unkempt beard was gone and he appeared to be in excellent health in a long white shirt and blue overcoat. He sat with legs crossed and eyes down, though as the six men entered – Paul Bremer and Lt Gen. Ricardo Sanchez, the coalition's top commanders, and four members of Iraq's governing council – Saddam raised his eyes. 'Shifty eyes,' recalled Mawfak Rubaie. 'He couldn't look any of us in the eye.'

At the moment of his arrest on Saturday, Saddam said little more than 'My name is Saddam Hussein. I am the president of Iraq and I want to negotiate.' 'President Bush sends his regards,' came the reply from a US soldier.

At the moment of his capture, the man behind the matted, greying beard and wild hair remained as inscrutable to Iraqis as he did during 35 years as a tyrant of the country.

But the following day, on Sunday afternoon when meeting members of the governing council, he revealed himself to be unrepentant, defiant and utterly beaten. 'His sacred halo was gone,' said Rubaie simply.

The ostensible purpose of the meeting was to confirm Saddam's identity, but that had already been achieved by the help of Tariq Aziz, apparently a fellow inmate at the military base the members were flown to on Sunday afternoon.

Instead, the purpose of the meeting was to have the chance to tell Saddam 'what a son of a bitch' he was, according to one official. But to begin with, the meeting was strangely cautious and respectful for all the emotions that must have been bubbling up inside Saddam's interrogators.

Mawfak Rubaie had been tortured under Saddam's regime in the late 1970s for political dissent. All four members of the council who were brought to meet Saddam – Mawfak Rubaie, Ahmad Chalabi, Adnan Pachachi and Adel Abdul Mehdi – had opposed his rule for decades.

'I asked him why he had committed so many crimes against the Iraqi people,' said Adnan Pachachi, who served as Iraq's foreign minister before the rise of the Baath Party. 'He said Iraq needed a just and firm leader. I told him he was an unjust and despotic ruler, at which he

just turned up his nose.'

Saddam proceeded to dismiss his role in gassing the Kurds and ordering the creation of mass graves for tens of thousands of Iraqis. 'These people are just thugs and hooligans,' he said, Rubaie recalled. 'He was diffident, uncaring but when I looked into his eyes I knew I was looking into pure evil. I could see it in his eyes and in his face.' Saddam only appeared genuinely flustered when cornered about his brutal suppression of the Shias following the 1991 Gulf War.

At that point he looked at Bremer and Sanchez, who up until then had remained silent. 'It was as if he was saying protect me from them. I think he feels safer with the Americans,' said Rubaie. 'He's probably right.'

Chalabi then asked him about his role in the post-war violence aimed at American troops, an aide to Chalabi said. Saddam responded that he gave a speech ordering the Iraqis to take up arms against the Americans and that is what they had done. He appeared to be back in dictator mode, at which point the party got up to leave. Saddam suddenly didn't seem to want them to go.

'"Is that all?" his expression seemed to say,' Rubaie recalled. But as the others left, Rubaie stayed behind. 'I had one last thing I wanted to tell him,' Rubaie said. 'I stood there and put the curse of God on him in this life and forever in the hereafter.' Saddam sat there swearing blindly, but then the door was closed and he was once again left alone with his thoughts and terrible deeds.

Yesterday, he was remaining silent, although his capture had led to the arrest of several top regime figures in Baghdad, US military officials said.

Documents found in a briefcase when he was captured have helped to unravel the workings of at least one terrorist cell in the capital. 'We've got Saddam's briefcase and a lot of leads,' a senior official said. 'So far we've tracked down the key players of one cell and we've learnt how other terrorist groups can operate.'

Officials would not give the name of the men arrested yesterday, but said they were prominent Baath Party members who had been under surveillance for some time.

Further raids are expected in the following days, officials said, but Saddam himself has shown little sign of wanting to spill the beans. Although Lt Gen. Sanchez, the top US military commander in Iraq, described Saddam as talkative, other officials dismissed suggestions that the former president was co-operating with interrogators.

At Baghdad International airport, where Saddam was held on Sunday, one military said: 'He's been just about as close to being defiant as he can be without getting into trouble.' The US Defence Secretary, Donald Rumsfeld, said: 'He has not been co-operative in terms of talking or anything like that.'

Some people believe Saddam has been moved to military facilities in Qatar, where interrogation will resume at improved facilities there, although this has been denied by a member of the governing council.

So far it is unclear what evidence, if any, troops uncovered of Saddam's possible operational control over the guerilla war being waged against the US-led occupation forces and those seen as collaborating with them.

Officials announced they found no communications equipment, maps or other evidence of a guerrilla command centre at Saddam's hiding place. But American officials are sure that Saddam has a wealth of knowledge on the resistance: it is a question of getting the information from him as quickly as possible before it becomes outdated. Officials remained confident Saddam would eventually crack under pressure.

Thirteen high-ranking figures from the list of the 55 most wanted of the deposed regime remain at large, including Saddam's deputy, Izzat Ibrahim al-Douri, whom US officials say may be directly organising resistance.

'I'm sure he was giving some guidance to some

*Saddam Hussein sporting a beard immediately after his capture, having been found hiding in an underground chamber near his home town of Tikrit, north of Baghdad; and after he was shaved by US military authorities. Photographs: Reuters/US Army.*

key figures in this insurgency,' said Brig. Gen. Mark Hertling. 'Put it this way, we know he's got the goods. It's a just a matter of time before we get them out of him.'

---

**WEDNESDAY, 14 JANUARY 2004**

# Spy Who Came Out of the Cold and Went Into the Kitchen

*Clifford Coonan, in Beijing*

What do spies do when there's no war left to fight? The end of the Cold War left Col. Steffen Schindler, head of military intelligence at the East German embassy in Beijing, jobless.

After the collapse of communism in Europe in 1989, fictional spy Ted Mundy, hero of John le Carré's latest novel, *Absolute Friends*, became a tour guide in Bavaria.

Schindler, the German Democratic Republic's top spy in the Chinese capital, swapped wire taps for a butcher's knife.

'One day they told me after 25 years of service that I didn't need to come into the work the next day. They said, you can go back to the GDR and sign on the dole,' says Schindler, speaking in the broad dialect of his native Saxony.

'I was 42 years of age – I had to do something.' A good-humoured man in his 50s with a ready smile, Schindler now runs a German food company and a popular restaurant called Schindler's Filling Station, near the Irish embassy in Beijing's diplomatic district.

Sipping a Wernersgruener pilsner in his restaurant on a sub-zero Beijing January evening, Schindler is happy to talk about his Cold War experiences but plays down the cloak-and-dagger elements of spycraft.

'Military intelligence is chiefly about analysing events and concepts and strategies,' he says. 'I was in a situation once where I was tailed by several cars. You have to make a decision: should I do something or do I let it go? Or should I just go home and drink a whiskey on my balcony? Which is what I did,' he says.

He rejects the popular perception that East Berlin was supporting groups such as the IRA and Germany's Red Army Faction in a bid to destabilise Western governments.

'Even in the worst depths of the Cold War there was no military link with groups like the IRA or the RAF. We saw them as separatist terrorist organisations. They didn't fit with the party's theoretical basis, they were anarchists and anarchists were undesirables. The IRA had no genuine national goals as far as we were concerned. And there was the whole religious angle. We weren't interested,' he says.

'We were interested in UNITA, SWAPO, the ANC,' he says, referring to the guerrilla groups of Angola, Namibia and South Africa. 'They seemed like real national liberation movements.' Schindler's job meant he knew Cold War legends such as master spy Markus Wolf, but strict hierarchies within the East German intelligence services meant it was unlikely that Wolf was aware of him.

When the Berlin Wall, or the anti-fascist protection barrier as it is known in the GDR, fell, he was surprised at the pace of change, with reunification of the two Germanys coming the next year. Too hasty, in Schindler's view.

'The euphoria of the Wall coming down should not have infected the government. It should have kept its foot on the brake a bit,' he says. There was no room in a unified Germany for former spies, leaving Schindler looking for something to do.

A group of top intelligence officers from several embassies, including the United States and Britain, would meet regularly in Beijing for informal talks and a few drinks. A cosy picture that contradicts the traditional image of Cold War hostilities.

*Emmet Kane, a woodturner from Castledermot in Co. Kildare, framed by Sky Burst, a carved oak with gold leaf at the Showcase Ireland fair in the Royal Dublin Society which was officially opened by Mary Harney. Photo: Cyril Byrne.*

It was through this loose alliance of fellow military attaches that Schindler found his new career. After a tip-off from his Algerian colleague, Schindler got into the slaughtering game and soon found himself back in Germany learning to be a butcher.

'The head of a German meat firm said I could re-train as a butcher in four months, which meant I wasn't qualified to make sausages – that takes much longer,' says Schindler.

He came back to China in 1991 where he managed a joint-venture slaughterhouse, then set up a butcher's shop in 1992. In 1999 he set up a company providing German food and in 2002 he opened Schindler's Filling Station.

Schindler enjoys talking about his restaurant, which serves central and southern German cuisine, with the occasional Berlin speciality, and beers from the former GDR.

But Schindler's first love was the military. 'I loved being in the military. I grew up with the army. It was a great career. I miss that.' Schindler is not what you expect a spymaster to look like, but then John le Carré would no doubt tell us that is exactly how a master of espionage should appear.

'I love John le Carré's books. I have them all. But what John le Carré describes is slightly different from my metier. The things that happen in le Carré happened once upon a time, but we now live in the age of satellite photography, high tech

*Former Fine Gael justice minister Paddy Cooney entering Leinster House to speak to the Oireachtas committee investigating the Dublin and Monaghan bombings of 1974. Photo: Frank Miller.*

communications equipment, infra red technology.

'The modern media works like an intelligence service – if something happens, it's around the world straight away. No intelligence service can compete.'

**SATURDAY, 17 JANUARY 2004**

# Call Me Mr President

*Frank McNally*

Following consultations with my family and a number of trusted advisers, I have decided to let my name go forward as a candidate for the office of president. I am fully aware that this is the greatest honour the people can bestow upon a fellow citizen, and seeking it is not a step I take lightly. I offer myself with a sense of profound humility, although I can't

promise this will last if I get elected.

I am also conscious of the greatness of former presidents in whose footsteps I hope to follow: presidents such as Douglas Hyde, Éamon de Valera, and that other guy in between them, whose name I can never remember. Not for one moment do I pretend to such eminence. But should I win the position of head of State, my only wish will be to serve others: at least in the event – admittedly unlikely – that my entire household staff is simultaneously indisposed.

It is now 14 years since Ireland had a male president. This has been a heady period in the life of the State. It has seen the greatest economic boom in our history, unprecedented cultural and sporting success, and the growth to adulthood of the Corr sisters. We have now entered a period of retrenchment, however; and with this in mind, mine would be a more sober presidency. I use the word 'sober' in the broad sense. Even a president is entitled to a social life.

My vision of Ireland is in keeping with our straitened times. The land which I would desire would be the home of a people who valued material wealth only as the basis for right living; a land whose countryside is bright with cosy homesteads (and not, during December, with garish, illuminated plastic figurines!); a land joyous with the contests of athletic youth, and the laughter of happy maidens (or *vice versa*). And a land whose firesides would be forums for the wisdom of old age, provided nobody rambled on too much.

Of course, many people will say that the presidency is meaningless. But I know that the €230,000 salary would mean a lot to my bank manager, for one. And besides, I believe the role's potential has not been fully explored by previous incumbents.

Among the few discretionary powers available to the president, for example, is the power to convene an emergency meeting of both houses of the Oireachtas. As president, in a gesture to my former colleagues in journalism, I would convene such meetings regularly, especially during August, when there's nothing else happening. At Christmas too. Trying to fill the paper on New Year's Day can be a real killer.

The role could be stretched in other areas as well. Take the notorious 'red carpet incident' during last year's Six Nations rugby decider at Lansdowne Road. It is generally accepted that the President Mrs McAleese reacted to Martin Johnson's snub with great dignity, and I agree. On the other hand, the President is supreme commander of the defence forces. Maybe it's a guy thing: but in her position I would have at least threatened war with England, to see how Johnson reacted.

Another area where I would have acted differently was her decision – at the request of the Taoiseach – to donate a parcel of Áras land to Dublin Zoo, for the African Plains Project. I deeply regret this. As president, I would work for the reintegration of the national territory, peacefully, and with the consent of a majority of the zoo's population. Also, if the Army was game, I'd be up for seizing the polo grounds. Who plays polo in a modern democracy, anyway?

The presidency now ending has famously been 'a presidency of embrace'. Again, I would not be found wanting in this department. As president, I would embrace everyone and everything, with the possible exception of any interns who found themselves working in the Áras during my time there.

As the head of State who would most likely have to host the first visit since independence of a British monarch, I would also extend the hand of friendship to Queen Elizabeth. I would not extend the red carpet, though; at least not fully. Suffice it to say it might – accidentally-on-purpose – not reach all the way out to the royal helicopter. Let her walk on the grass, for a change, and see how that big gorilla Johnson likes it.

My campaign slogan will be 'A Presidency for the People'. However, if the right sponsor becomes available, the bit about 'the people' is

*Gordon Crockard from Newtownards in Co. Down takes to the air during the World Motocross Championship at the Point Theatre in Dublin. Photo: Alan Betson.*

negotiable. I'm not going to get hung up on details. The main thing is that I have a strong sense of priorities.

If I had to say what single thing I would hope to achieve during my seven years in office, it would be this: free All-Ireland final tickets every year!

Although I will accept support from all quarters, my presidential campaign will reach out in particular to the little guy. The message is: give me your tired, your poor, your huddled masses yearning to breathe free. But don't give them to me until after I'm elected. And even then, make sure and ring first, to see if I'm in.

**TUESDAY, 20 JANUARY 2004**

# Verdict on Bridge Evidence Causes a Stir

*Court Sketch: Carl O'Brien*

As the packed courtroom gasped, Ian Bailey closed his eyes, leaned forward slightly, and whispered to himself. It was a rare and revealing moment.

For most of the case he stared impassively into the middle distance as witness after witness gave their evidence. Under fierce cross-examination over five days he rarely lost his composure. Even the judge, a seasoned observer of Circuit Court cases, was moved to comment that he was an exceptionally 'cool witness'.

But even Mr Bailey could not prevent an emotional flicker from registering when it became clear he was going to lose the majority of actions he had taken to restore his damaged reputation.

From early in the day the sense of anticipation was building up inside the old Atkins garden centre, the temporary headquarters of Cork Circuit Court.

For two weeks before Christmas the sight of Mr Bailey and his partner, Ms Jules Thomas, accompanied by a scrum of photographers

and cameramen, had stopped traffic outside the courthouse.

Yesterday morning, without his partner, he evaded an even larger throng of Irish, British and French media by arriving early through a side entrance at around 9.15 a.m. By the time Judge Patrick J. Moran arrived it was packed with media, gardaí involved in the original murder investigation, barristers, members of the public and the local French consul, Françoise Letellier.

Judge Moran began his 40-minute judgment and listed the evidence given by individual witnesses and neighbours, contradicting statements made by Mr Bailey earlier in the case. When the judge said he accepted that Mr Bailey was a violent man, there was quiet murmuring around the room. When he said Mr Bailey 'liked notoriety' and 'courted publicity' there were more glances exchanged.

But the key moment came when the judge listed the evidence of Mrs Marie Farrell, one of a procession of neighbours, former acquaintances and shopkeepers, who told of their experiences with Mr Bailey. She was the woman who, in a nervous but determined voice a few weeks earlier, told the court she saw him at a bridge close to Ms Sophie Toscan du Plantier's house early on the morning of the murder.

'Mrs Farrell said she came here reluctantly,' Judge Moran said, and paused briefly. 'On the balance of probability, I accept Mrs Farrell's evidence that who she saw around Kealfadda Bridge was Ian Bailey.'

An audible gasp went around the court. Solicitors looked up from their furious note-taking. And Ian Bailey closed his eyes, moved forward, and whispered to himself.

Whatever he felt like on the inside, by the time he left the courtroom yesterday, Mr Bailey seemed to have regained his old composure. Once again he stared impassively into the middle distance, battled his way through the hordes of media, and into a waiting car.

*Ian Bailey, who was interviewed by gardaí investigating the 1996 murder of Sophie Toscan du Plantier, leaves Cork Circuit Court after winning a libel action against two newspapers. However, he lost his case against six others and was branded a violent man by the judge. Photo: Haydn West.*

**TUESDAY, 20 JANUARY 2004**

# PS, I've Made a Fortune

*Kathy Sheridan*

OK, let's cut to the chase. Your first 10 chapters charm a UK publisher into parting with £150,000 (more than €200,000) for a two-book package. In a separate deal publishing house Hyperion lays out $1 million (about €800,000) for the US rights. Meanwhile, publishers from 22 countries around the world are ripping out their chequebooks to grab the rights for their territories. Then one day you're out shopping, excavate the mobile from your bag and, hey, it's Wendy Finerman, the Hollywood producer who made *Forrest Gump*. She just wants to congratulate you on the book and mention that her screenwriter might be in touch for a dig out with characterisation. That's another $100,000 up front for the film rights – oh, and $500,000 more if they make it to the first day of filming.

Of course, no 22-year-old first-time novelist would get away with a plot like that. In fact, plenty of people say no 22-year-old should get away with that kind of thing in real life. It stands to reason that it's only because her father is Bertie Ahern. As theories go, it makes little sense. A nanosecond's consideration of a typical chick-lit reader in Tennessee or Thailand, never mind a hard-nosed Hollywood producer (whose screen-writer, Steven Rogers, is into his second draft and hasn't troubled the author so far), should quash it.

*Cecelia Ahern. Photo: Bryan O'Brien.*

Cecelia Ahern shrugs in the manner of someone who has heard it all. 'I'm really proud of Dad, and it's great to be linked to him, and I can understand that in marketing you need a whole new angle, but it's an insult to the publishing world to say that they would buy something simply because of that.'

What must it be like for her father to have two daughters who are richer than him? (Ahern's sister, Georgina, is married to Nicky Byrne of Westlife.) 'Poor Dad,' she laughs. 'And he works harder than the two of us put together. But politics is his absolute passion and he's reached the job, and I can understand … It makes him happy. He does it 24/7. With Dad, for the amount of time he puts into it, it has to be the passion.'

It is immediately clear when she is uncomfortable with a topic; her face flushes bright pink, to match her loose-fitting jumper. Sitting in a comfortable bedroom in the Merrion Hotel in Dublin, she has presented herself for interview without a minder or tape recorder, with minimal make-up and looking not a day over 16.

She signs the chit for the coffee rather awkwardly, betraying nothing of the flash, been-there-done-that persona one might expect of someone who has already been fêted around US booksellers, hitting four states a day, and who has been interviewed, flattered and photographed for everything from *USA Today*, *Vogue* and *Marie Claire* to *Time* and *People* magazine, as well as sharing the spotlight with nine other 'rising artistic talents' in the *Observer* magazine's edition on the best and brightest of 2004.

She is persuasive in her repeated insistence that she is a 'shy' and 'very solitary' person. The odd thing is that this woman who grew up in the media shadow of a high-profile father chose to study journalism and communications, of all things, at Griffith College, Dublin. 'What I've learned is that I crave privacy. It's the kind of person I am. I think privacy is the most sacred thing ever, and once you've lost it you've lost something very special. I have such a private life. I just want to talk about my book. And it is just a book. I'd really be at home if it was not for this book.'

And although she might flush bright pink while refusing to comment on unwelcome topics, she is resolute. 'I'm well able to say "no comment" when I don't want to talk about something. I've grown up reading awful things about Dad, and, yeah, things do sting a bit, but it wears off. I just feel sorry for Dad. He is such a nice man, it's horrible.' She is equally adamant, however, that

people cannot be dragged into the limelight by the media unless they choose to be. 'My mother stayed out of it. I think you can walk into it … it's completely by choice.'

Her words are borne out by her actions. She ignored the old first-time-author dictum that you write about what you know. 'It's called imagination,' she says brightly. 'I was very conscious that people would be looking for autobiographical stuff. I went out of my way to make this different [from my life], and I was showing it to my mother and family members all the way through. You don't put family members in a book – and Holly [the central character] is nothing like me. It's not a diary, it's fiction.'

So how did she garner her insights into, say, bereavement? 'I don't know anyone who's lost

*Northern Ireland's education minister, Jane Kennedy MP, announcing changes to the North's secondary school exams, and the abolition of the 11 Plus test. Photo: William Cherry/Pacemaker.*

anyone that I'd be even close enough to to talk about it. I'm alone a lot. I think a lot. I question myself a lot. I went into the depths of my imagination. You look at people around you and you learn.' The large family scenes? 'That's just fiction.' The incredibly united, calm, supportive parents? A tad unrealistic, perhaps? 'It's not about them. It's about Holly, and they are among the people who were there for her.'

We tease this out and she holds her ground. 'I see older people all the time holding hands … don't you?' But is this marriage not somewhat idealised? 'I don't go into their … into their … It was about Holly, and they were there for her and that was their role in her life. If it was a book about her parents, then perhaps I could go into things that happened over the years, problems in their own marriage; there could be a story there. But, generally, I think there are some people who have happy marriages. I think in some cases it can work. I think in a lot of cases it just can't. People change, people grow apart, and it does happen. And you can fall out of love just as easily as you fall in love, so … it happens.'

She also defends her rather featureless portrayal of twenty-first century Dublin. 'There is nowhere recognisable in there because it puts a time on a book, and I want this to be timeless … It was never important where Holly was.' How about the strange but true fact that it is a chick-lit novel without sex? 'I didn't think it was important for the book – and I would have been really embarrassed writing it.'

Ahern's confidence is high, so high that it will take something unusual to buckle her. She has scanned the Irish reviews so far and adjudged one to be 'not a review at all', while the others, though by no stretch ecstatic, were inoffensive, with one even somewhat favourable. 'I'm under no illusion whatever that I'm the only author who's going to be loved by the world. If there is constructive criticism I'm going to take it if I agree with it,' she says modestly before adding cheerfully: 'So far there's nothing I agree with.'

So there is nothing she would have done differently with the book? 'No, there's nothing I feel I could have done better. Nobody can touch me on it. I'm delighted with it … really, really proud.'

She has always written stories, she says, recalling that as a 14-year-old she tried to write a book in which the central character was 16. So money was 'definitely, definitely' never the driver. 'I think this book is written so well because it's written completely from the heart. All this' – the money and so on – 'comes to people who don't go looking for it.'

And it's still not about the money, she insists. 'It's not important to me. I'm not a flash person at all. But it's an incredible bonus. It means I can help out friends and family, and it has allowed me to move out and get my own place, an apartment.' She would like to live beside the sea. 'I love the seaside, but prices are crazy.' But hasn't she wads of money now to indulge that? 'People keep reminding me of that, and it's true. But I'm such a careful person. I don't splurge out.'

She works when others of her age are out clubbing. She wrote *PS, I Love You* in three months, in the family dining room, to the exclusion of sunlight, friends and family, writing in longhand from about 10 p.m. until 6 a.m. or 7 a.m., typing it up the next day.

She was also lucky to have two indulgent parents, at that juncture between getting her degree and starting a master's in film studies, when the gift of time left her free to pursue her goal. And her run of luck culminated in finding an agent of the calibre of Marianne Gunn O'Connor.

For a 22-year-old she seems solidly settled. Her drink of choice, she claims, is 7 Up. 'I get too hungover. It's not worth it.' Her boyfriend of nearly three years, David Keoghan, is an athlete and shares her restraint. 'It'd be one or two drinks every few weeks.' And he is the love of her life. 'He's the one. I can see forever with him. I have no plans to be leaving him any time in the next 80 years.'

*Irish troops patrolling the streets of Monrovia, capital of Liberia. Photo: Declan Walsh.*

**WEDNESDAY, 21 JANUARY 2004**

# Dealing with Liberia's Lost Generation

*Declan Walsh, in Monrovia*

Stephen swung his legs idly on an upturned canoe on Monrovia's rubbish-strewn beach, staring out to sea. During the war he had respect, he said.

As battles blazed around the city, the 16-year-old fighter strutted the streets with a joint between his lips, an AK-47 over his shoulder, and a nickname inspired by movie-star violence – Judgement Day.

But now people treated the ex-fighters like beggars or criminals, he moaned, his small eyes glazed over with marijuana. 'You say you have no chop (food). They say go away,' he said. 'They say suffer and die.' His AK-47 remains buried under the rough shack he shares with another fighter. He will surrender it only in return for money or a living.

'We want the UN soldier to take the guns away. But we need to find a way to live. Time is running out.' Liberia has tens of thousands of volatile, drug-addicted gunmen like Stephen. Yesterday the UN relaunched its programme to disarm them, a critical step in the ongoing peace process. It is a mountainous task.

'It's going to be a very difficult process, every step of the way,' said UN spokeswoman Ms Margaret Novicki.

*Demobilised girls at the Samaritan's Purse Interim Care Centre near Monrovia. Photo: Declan Walsh.*

Irish troops assisting with the process know at first hand how tricky it can be. As they arrived in Liberia in December their convoy passed the chaotic scenes of the UN's first disarmament attempt.

Thousands of fighters descended on an ill-equipped UN camp, demanding to be paid in dollars immediately. Refusal sent the soldiers on the rampage, storming through city suburbs, shooting in the air and looting. At least eight people were killed. 'They called it happy firing but it wasn't very funny,' recalled Comdt William Dwyer.

The UN ended the crisis by paying the soldiers $75 each, and destroying as many weapons as possible. 'Sure there were mistakes,' admitted Ms Novicki. 'But all sides were under pressure to

demobilise quickly. And in the end there were 12,000 less combatants and 8,000 less guns.'

This time the UN is starting with an information campaign aimed at the ex-fighters. About 9,500 peacekeepers, mainly from African and Asian countries, are in place. And actual disarmament will not start until the entire 15,000-strong force has arrived, probably next month.

But presuming the fighters lay down their arms, the next problem is what they will do next. For years Liberia's undisciplined fighters lived through theft at gunpoint, popularly known as 'Operation Pay Yourself'. Now they must get by in a devastated country with little money or jobs. 'We want to learn a trade, to work for our own money,' said Stephen's colleague, 18-year-old Joseph.

The psychological damage could be even more difficult to resolve. All sides snatched teenagers from their homes, and forced them to fight. Now that lost generation is struggling to adjust to life without violence.

A sparsely-furnished house on the city outskirts, near a villa owned by Liberia's soccer hero George Weah, is a half-way house for 26 recently demobilised girl fighters. The youngest is an 11-year-old who carried her brother's ammunition into battle; the eldest is a combat-toughened 19-year-old with a bullet wound in one leg. Staff say they can be aggressive, even dangerous.

One girl tried to stab a social worker during a quarrel; another tried to push a rival from a second floor balcony. 'Most of these girls have spent their formative years in war. It's going to be a long road for them,' said centre manager Mr Thomas Jeffrey. Two years ago Yei Dahn (14), was snatched as she walked home from school and forced to fight with a notorious militia known as Jungle Fire. She was taken to Gbarnga for training, where the Taylor army fashioned her into a killing machine with brutality and drugs.

'They used to force us to smoke (marijuana), to make our minds strong for the fight. If you refuse, they kill you,' she said. To eat, they used Operation Pay Yourself. 'I had a gun so I had power. We used to beat people, kick them and then take their food.' Now the night brings fearful images. Yei has nightmares of people with their throats slit. She wants only to go home. 'I don't want to fight no more war. I just want to see my mother,' she said.

The Irish Minister of Defence, Mr Smith, is due to arrive in Liberia this evening for a short visit to the Irish troops and the President of the transitional government, Mr Gyude Bryant.

Destroying Liberia's guns could help stabilise all of west Africa. Recent wars in Sierra Leone, the Ivory Coast and Guinea have been fuelled by floods of guns and itinerant fighters that wash around the region. Under Charles Taylor, many originated in Liberia. For now, the key is to ensure all factions are disarmed simultaneously.

On Monrovia's filthy beach, ex-fighter Joseph said: 'We put our arms down. The UN must make sure the others do the same.'

**SATURDAY, 24 JANUARY 2004**

# TV Review

*Shane Hegarty*

'Waiting For Houlihan' was a tribute to the writer that mixed interviews with autobiography. He is from Castleisland, Co. Kerry; proud to be branded a mountainy man and

*Sports writer Con Houlihan at the unveiling of a statue of himself on the main street of his home town, Castleisland in Co. Kerry. Photo: Don MacMonagle.*

peasant, who grew up in a part of Ireland that was unnoticed, 'a world that has fallen off a cliff of silence'. During the early part of his career he was a teacher. When Brendan Kennelly was 16, he sent some poems to Houlihan, who replied with a single line: 'Dear Brendan, You make all the right mistakes.'

Houlihan's accent is thick, his voice the sound of turf being cut from a bog. He writes in stubby sentences on white butchers' paper. The words, though, have always conveyed events with an awesome clarity. You hope that the former Dublin goalkeeper, Paddy Cullen, has come to appreciate Houlihan's precise dissection of the moment in the 1978 All-Ireland Football Final when he chased back to his goal 'like a woman who smells a cake burning. The ball won the race and it curled inside the near post as Paddy crashed into the outside of the net and lay against it like a fireman who had returned to find his station ablaze'.

As an aside, isn't it interesting that this journalist featured in a series titled *Arts Lives*? Perhaps there should be some tax exemptions after all.

*(Edited from a longer review)*

**TUESDAY, 27 JANUARY 2004**

# Fathers and Sons

*Mind Moves: Marie Murray*

Fatherhood is special. The relationship between fathers and sons is special. It is a unique connection of exquisite gruff intricacy. It is central to emotional development and mental health.

It is a significant factor in the development of the baby, the exploration of the infant, the courage of the child, the strivings of the adolescent and the success of the adult.

It may make and shape a young man's attitudes, values and beliefs. It is one factor which determines his tolerance or prejudice, his behaviour towards women, his expression of aggression, his views of

marriage, of divorce, of love, of sex-roles, of self-esteem. It is one key in his capacity for compassion and his acceptance of the splendour of manhood in its most honourable manifestations.

The father-son relationship is the exclusive domain of men. It has sometimes been privileged, often derided, occasionally obsessed about and frequently fought about in ridiculous, unnecessary and illogical competitive disputes about the influence of motherhood versus fatherhood on the child.

This is because fatherhood, like motherhood, is a socially constructed role. In the past it confined itself almost exclusively to patriarch, protector, provider, decider and disciplinarian encapsulated in the catch-cry of many childhoods: 'wait 'till your father gets home'. It disparaged men who wished to child-care with caricatures of apron-bedecked pram-pushers, equally deriding the role of women at that time. It denied many men their capacity to nurture and know their children. If, tragically, parents lost a child, a father grieved silently as if this dead child was not his child, swallowing the exclusion of the question 'how is your wife coping?'

When their own fathers died, denied the chance to show the craggy compassionate care that many men express wordlessly to each other, sons also grieved silently; grieved for what might have been, for time not spent together and for words that were said or not said to each other, for memories of the texture of a coat, the fixing of a toy or the tallness of paternal protection. Indeed, sons whose fathers die young or who leave, neglect or reject them in childhood, move into high-risk categories for later adolescent and adult depression unless the loss is acknowledged and addressed.

Fatherhood also has a unique impact on men. It is not just mothers' hormonal levels that change with childbirth. Fathers' testosterone levels plunge by as much as one-third when the new baby comes home. This conflicts with the many images in Irish literature of the absent, ineffectual, feckless and violent father. In sport, men march on the football pitch with miniature versions of themselves. In word and song Father is Father, Da, the Old Man, Papa and Pa.

Psychodynamically, Freud's famous Oedipus Complex represents sons as incestuously inclined, envious, in anxious competition with their fathers for their mothers' love. This was beautifully expressed by our own writer Frank O'Connor, whose short story on the matter resolved it better, perhaps, than Freud, by father and son colluding as comrades in adversity when the new baby arrived to replace them both in 'mother's' affection. And who could ignore Adrian Mole's description of his father's definition of the 'perfect son', plunging the boy into adolescent angst at the impossibility of being what his father wants him to be?

But how do fathers determine what their sons will be? The accumulated research evidence of three decades confirms fathers who are warm, supportive and involved can assist the cognitive, academic, social and emotional well being of their sons. Self-concept, stability, conduct, school behaviour and substance use are amongst the factors researched. Rejection by fathers has been associated with

*A male adult blackbird feeds a chick in a nest in a Christmas tree in the grounds of St Joseph's Hospital in Limerick. The blackbird built the nest before Christmas and hospital authorities decided to leave the tree* in situ *until the chicks hatched. Photo: Kieran Clancy/PicSure.*

adolescent delinquency, polydrug abuse and, most especially, with dissatisfaction with life and high levels of depression. Boys usually imitate their fathers. Good and bad they imitate them.

If fathers are not there, whom can they imitate? Many boys from fatherless homes have been found to be less well-adjusted, less competent in forming friendships and frequently to confuse masculinity with violence.

Conduct problems often mask the yearning of a son for his father's attention and approval. Sons usually love and admire their fathers more than their fathers may know. Fathers often love and admire their sons more than their sons know.

Clinicians often observe from professional sidelines the yearning for attention and acceptance between fathers and their sons that gets diverted into anger and hurt, destruction or depression. Women therapists observing this process must also acknowledge we do not know what it is like to be a boy or man, a father or son, but that this is of immense dimension in relationship terms. It is the most significant male-to-male relationship. It has little to do with 'begetting' and everything to do with commitment; it unfolds in everyday communications and conversations. It is made.

So what kind of relationship have you made with your son? How much time do you spend with him? How does he know that you love him? What qualities do you admire in him? What is the nicest thing you ever said to him? What, if anything, is the worst? What does he admire most in you? What, if anything, does he wish was different in your relationship?

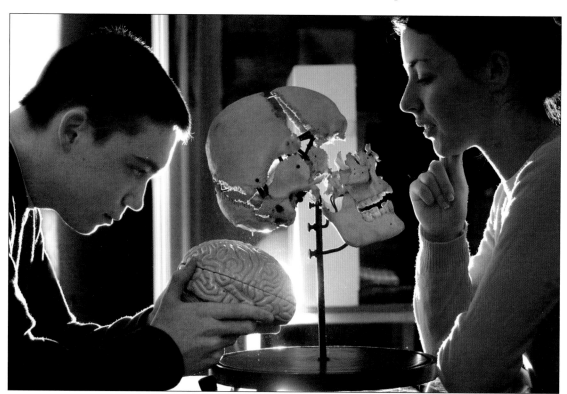

*Peter Barrett (left) from Presentation Brothers College in Cork with Eimear O'Hanrahan from Loreto High School in Rathfarnham, Co. Dublin, examining a skull and brain in the anatomy display at the Royal College of Surgeons in Ireland open day in Dublin. Photo: Matt Kavanagh.*

*Arts, Sport and Tourism minister John O'Donoghue with larger-than-life puppets from Bui Bolg in Wexford, at the launch of the Cultural Programme for Ireland's presidency of the European Union. Photo: Eric Luke.*

What do you think he would answer if asked those questions? The father-son dyad is as intimate as a 'scrum', as triumphant as a 'try' and as celebratory as a 'conversion', when fathers and sons are in warm relationships with each other. But it cannot succeed without time, tactics and commitment.

When the opportunity is lost, the 'match' is lost. This is a cruel defeat. Time spent, not money spent is what sons remember. Fathers too need recognition for what poet Hayden calls 'love's austere and lonely offices' so that their sons will not regret, as the poem 'Those Winter Sundays' regrets that 'no one ever thanked him'.

*Marie Murray's column appeared in the first issue of* The Irish Times' *new Tuesday section, Health Supplement, which was launched on 27 January 2004.*

**WEDNESDAY, 28 JANUARY 2004**

# We Are Left to Work Out Who has been Blessed and Who Shall be Blamed

*Tom Humphries*

It's hard to know precisely what to feel when the latest shiny-suited sports minister stands up and announces the Government's freshest grand plan for Irish sport. Déjà vu? Ennui? Winter vomiting disease? Irritable bowel syndrome?

So the Government has decided to do what intellectually unremarkable dogs on the street have been telling them to do for half a decade. They have decided to redevelop Lansdowne Road. For this small mercy we are supposed to shake our cha-chas in exuberant celebration and give much thanks. We are supposed to grant general absolution for the crimes prompted by the Taoiseach's dementia of the ego, the years wasted as the Government dreamed of a stately pleasure dome with velodromes measureless to man.

Is it churlish to point out that since 1998 we have had so many receptions, launches, press conferences, reports and briefings that the aggregated monotony and banality amount to nothing less than a glimpse of hell? There seems to be no Governmental embarrassment at the fact that all these years haven't produced so much as an upturned sod.

Perhaps when Lansdowne is rebuilt we could incorporate some of the grandiosity which Abbotstown reached for by engraving some of the more memorable quotes from the past five years on to marble slabs and placing them in the walls.

The words, after all, are what we are left with after half a decade of hubris and nonsense. Speaking of what Michael McDowell called a Ceaucescu-era campus and stadium, An Taoiseach chastised his doubters once by saying: 'As a nation not only can we afford this undertaking; we cannot afford to let it slip.'

Such a moment, like the vision of a great dam at Ardnacrusha, deserves commemoration. In the meantime we are left with a modest proposal and the task of deciding who has been blessed and who shall be blamed.

The decision, of course, marks a big win for Irish soccer. The sports association with the least competence and the most exaggerated sense of its own entitlement finds itself with a tureen in its hand just as it begins to rain soup.

The people who mislaid Flower Lodge and Glenmalure Park, who turned Dalymount Park into a rustbowl and in the Shamrock Rovers stadium in Tallaght have created a latter-day Pompeii, the people who 'almost' gave us Eircom Park and the Euro 2008 championships – these are the blazers who will benefit the most.

Good luck to them. It is not the fault of those kids who dream of the big time that Irish soccer has never built a venue in which to have a big time. It is soccer's fine fortune that the Taoiseach is a Manchester United sort of guy from whose lips phrases like 'Theatre of Dreams' find a ready launch area.

Soccer wins out, and the Government will help build an Irish home for the world's richest professional sport. In rugby headquarters the celebrations will be somewhat less dizzy. Had the IRFU known half a decade ago that the governmental huffery and puffery about stadiums would amount to this they might have refurbished their own place by now at less cost and with greater efficiency.

And then there are all those other sports who will be invited to huddle under the fig leaf that is the diminished Abbotstown dream. How they must regret not following the example of the Golf Union of Ireland who last year just gave up on the Taoiseach's big dream of an Abbotstown Golf Academy and set about providing one for themselves at Carton House.

Once upon a time the plans for what was to be built off the M50 would have taken a volume to compile. The sporting metropolis would be all things to all sports people. It would have a sports science and medicine centre, a tennis centre, golf academy, velodrome, indoor arena, Bertie bowl, aquatic centre and so on.

What is remarkable is that we believed it for so long. Two years ago this week, Mr Des Allen, speaking on behalf of 65 Irish sporting bodies, embraced the whole idea in a cautious way: 'The Federation of Irish Sports welcomes wholeheartedly the decision to build the facilities in full and as originally proposed, but obviously it would be very disappointing for the 65 sports we represent to see reduction and disastrous to see the elimination of some of the facilities. To suggest reviews at this stage would appear to be stepping back.'

There has been stepping back of course. More stepping back than a beaten boxer. Still the

*Architect's drawing of the proposed new stadium for Lansdowne Road superimposed on a photograph of the site.*

Government rolled on. In a way the finality of yesterday's sudden U-turn into the realms of common sense means that we will miss the whole show.

The production survived the High-Point Rendel Report which contained judgments so damning of the whole business that it should have brought forth a sheaf of resignation letters rather than the grim pathos of Paddy Teahon of Sports Campus Stadium Ireland fulminating that we had his personal guarantee that he'd get the Bertie bowl built for the price of a Happy Meal.

Then the soiled and flimsy tissue of hope that was the joint Euro 2008 bid was pressed into service to help dry away our tears. We were urged to stomp and cheer for the vision and acuity of our leaders who would prepare the nation so wonderfully for its putative co-hosting role.

Of course UEFA, the only people we needed to impress more than ourselves, didn't see it that way. It was one thing to get the nabobs and panjandrums of the FAI on board; another thing entirely to convince folk from the real world that we were a serious sporting nation.

And through it all the Progressive Democrats were never for turning. By interring the Bertie bowl dream yesterday the Taoiseach quietly ceded one of the key prestige battles of the Coalition years. A personal calamity given the political weight he had put behind Abbotstown, but not an unexpected calamity. One shambles had begotten another over the years.

A quick leaf through our back pages is once again in order. In far distant 1998 and in the midst of the solemn deliberations of a governmental

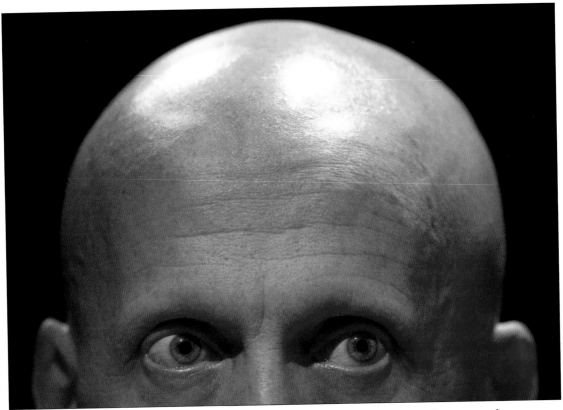

*International football referee Pierluigi Collina during a Euro 2004 promotion event and question and answer session at Dublin City University. Photo: Dara Mac Dónaill.*

committee to examine the feasibility of a national stadium the FAI with perhaps six fixtures a year to contribute to such a stadium decides that it must have its own place in which to decently stage these. This place would have retractable roofs and would look very similar to a stadium in Arnhem in Holland.

By the following spring the government was offering cash (€11 million in grants) if the FAI scrapped the idea. For a brief and glorious period the city prepared itself (not really) for the day when its citizens would be able to stand in the upper deck of the 80,000-capacity Croke Park and gaze across at the 70,000-capacity Bertie Bowl and then take in the distant splendour of the 45,000-capacity Eircom Park.

Eircom Park shrank again and again until finally it disappeared. Abbotstown was shelved and

relaunched more often than a beloved book. The GAA on the verge of opening the gates of Croke Park was suckered by an offer of £60 million to keep the place to itself and thus enable the Bertie Bowl.

And so it went. Architects were commissioned. Reports were published. Abbotstown was damned and ridiculed but never truly scrapped. The costs mounted. Attitudes hardened.

Yesterday's announcement of a new 50,000-seat Lansdowne Road isn't quite too little, too late, but is certainly the bare minimum, delivered much too late.

The GAA, not unlike the IRFU, has been used and abused throughout the entire process and for a sporting body which formerly was not averse to considering itself the sporting wing of Fianna

Fáil, that process has been distressing. The final bemusement came yesterday with the Minister's casual claim that the GAA could use Lansdowne Road if they wanted to.

As such, of course, the Minister was reclassifying himself as a 'nit wit' or some unspecified part thereof, *vis-a-vis* the rules of nitwittery as established by An Taoiseach three years ago when he announced that 'if you believe that soccer, rugby, gaelic football, ladies football and camogie and other sports can all be played on the same pitch you have to be a bit of a nitwit.' The contention yesterday by the Minister that the dimensions of the new ground would be adequate to accommodate Gaelic games is worrying. The pitch in Croke Park is 145 metres long and the GAA minimum-length pitch is 130 metres. The maximum length of an international soccer pitch is 110 metres, and a rugby pitch is 10 metres shorter.

Better perhaps to point to another engraved marble slab. The FAI and the IRFU in a joint statement 2¹/₂ years ago worriedly pointed to the issue of pitch dimension. Both organisations are conscious of the negative impact evident in stadia around the world where soccer and rugby are played on a pitch far removed from spectators, normally as a result of a surrounding athletics track.

The statement went on to give the specific dimensions of the three types of pitches and pointed out that in the event of Croke Park becoming the National Stadium 'this would leave spectators at rugby and soccer matches a minimum of 15 metres from the pitch side and 25 metres from the goal line.' So is Mr O'Donoghue telling us that we are to build a world-class, state-of-the-art stadium which is unsatisfactory for its two principal tenants but may just suit the GAA which has no real interest or incentive to use the facility?

One suspects that we won't be seeing much hurling on the sward of Lansdowne Road for some time. Neither, of course, will we be seeing anything else for a while. It is hoped that, with the unlikely quiescence of the residents of Dublin 4,

the Stadium project will be completed by 2008. That's four years, or 12 months less than the Government has wasted on the debate so far. Soccer and rugby will spend part of that period looking for alternative homes.

With the mood as it is in the GAA at present Croke Park will be remaining locked. Perhaps the final stage of the metastasising scandal of the national stadium will be the sight of Irish teams playing home internationals in Britain. For this the Soldiers of Destiny have shimmied and stroked for so long? When it happens the GAA will most likely shoulder the blame, and certain profiles along the Drumcondra Road will be kept discreetly low.

And in the Fianna Fáil offices in Mount Street there will be quiet, wondrous realisation that this is a country which merely loves the idea of itself loving sport, a country that loves the last good time more than it loves anything else.

We are a people who will tolerate any class of a shambles if it has to do with sport, because at the end of the day it's only sport. The Taoiseach, who loves the idea of loving sport more than any of us, knew that all along, of course.

**SATURDAY, 31 JANUARY 2004**

# To Goa or Not to Goa

*Róisín Ingle*

The smell of human effluent floats through the mosquito-proof grids on the window, and I marvel again at the incredible power of India to project your moods directly back onto you. The brother and I have had a row. One of those silent ones, full of wounded stares and meaningful pauses that insert an impenetrable canyon of mistrust into an already stilted conversation.

He has just gone roaring off on his Royal Enfield Bullet, his machismo Royal Enfield Bullet to be precise – the same motorbike we were supposed to travel north to Goa on. He needs some space and so do I. And it doesn't matter if some of what I'm smelling through the window is my own effing effluent. I hate this country right now.

He has been asked to be the yoga teacher on a 10-day silent retreat in Bodhgaya. This is the place in Bihar where the Buddha sat under a tree and declared that he wouldn't move until he became enlightened, which he eventually did. Bodhgaya means camping out in a Thai temple and sharing sleeping space in a women's dormitory. It means cold, early mornings and intense meditation, with extra helpings of emotional duka (suffering) thrown in – very welcome madam, pukka duka it is too, no extra charging. It means yoga at the crack of dawn every morning. Taught, of course, by the brother.

Goa, ah Goa, the land of golden beaches, left-over hippies, luxurious beach huts, yoga at a reasonable time on the sands and maybe, just maybe, my first sun-tan in years. We have to make a decision by the morning.

I tell him a retreat sounds good, but I really want to go to Goa. Do the beach thing. Have a regular holiday. I want to do more of India than just the spiritual thing. What could be more India, he retorts, deliberately mishearing me, than meditating in the place where the Buddha first became free? (He had me there, you have to admit.)

There is silence and a wounded stare (him), some more redundant conversation (me), before the front door shuts quietly behind him and I hear the Enfield starting up.

He told me this trip would be an assault on the senses, an unforgettable lesson in how to live life in the moment. He wasn't lying. Life hits you in the face here as soon as you walk outside the door, whether it's little girls smiling and pooing at the side of the road, or toothless old women raking through piles of rubbish for food, or a one-legged dog picking a fight with a family of cheeky monkeys. The monkeys always win, by the way.

And then there are the smells – the excrement smells that shift direction with the breeze, the scorched earth smells, the heavenly perfume of butterfly-covered bougainvillea, the hellish odour of thousands of bodies sweating and eating and pissing and shitting together, all of them taking life by the scruff of the neck and eating it with their *dosa* for breakfast. No wonder I'm in bed by 10 p.m. most evenings.

On our first day here we did Pradakshina, a holy walk around a holy mountain, which takes around four hours. I saw only what my light heart wanted me to see. The cute kids pestering you for a pen when what they really want are pennies. The old *sadhus* lying in improbable positions snoring in the sun. The little boy slicing the top off a coconut and handing it to you to drink deep from a pink plastic straw. The crazy, chaotic temple where a girl selling flowers wouldn't take no for an answer and pinned an arrangement of daisies on my hair. The gappy-toothed lepers who clung to us as we pushed through the throng.

In a bad mood, India's extreme sights and sounds play out like the worst kind of nightmare; in a good mood, they make for an awfully big scratch-and-sniff adventure.

The brother doesn't return until 2 a.m. and we don't speak again until he hunts me down in the Internet cafe the following morning. Tempers briefly flare, but we soon bury the hatchet and over lunch do what our mother always told us to do when making important decisions. We write down the pros and cons. Goa, of course, wins hands down.

Then the brother starts reminiscing about the last time he went on the Bodhgaya retreat. On the final day, he bunked out of the temple by scaling the perimeter wall. He experienced a deep urge to sit under the Bodhi tree where the Buddha was enlightened. It was, he said, kind of like the time he bunked into the RDS to see The Kinks.

As he climbed a second sacred wall, he was caught by four security guards, who, to eject him properly, had to lead him past the Bodhi tree. As he passed, he bent down and picked up a leaf, a spiritual groupie to the last.

*Enjoying a walk to Bull Island early on a February morning. Photograph: Bryan O'Brien.*

His meaningful pause 'n' stare combination seems like it will never end. We toss a five-rupee coin. I'm so glad I remembered to pack my swimsuit.

---

**MONDAY, 2 FEBRUARY 2004**

# 'He has Been Through Some Extremely Chaotic Events …'

*The Children's Court: Carl O'Brien*

When the garda eventually caught up with the joyrider, the boy was crouching behind the driver's seat, wearing a black wig as a disguise, hoping he had evaded the police. He had just driven at high speed against the flow of traffic on Finglas's Tolka Road.

A double-decker bus and several cars swerved out of the way. Next he broke some traffic lights. By the time he sped up onto a footpath, he was being pursued by a patrol van and the garda helicopter. The 17-year-old later brought the car to a halt amid the concrete and metal sprawl of a scrapyard in Finglas.

'I was in the patrol van and couldn't keep up with the car,' said Garda Alan Govern, in soft, measured tones, in contrast to the drama of his description. 'Motorists were able to direct me to where he had driven. When I drove past a yard with scrap cars, I saw a car abandoned. The passenger had run off, but I found the driver crouched behind the driver's seat.'

The blue estate car had no tax or insurance and the youngster did not have any driving licence. When he later gave a urine sample to the garda, the results were well over the legal drink-driving limit.

His mother came down to the station and co-operated fully with the gardaí, he said. The 17-year-old did not have any previous convictions of this kind, the garda pointed out, helpfully.

'Well, he has certainly made up for his history,' said Judge Angela Ní Chondúin, looking across to the accused, who, dressed in a grey tracksuit and blue sports top, ran his fingers nervously over a gold ring on his finger.

Like many of the children who pass through the Children's Court in Smithfield, he was staying with his grandparents. His father died when he was just four years old. His mother had rung the solicitor to say she could not be in court because of a 'problem'. For years, the accused's solicitor pointed out, he had been leading a chaotic, drink-fuelled lifestyle.

'He has been through some extremely chaotic events which I won't go into,' said his solicitor, Ms Michelle Finan. 'He has had a very difficult time for a boy of his age.'

Alcohol appears to be the main source of his problems, she said, and his mother and grandmother were hoping he could go to a residential centre for the treatment of alcohol.

'I know this is an extremely serious offence. He has special problems,' his solicitor said, pleading for mitigation. 'He could have killed any number of people,' Judge Ní Chondúin pointed out, adopting a stern tone as she looked towards him again through her black-framed glasses.

Noting the solicitor's submissions, she agreed to adjourn the case, on bail of €100, to allow for the possibility of sending the boy to a residential treatment centre for addiction.

The 17-year-old, whose legs shook under the witness stand partly in nervousness and partly to keep warm in the chilly courtroom, looked relieved. He smiled weakly as he walked out of the courtroom.

Later in Court 55, another 17-year-old shifted uncomfortably in the witness stand, having been arrested in the early hours of New Year's Day in Ballyfermot under the Intoxicating Liquor Act. His solicitor pointed out that he had left school, was on the waiting list for a FÁS course and had no income.

'He might be fond of his grandmother, but he's causing her grief. And if he gets into any more trouble, he'll get grief from me,' she said, before deciding that he be bound to the peace for 12 months.

'Say thank you to the judge,' the youngster's grandmother piped up from the back of the court-room.

'Thanks,' he said, looking embarrassed, as he sat with his arms folded on top of the witness stand.

**MONDAY, 16 FEBRUARY 2004**

# 'He Comes Home at Night, Out of his Head on Drink, and Breaks up the House …'

*The Children's Court: Carl O'Brien*

The middle-aged mother stood up in court, clasping her black handbag tightly underneath her arm, and broke into tears.

'I'm afraid of him,' she said between staggered breaths, not looking at her 17-year-old son who sat in the corner of the room with expressionless eyes.

'He comes home at night, out of his head on drink, and breaks up the house and calls me terrible names. He's been thrown out of school. I organised for him to go back to school, but he wouldn't go back,' the mother said, reaching into her bag for a tattered piece of tissue to wipe her eyes.

The boy, wearing a green Reebok tracksuit top, leaned back in his chair, let out a loud sigh and scratched his head. Judge Bridget Reilly asked the mother whether the incident had been an isolated one.

'It's been building up over the last year,' she said, as her voice trembled.

'And did you seek any help?' the judge asked.

'Where do I get help from?' the mother asked.

'It's clear the boy needs help. This doesn't happen over night. You yourself say he is not well,' the judge said.

'Everyone has tried to help him,' the mother answered later, 'but he doesn't want it.'

The garda, who gave evidence of the arrest of the boy in the early hours of the morning, said the boy had been arrested under the Criminal Damage Act.

The boy's solicitor, who was appointed for him by the judge under the legal aid system, said his client's parents were separated and that the boy wished to stay with an uncle. The judge took the uncle's details and organised for him to re-appear before the court in a week's time.

'I hope you can find a way of dealing with your problems at the moment,' the judge said to the boy, who stared intently at the wood-panelled floor. I don't know if you feel they are over-whelming you or if they are too much to deal with, but things can change,' the judge said sympathetically, before concluding the case. The boy stood up, while his mother turned her back on her son and walked out of the courtroom.

The case was not the only case heard by the judge last week regarding a parent being terrorised by a child.

A day earlier a girl appeared in Court 55 of the Children's Court after spending a week in Mountjoy jail having allegedly assaulted her mother, brother and sister.

A week before, the 17-year-old girl with wild hair and red eyes shrieked at her mother and had to be removed from the courtroom as she unleashed

The director of Women's Aid, Margaret Martin, with Irish Rugby International Shane Horgan at the launch of the Women's Aid national advertising campaign to raise awareness of domestic violence. Photograph: Matt Kavanagh.

a tirade of abuse at the judge.

A week later the girl stood before the judge looking elegant with her hair tied up and wearing a black trouser suit, although her eyes looked tired and aged. Her well-dressed mother, accompanied by her son and older daughter, were in court to say they were willing to take the 17-year-old back into their home on condition she did not take drugs or alcohol.

'I'm sure this has caused a lot of stress for everyone and I'm sure that you are in some dis-tress,' the judge said, before asking the girl if she could change her behaviour.

'Yes,' the girl said meekly. The judge issued strict bail conditions, including provisions that she

*Garda recruits celebrate their graduation at Templemore, Co Tipperary. Photograph: Catch 22.*

sign on at a garda station once a week, obey a nightly curfew, and not threaten or assault any family member.

*Carl O'Brien's series ran throughout February and provided a rare insight into the working of the children's court.*

**TUESDAY, 3 FEBRUARY 2004**

# Architect of the Peace Process Who Broke the Murderous Cycle

*Gerry Moriarty, in Belfast*

John Hume was accepting handshakes from SDLP supporters, preparing for one-to-one camera interviews in the Wellington Park Hotel in Belfast yesterday after his noon announcement that he is bowing out of political life.

His sometime rival but steadfast ally, Séamus Mallon, looked on rather wistfully. Fancy a job in Europe, Séamus, as John Hume's replacement? we asked. 'John the Baptist came before Jesus, not after him,' the Armagh man said.

Mr Mallon wasn't being blasphemous, just a little mischievous, while at the same time paying solid tribute to a truly giant Irish political figure of the twentieth century.

He could have chosen as a better comparison Charles Stewart Parnell, another politician who fought the age-old Irish battle for constitutionalism against violent means of pursuing political objectives.

In the end, Parnell failed as later Pearse and Connolly and Collins and de Valera opted for the violent route after the repeated Home Rule failures in the face of the Orange card, carving out the Free State and later the Republic, but leaving a divided island and people.

*Sisters Theresa and Maureen Maguire from Taney in Co. Dublin standing at the new Luas bridge in Dundrum, with Harcourt Street line tram tickets from 1958. Theresa and Maureen took a ride on the Luas when the light rail system underwent its first test. Photograph: Bryan O'Brien.*

The same battle was fought in these Troubles, with the Armalite and the AK 47 of the IRA continuing the violent struggle to force the creation of a united territory.

It's all part of the peaceful/violent cycle of Irish history and it took a historian, Hume, to find strategies to break that murderous circle – which is his crowning achievement. He said at the press conference yesterday that it was 'the historian in me took on the IRA'.

He explained how in advance of the Anglo-Irish Agreement of 1985 he tried to persuade Margaret Thatcher to effectively declare Britain neutral on the future of Northern Ireland.

Those words of Britain having no 'selfish, economic or strategic' interest in the North were made fact in the Downing Street Declaration of 1993, a document that flowed from the earlier Hume-Adams negotiations. That simple phrase

destroyed the IRA's argument for violence because to continue the war meant that the IRA was not killing to expel the British but to kick out those they claimed were fellow Irish people, the unionists.

Republicans continue to claim that the violence of the IRA played the major part in convincing the British to make commitments they never wanted to make.

Hume's response yesterday was, 'I am very pleased that Sinn Féin have changed their mind and their approach because for the last 30 years were they right or wrong? I mean, that's the real question. Was violence right or wrong?' Equally, he set the agenda for the negotiations that led to the Belfast Agreement almost six years ago: resolving the three sets of relationships at the heart of the conflict – between unionist and nationalist in Northern Ireland, between the North and the South, between Britain and Ireland. That remains

*Skiers are pulled by horses in St Moritz, Switzerland. The men and their horses race over the frozen lake of the mountain resort of St Moritz. Photograph: Ruben Sprich/Reuters.*

work in progress but odds are we will get there – eventually.

He is justifiably called the architect of the peace process. The SDLP may suffer further travails in the months and years ahead but it can remain proud it stuck to its peaceful principles – spilling sweat not blood, as Hume said *ad nauseam* – and more importantly, even if some members faltered during Hume–Adams in the early 1990s, holding its nerve.

The old teacher as well as the historian in Hume believes in repeating a message until it is hammered home. Effectively he has been arguing his 'agreed Ireland' since he entered politics on civil rights platforms in the 1960s.

He travelled Europe, the US, the world, persuading high-stature international friends to support his endeavours, while at the same time, like no other Northern politician, instilling nationalists with a formidable self-esteem and confidence.

Hume was always obdurate. His opponents, and sometimes his friends, could mock his repetitiveness of language but he didn't care. He joked again yesterday about his 'single transferable speech' or 'Humespeak' but it was the intellectual and rational force of the case behind it that mattered and in the end carried the day.

That's a remarkable achievement because republicans – if they have learned anything over the past 10 years – learned that it was when they stopped killing people that they started making huge political gains. The trouble for the SDLP and Hume was that it was at their expense.

But, and here's the essence of Hume and to a point the other party visionary, Séamus Mallon, they were prepared to make that sacrifice if it meant creating and sustaining the peace.

'True republicanism is real agreement between Protestant and Catholic, and real mutual respect, not victory by one side over the other,' said Hume yesterday, encapsulating his philosophy.

Fine words but no consolation for new party leader Mark Durkan. How do you replace such a candidate for the European elections in June, and at such short notice? That certainly was a failing of Hume's: he did not prepare the succession and he did not pay attention to organisation, as is glaringly evident by Sinn Féin's superiority in this regard.

Sinn Féin could take Hume's seats in Europe and Westminster but it won't undermine Hume being up there on a high political pedestal with Parnell – and being more successful – or the fact that if Sinn Féin politicians further undermine the SDLP it will be because they are diverting to the constitutional path charted for them by John Hume.

**SATURDAY, 7 FEBRUARY 2004**

# Makes You Want to Emigrate

## *The Last Straw: Frank McNally*

Nostalgia was rampant at the Planxty concert on Wednesday night. Everywhere you looked in Vicar Street, you could see people having misty-eyed memories of the 1970s. A man beside me in the gents' toilet summed it up when, pining for lost youth, he sighed: 'God, I feel like emigrating again.'

My own mind wandered back to the first time I went to see the band, the summer I left school in

1979. I bought a tent with the savings from a factory job, and with my friend, Damien, headed west in search of music and women – not necessarily in that order.

As we would learn, the tent was not waterproof. Fly-sheets were extra, and my savings weren't extensive. Anyway, with the optimism of youth, we knew it wouldn't rain.

It rained non-stop in Galway – what were the odds? – but every cloud has a silver lining. And the absence of a silver lining, or any kind of lining, on the tent meant that you didn't waste mornings sleeping in. Around dawn, the water dripping through the seams would force you to get up and wring your hair out. By then, you'd be wide awake and ready for the day.

We quickly tired of the Galway climate, however, and instead of heading for Clifden, changed course for Sligo and the Ballisodare Folk Festival. As I recall, the event was to be headlined by the well-known folk guitarist Chuck Berry, as well as Planxty. And even though, in a major surprise, it turned out to be raining in Sligo (and had been since about 1977) the place was buzzing.

A particular memory I have of Ballisodare is buying a steak-and-kidney pie from a chip van, and finding the inside still frozen solid. You were reluctant to complain about food in the 1970s, but I steeled myself somehow. The chef frowned at me for being so picky and threw the pie back in the frier, out of which, when he eventually rescued it, it emerged looking like debris from an accident in a nuclear plant. I might be making this up, but I think the van was called 'The Gourmet Diner'.

The main thing is that the Planxty gig in Ballisodare was fantastic. I imagine so, anyway. I wasn't actually at it. It was either sold out, or we couldn't afford the tickets, or both. Anyway, as I say, music wasn't the priority. In fact, I think the main reason we went to Sligo was that Damien had an older sister living there, in a house. Like Janis Ian, I learned the truth at 17. Which is that, fun and all as it is waking up in a wet tent, there's a lot to be said for a roof.

I did see Planxty once before they broke up in the early 1980s, and it was sobering to recall on Wednesday that way back then I thought they were oul' fellas, although they were younger than I am now. But what was really reassuring about this week's concert was that, incredibly after all this time, the age difference between the band and me is still exactly the same. It was just a bonus that they were still brilliant, too.

What was even more sobering about the concert was the fact that Vicar Street imposed drinking restrictions during the performance. A few fans had clearly taken the precaution of filling up beforehand, allowing Christy Moore to prove that, while he's lost his hair, he hasn't lost the high-velocity wit that can put a heckler down, permanently, from 500 yards. But the relatively abstemious audience, combined with the strict smoking ban and excellent air conditioning, made the event a lot healthier than Planxty concerts past, which was just as well given the infirmity of the audience.

The only throwback to the 1970s was a very persistent fly that dogged the band for much of the night. There were a lot of flies in the 1970s, as I recall, especially around folk musicians. The one on Wednesday was the subject of so much entertaining banter that you suspected he was on the

At the Planxty reunion at Dublin's Vicar Street were (right) Christy Moore, Liam Óg Ó Floinn (centre) and Andy Irvine. Photograph: Alan Betson.

payroll. But either way, he provided a crucial link with the past.

Of course, Ireland itself is unrecognisable from the country in which Planxty first performed their songs of love, loss, adultery, murder, dispossession, and the emigrant ship. The same gents' toilet the other night had a polite attendant, apparently African, with a liquid soap dispenser in one hand and towels in the other. I'm fairly sure this service was not available at the Ballisodare Folk Festival. A little embarrassed, I took the soap and towel and left a tip. But you'd miss the hard times, all the same.

**SATURDAY, 7 FEBRUARY 2004**

# Ambitious Document Craftily Turns the Tables on Party's Critics

*Frank Millar, in London*

The Rev. Ian Paisley's Democratic Unionist Party will (eventually) be able to do business with Sinn Féin.

And if Ulster Unionist leader David Trimble's survival strategy requires the DUP's chief strategist Peter Robinson to fall on his face, then he would do well to find another one.

These are two key conclusions to be drawn from the DUP proposals. For sure, the document published yesterday represents an opening gambit at the start of what will inevitably prove another protracted and difficult negotiation.

But it is a clever one and – notwithstanding some predictable knee-jerk reactions from SDLP and Sinn Féin quarters – there is discernible excitement within the British government about what it clearly considers impressive evidence of the DUP's serious intent.

This is not to suggest an absence of doubt – either about Sinn Féin's response to the particulars of this DUP blueprint, or more generally about the ability of the two parties to seriously engage any

time soon. Sinn Féin president Gerry Adams voices a widely held suspicion that such an engagement may have to await the 'post-Paisley' era.

Similarly – for all its public insistence that the suspension of the Stormont Assembly be lifted immediately – some British officials suspect Sinn Féin is content to play things along, in anticipation of electoral advances in the Republic come June and the final destruction of the SDLP come next year's expected British general election.

As one seasoned Whitehall observer puts it: 'Wouldn't it be ironic if the DUP was climbing aboard the peace train just as the wheels come off?'

Yet on the evidence of yesterday's DUP presentation one thing seems certain: Dr Paisley and his colleagues do not intend to offer themselves as an easy scapegoat in any new 'blame game'.

To the contrary, this negotiating document – bearing all the signs of Mr Robinson's considerable craft – has, at least temporarily, turned tables and left others with questions to answer.

During his Powerpoint presentation for Mr Blair on Thursday (which the prime minister reportedly found impressive, for its novelty as well as its substance) Mr Robinson insisted the DUP could not be counted among those unionists who – in Martin McGuinness's memorable phrase – 'don't want a Fenian about the place'. And he doubtless took particular pleasure in highlighting page 15 of the DUP Concept for Devolution which makes clear the party 'will not operate the Mandatory Coalition with Sinn Féin before it meets the Blair necessities' as spelt out in the prime minister's famous speech in October 2002 demanding paramilitary 'acts of completion'.

Here was the original 'Protestant Unionist Party' signalling that in fact all the Fenians – including Sinn Féin – could be made welcome provided the IRA conforms to the demands of the British and Irish governments as spelt out in paragraph 13 of last year's Joint Declaration.

Having affirmed their power-sharing credentials, the DUP now wants to know why won't

*The Rev. Ian Paisley, leader of the Democratic Unionist Party, during a press conference in Belfast where his party put forward proposals for the restoration of devolution in Northern Ireland without prior IRA weapons decommissioning. Photograph: PA/Paul Faith.*

the SDLP join a voluntary coalition pending delivery by the IRA?

And if a break in pan-nationalism is inconceivable, why not devolve power to the Assembly (as opposed to ministers) and allow the Assembly to discharge many of its responsibilities by means of a weighted-majority voting system following a local government model?

Mr Trimble complains this would actually permit the restoration of devolution prior to paramilitary acts of completion. His problem is that Mr Blair might be attracted by a scheme which offers to remove the twin issues which have dogged the Trimble years – prior decommissioning and 'exclusion'.

Mr Trimble's other problem is that many of his Assembly members will now be willing the DUP to succeed.

**TUESDAY, 10 FEBRUARY 2004**

# Western Ways

## The Bigger Picture: Shalini Sinha

Love is in the air. It's either that or a deep sense of loneliness. Believe it or not, your loneliness might be pointing towards a more rounded life.

Our current society teaches us to think of love in very limited ways. Many people feel desperate about finding the 'one person' who will save them, fulfilling all their needs. This desperation makes us afraid to discuss views on commitment, babies, jobs and life, let alone expectations for each other and the relationship. We rigidly define our relationships: 'just friends', 'dating', 'going out' and so limit how we can love. Having been raised in an arranged marriage culture, I've come to call this 'Western, compulsive, heterosexual coupling-off'.

Adults ask children as young as two and three about 'boyfriends' or 'girlfriends' (whichever they find acceptable to the defined gender of the child). We learn that coupled relationships are a sign of maturity and the only acceptable place to express affection on a moment-by-moment, day-by-day

basis. As early as 10 years old, we're forced to limit our ways of loving. What a shame.

What sets our relationships apart from common friendship is an unspoken agreement to engage in sexual affection – kissing, holding, even intercourse. Sex, however, was only meant to be one expression of love, not the definition of it. Establishing a rigidly defined, sexual relationship before we get to really know someone seems to me to be a recipe for heartbreak and a mistake.

Being in a relationship seems to define our worth and lovability. In reality, however, most of us have been heartbroken, disappointed, betrayed and rejected all before the age of five, by people who loved us but eventually showed themselves as

*Princess Kasune Zulu of Zambia and Senator David Norris at the Living with Aids, Dying of Hunger conference in Dublin. Photograph: Dara Mac Dónaill.*

*Bob Geldof (left) and retired South African Archbishop Desmond Tutu in Dublin for the Breaking The Barriers Aids conference organised under the auspices of the Irish presidency of the European Union. Photograph: Maxwells.*

fallible. It is this heartbreak that limits, even ruins, our attempt to be close. We need to uncover it, feel it fully, reclaim our power and emerge from it so we can indeed know our own hearts and minds, and understand how deeply we can touch another.

Until we do this, no relationship will ever fill that hole. Disappointment is inevitable when our one-and-only is revealed as mortal. We blame them, hate them, and even leave them. Because infatuation and feeling 'in-love' come before commitment, our whole relationship is shaken if the infatuation and 'in-love' feeling disappear for a moment.

Our narrow view of relationships keeps us isolated and holding back from loving everyone in our lives fully and knowing them completely. What a world we would have if love was fostered and encouraged on every corner and in every relationship!

First, there would be no need to 'gain experience' from a number of relationships. In my experience, most people who have many different relationships never learn from them. Closeness, trust and intimacy are certainly not practised. They grow in the most difficult of times when all you have to hold on to is a commitment to believing in each other and hanging in. What we really need to learn is not to be found with multiple partners, but inside our own hearts. And it is difficult to know until we feel the full depths of our loneliness.

Human love was meant to be fluid, relaxed, and in every interaction. We can love each other openly and in every encounter – not simply displaying sexuality, but real love. And the closer and deeper our connections become, the more our childhood loneliness will surface for healing, allowing us to become clearer and more able to plan and go after what we really want.

Breaking open our relationships also means relaxing around sexual orientation. The connection might not be apparent, but society's oppression against gay, lesbian and bisexual people is an extension of sexism – keeping us in rigidly defined relationships, limiting human love and affection. Whatever your orientation, when you express yourself outside the prescribed roles – be a warm, affectionate man or a physically powerful woman – you're isolated and ridiculed. It has nothing to do with sex. Gay culture could teach us to be more open and welcoming towards each other.

The more we insist others be less than themselves, the harder it is for us to be all we want to be. It is love we need to learn about, not sex. Sex is best when two people are completely empowered, vulnerable, and can express themselves fully. This can't be achieved when you don't know each other well, have no commitment to love each other completely, or play games to please each other in the hope of feeling close to and loved by someone.

But, deep-reaching, widespread commitments can teach us a lot about the human heart. Only when we decide never to give up on someone can we be free to love them completely. And we have every right to expect this in return from anyone who is good enough to grow with for the rest of our lives.

**SATURDAY, 14 FEBRUARY 2004**

# 'Nothing Can Replace Our Son'

*Ian Kilroy, in Boston*

On a crisp day last spring, Steve Sammis, from Massachusetts, looked on as his son, Benjamin, was laid to rest. A soldier kneeled before him and presented him with the red, white and blue American flag, taken from where it had been draped over his son's coffin. A bugle played. Then, as Sammis stood amid the sea of white crosses that is Arlington National Cemetery, Virginia, he was momentarily shaken out of his numb grief by an aircraft speeding by overhead, an overfly for his fallen son.

'He was buried with full military honours. It was extremely reverent, extremely symbolic. It was an overwhelming experience,' Sammis says, his eyes full of emotion. 'That day has left a lasting impression. It will stay with me forever.'

Twenty-nine-year-old Benjamin W. Sammis was flying back to Kuwait on April 4th last when he learned of a group of US marines separated from their main unit. They were pinned down under heavy fire 40 miles south of Baghdad. Sammis turned his Cobra helicopter around and, with two other helicopters, returned to provide cover as the marines withdrew.

It was a battle zone. There was smoke and fire everywhere. Billowing flames made night-vision equipment useless; it was impossible to see. In the confusion, Benjamin flew directly into a Republican Guard observation tower. DNA samples were required to identify his remains.

Ten months later, Benjamin's father is still reliving the moments he first heard the news. 'It's that call that you never want to think you're going to get,' he says. 'That's when it comes. There's a knock on the door and you go to the window and it's 11.45 p.m. Eastern Standard Time. There's a marine major and sergeant standing out in front of your house. I look out the window and I say to my wife: "Beth, there's a marine officer out in the yard." We know at once what has happened.'

What had happened was that Benjamin Sammis – like 536 or so other US soldiers to date – had been killed in one of the most controversial wars of recent times. He left behind him a young wife, Stacey, and two brothers, as well as his parents. He had been an athlete and competitive sailor. He had loved soccer and had fulfilled the wish he'd had since the age of 10 to fly. Now his

*A 3rd US Infantry bugler plays Taps during the burial service for US Army Sergeant Chad. Photograph: Joe Raedle/Getty Images.*

life was over. And since hearing of his death, life has been an agony for those closest to him.

'The only way to describe it is emotional torment,' says Sammis. 'Mostly it's torment. There's nothing you can do. Your life is never going to be the same again. We lost a son. Nothing can replace that.'

Sammis wears a yellow ribbon as a constant reminder of his son. It is pinned to his clothing with the miniature crossed flags of the US and the US Marine Corps. The yellow ribbon means he wants the troops 'to come home soon and come home safe', he says. It is a sentiment increasingly heard in small towns and on local radio stations across the US. Apart from campaigning groups such as Military Families Speak Out and Veterans Against the War, ordinary US citizens are questioning in greater and greater numbers the validity

of being in Iraq. Sammis, however, remains supportive of US actions there.

'I believe in what we're doing,' he says. 'I know that Ben was doing his duty, what he was trained to do. Because of his actions there are countless marines alive today. I'm very proud of what he did. I'm very proud of how he stood as a person. I hold that same sense of pride and affection, that same support, for other American service personnel as well.'

Sammis sees his son as a hero – as do the vast majority of Americans, both those in favour of and those against the war. He agrees that, in the context of public criticism of the war, his son's death is more difficult to bear than it would otherwise have been. But he is not prepared to join the growing chorus of criticism yet.

'There was an intelligence failure, apparently,' he says. 'But I don't think we have enough

*Kim Hitzges receives the American flag at the grave site of her son US Army Sergeant Chad Keith during his funeral at Arlington National Cemetery in Arlington, Virginia. Photograph: Joe Raedle/Getty Images.*

information to turn around and start pointing fingers yet.'

For Sammis, the war in Iraq is about freedom and the prevention of terrorism. 'The reason that you and I can sit here and talk like this is because people are willing to put their lives on the line,' he says. To fight terrorism, he adds, 'means you've got to find out where they are, where they're planning their activities, who their leaders are – and kill them. Let's not be polite about it. You've got to find out who's supplying them, and get them. Unfortunately, you probably have to kill them too.'

His words are never spoken with anger, only with sadness. 'As a son, well, I couldn't have asked for more than Ben,' he says. 'We shared a lot of good times.'

While Steve Sammis may not be angry,

Rosemarie Dietz Slavenas certainly is. Her 30-year-old son, helicopter pilot Brian Slavenas, was shot down over Fallujah in November. 'George Bush killed my son,' she says. 'I believe my son died not for his country but because of our country's lack of a civilised foreign policy.'

On 2 November, Brian Slavenas was flying over a civilian area of Fallujah that had been searched by the US army the night before. There was anger in the area about the search and as Brian flew over the next morning his helicopter was hit by a missile fired from a shoulder-held weapon. The massive helicopter went into a spin. The rear propeller was damaged and the back of the helicopter was a fireball. The aircraft crashed and 16 people were killed. While 20 others survived, Brian died half an hour after being admitted to a hospital in Fallujah.

'I was coming home from church when I heard that a helicopter had crashed in Iraq and that there were injuries,' says Rosemarie Dietz Slavenas. 'Then when I came home there were two men in my yard. It was dark and they came towards my car. I could see one was a police officer and I asked him what happened. "The worst, the worst," he said. And I just began screaming "no, no, no".'

Slavenas had been an active member of an anti-war group before her son went to Iraq. She still takes part in an anti-war/anti-occupation vigil every Friday in her small Illinois town. She says she cherishes the memories of her son, and cherishes too the letters she received from him only days after he died.

It is moving to hear her read from one of those letters. It is an ordinary letter, full of inquiries and hopes. He asks about the new home his mother has moved into and about their 17-year-old dog, Pepper. 'Pepper will have an 18th birthday in a few months,' the letter says. 'Maybe that old peppery pooh will make it to 20.' The letter is dated 26 October. 'Things are going well,' it goes on. 'Maybe we'll be home in April. I'm not sure.'

A week later, Brian was dead, a year to the day before George W. Bush has to seek re-election.

Slavenas says her son tried and failed to get discharged from the military when he learned he was being deployed to Iraq. Her husband, from whom she is separated, contests this. She says that if her son had gone AWOL he would have spent two years in prison and be alive today. It is with bitterness that she now reads of her president's military career.

'It just came out in my local paper about the president and all the time he went missing from the military. I guess there's different rules for different folks,' she says.

Her heart goes out to other families who have lost loved ones in Iraq, she says, a great number of whom have been killed since an end to hostilities was proclaimed on May 1st last. She thinks, too, of Iraqis who have lost their lives. 'They call it "Iraqi Freedom",' she says. 'But who knows how many Iraqis have been killed?'

Up to 10,000 Iraqi civilians, according to the latest estimates from independent think-tanks. The nature of US television coverage means that most Americans are unaware of this. There's even a prohibition on showing US coffins coming home. But as more and more of those coffins do arrive, people are starting to utter the most feared word in the Pentagon: 'Vietnam'. As in that earlier conflict, Americans are starting to question the motives behind US involvement.

'They've been sent there because we have an economic interest in Iraq,' says Slavenas. 'I think the loss of life is obscene, what's being done is obscene. It's more than needless.'

She says that while she marched against the war with thousands all over the world this time last year she had no idea that so many would be dead only months later. The fact that one of those is her son has changed her life forever.

'He was such a beautiful, healthy young man,' she says. 'He never even smoked or drank. He was always a very athletic, positive person. When I saw the pictures of his helicopter, here he was, his beautiful, beautiful body broken. I couldn't look at it. I would have lost my mind.'

Next Friday, like every Friday, Rosemarie Dietz Slavenas will again be demonstrating.

**FRIDAY, 20 FEBRUARY 2004**

# Meddling Monster or Concerned Parent?

*Miriam Donohoe*

Pass my flak jacket, please. The war has begun. It seems only a few short years since I said goodbye to the terrible twos. But the battle lines have been drawn again as I launch into the terrible teens and enter combat with my 14-year-old son over what he claims is his right to privacy.

I always swore I would be a cool, hip, no-nag mother. A model mum with an honest and open relationship with my son. A mother he would be proud to bring his mates home to. Sadly, all those rose-tinted dreams of mother-son heaven have been thrown out of the window these past six months. I have become 'super nag', a monster daily accused of being a snoop, a nosey parker and a meddler. I have even been called a weapon of mass destruction, the current favoured nickname (grrrrrr). And all I'm doing is trying to keep tabs on my teenager.

Twelve months or so ago we were guaranteed to be told everything. We knew about any problems Stephen was experiencing at school, his successes or defeats on the football or rugby pitch and what his mates were getting up to. I even got a detailed report on his first disco, last June, and the girls he chatted up. He was at his second disco recently – and I wasn't told a thing.

Overnight he has clammed up. He now gives us information only on a need-to-know basis. What he thinks we need to know, by the way.

Like every other teenager in the country, Stephen does most of his communicating via mobile phone and e-mail. We are not the recipients of too many messages from him, just the occasional text wondering if we can pick him up from school, as it's raining, or asking what time we'll be home ourselves (a not-too-subtle ploy aimed at extending his time on the computer to the moment we turn the key in the front door).

The delete button on the computer keyboard is a great weapon in his armory. So is the erase function on the mobile phone. It means we are missing whole conversations he has with people, and all we get is an innocent shaking of the head when we ask if there's stuff he is not being forth-coming about.

I accept the Internet is a fantastic learning resource and source of entertainment for children. But what about the real dangers for children online? Aren't parents constantly warned to watch out for Internet predators? Look at the shocking case last week of the US marine who wooed a 12-year-old British girl over the Internet and con-vinced her to run away from home.

The problem is that most teenagers go online at home, right after school, when we and other working parents are not at home.

It all came to a head recently when I asked Stephen for his e-mail password. With all this talk about Internet predators I wanted to be a responsi-ble parent and check on whom he was e-mailing. And who was e-mailing him. No threat under the sun could prise the magic password from him. He was entitled to his privacy, he insisted.

And when I picked up his mobile phone the other week and started to casually check his messages, he grabbed it from me, switched it off and refused to give me the PIN. He pulled the privacy line again.

I trust and have every confidence in our eldest child, of course. I couldn't possibly believe any-thing untoward goes on in these electronic com-munications channels. But where do I draw the line between wanting to protect, help and educate on the one hand and wanting to respect his desire for privacy and independence on the other? God knows we are entitled to know what our son, at 14 years of age, is up to, who he is mixing with and where he is going. But we aren't into this business of snooping either.

His idea of snooping can often amount to just a polite inquiry on our part about his activities. There are moments when he does open up and when the pre-terrible-teen lad emerges once again. And during these moments he gushes forth with his innermost views on everything from his hopes to capital punishment, George Bush and the war in Iraq. We get the full version of 'I'm a teenager with attitude'.

We just want to reserve the right to ask ques-tions about important issues such as sex, drink and drugs as he heads towards young adulthood. We are reassured by friends who have been here that this obstinacy is part of the growing process. These

*Miriam Donohoe at home with her son, Stephen.*
*Photograph: Alan Betson.*

FRIDAY, 20 FEBRUARY 2004

# Stop Breathing Down My Neck All the Time, Mum

*Stephen Murray (Miriam Donohoe's son)*

I am a 14-year-old second-year student who has embarked on a new expedition in life. That expedition includes changes and my huge need for privacy.

As a teenager I expect to have privacy at home. Privacy is something that everyone has a right to. We all need it in order to stay sane. You cannot live with someone breathing down your neck the whole time.

Maybe this is the case in the early stages of life, from age one to 10. But I have entered the second decade of my life, a time when a lot of changes occur.

Privacy is up there with my biggest need. It is like gold dust for me at the moment, and I just can't get enough of it. But privacy and being on my own are scarce around here.

My parents are constantly interfering with my personal issues. If my mobile phone is lying around they will swoop like vultures, open the phone book or in-box and go in for the kill.

Any girls' names will bring thorough interrogation, but I have learned the short cuts and tricks. Totally ignore them or come up with a mantra and constantly say it until the vultures leave. But do they leave successfully? I am afraid not.

The vultures use this lethal approach with my e-mail as well. If George Bush is on the lookout for weapons of mass destruction, then he need look no further than my house – or probably most family homes.

My room is a place that should be for me to go home to after school, to think about matters, and a place I and nobody else has access to.

My parents will often come up to my room to talk to me about irrelevant matters (like homework and stuff). I wish to be left alone, without constant

same friends have emerged from the terrible teens with their children intact. All their warnings about what lay ahead have not prepared us, however, for the testosterone and hormonal force about our house.

I am convinced there must be a middle ground, somewhere that allows me peace of mind and allows him the space, privacy and independence he craves. No doubt I will eventually find it and the rows about what's his, what's ours and what's allowed will become less frequent. In the meantime the battle rages. And the book title is already in my head: How I Survived His Teenage Years, by a hassled mother.

interruption, in my room, the only place in the house that I own.

Sometimes, after interruption from my parents, I begin to understand my religion teacher telling us about meditation and the seven circles of faith, which include silence and space, both being factors of privacy.

I get space in my room, but silence is a different story. Shouting 'shut up' down the stairs works for about five seconds. Closing the door usually makes my parents and sister even louder.

Sometimes I consider saving up to soundproof my room and be rid of all noises from downstairs. But I get my peace when they leave the house, which comes around every now and then. At this time I am free to roam about my house, use my phone, check my e-mail and, most importantly, think with a clear mind without the usual interruption.

Privacy is so important at this stage of my life. I would nearly be tempted to use my pocket money, if possible, to buy some of it.

*Environment Minister Martin Cullen at the launch of an information campaign on electronic voting at the Mansion House in Dublin. Photograph: Frank Miller.*

**TUESDAY, 2 MARCH 2004**

# Truth is Essential for Peace

*Fintan O'Toole*

One of the mysteries of Sinn Féin's finances is the gap between the vast sums it raises in the US and the amounts it spends on elections in Ireland.

But there is a perfectly logical explanation: the cost of keeping Gerry Adams in trousers. Every time he denies that he was ever a member of the IRA, his pants catch fire. As the questions, and the denials, become more frequent, this act of spontaneous combustion takes place on an ever more regular basis.

In the old days, when he dressed from Dunnes Stores, this wasn't so bad, but ever since Tiochfaidh ár Lá became Tiochfaidh Armani, we are talking about serious money.

The real question, however, is whether Gerry Adams's inability to acknowledge his past matters at all. The point of a lie is to deceive, and in this case the deception is scarcely perceptible. The evidence of his having been a senior IRA member is so overwhelming that it is impossible to find anyone who actually believes his denials. As early as July 1972, when Adams was just 23, the British government arranged talks with the IRA leadership in London. One of the IRA's conditions for agreeing to take part was that Adams be released from

*Amanda Coogan, winner of the Allied Irish Banks Prize 2004, an award for promising artists, with her work Reading Beethoven at the RHA Gallery in Dublin. Photograph: Bryan O'Brien.*

custody to join its negotiating team.

In January 1973, the US embassy in Dublin reported to Washington that the IRA was led by a 'Troika', namely Dáithí O'Connell, Joe Cahill and Gerry Adams, 'who is still an active Belfast military commander'.

In 2002, Dolours Price, who was convicted of involvement in the planting of four IRA car-bombs in London in March 1973, described Adams as 'my commanding officer' at the time.

In the mid-1970s, Adams, then a prisoner in Long Kesh, wrote for *An Phoblacht* under the pseudonym 'Brownie'. In a column in May 1976, he made his only public admission of IRA membership. 'Rightly or wrongly, I am an IRA Volunteer and, rightly or wrongly, I take a course of action as a means to bringing about a situation in which I

believe the people of my country will prosper,' Adams wrote. 'The course I take involves the use of physical force.' So in one light, Adams's denials can be seen merely as the kind of meaningless gesture that politicians sometimes find necessary. They are the equivalent of an old-style Irish politician beginning a speech with a 'cúpla focal' of Gaelic, or Tony Blair singing The Red Flag at a Labour Party conference.

Since only a fool would believe that the 'cúpla focal' merchant is committed to the Irish language or that Tony Blair is a socialist, the lie is not so much a deception as a ritual fabrication. It is almost a form of good manners, like telling your granny that you just love the hideous jumper she knitted for you.

In Adams's case, democratic politicians needed someone from the IRA to deal with and it suited

*Naturalist David Bellamy shows a lobster to two-year-old Liam Clarke from Moycullen in Co. Galway during his visit to the Martin Ryan Institute at NUI Galway. Photograph: Joe O'Shaughnessy.*

everyone to pretend at the same time that that person wasn't really from the IRA. Adams himself in that sense was a necessary fiction. The problem is, though, that the fiction has become a real lie. For quite separate reasons, North and South, it has grown into a boil that needs to be lanced.

In the Republic, Adams has become, according to the polls, the most respected party leader. Here is a society which is obsessed with the sins of the past. We have tribunals inquiring into the financial misdeeds of politicians and businessmen 15 years ago. We have a Church wracked with the guilt of institutionalised abuse stretching back half a century.

And yet we seem to deeply admire a politician who has been accused by a highly respected journalist, Ed Moloney, in his book *A Secret History of the IRA*, of having established and controlled the cell within the IRA that kidnapped, tortured and 'disappeared' Jean McConville and others. It is surely quite reasonable for, say, Liam Lawlor to wonder why he has gone to jail for his evasiveness in relation to land deals and planning in the 1980s while Gerry Adams, who has not dealt in any open way with these infinitely more serious allegations, is a political saint.

And at the same time, Sinn Féin has not adopted a policy consistent with Gerry Adams's personal position of drawing a veil over all the hideous deeds of the Troubles.

It has supported or demanded inquiries into Bloody Sunday, the Dublin and Monaghan bombings, the murder of Pat Finucane, and collusion between the security forces and loyalist paramilitaries.

*Jockey Jim Culloty in high spirits after his third Cheltenham Gold Cup win in a row, riding Best Mate. Photograph: Brenda Fitzsimons.*

And this double-standard isn't just regrettable hypocrisy. It cripples the peace process by making reconciliation impossible. It creates two categories of victims – those murdered by the state and/or loyalists, whose families deserve a full accounting, and those murdered by the IRA who do not.

The best way to cope with these real problems is not to focus solely on Gerry Adams but to do what should have been done as part of the Belfast Agreement: establish a proper Truth and Reconciliation Commission.

Only thus can we recognise that reconciliation without truth is just as false a concept as truth without reconciliation.

# High-Stakes Showdown at Deadman's Inn

*Joe Humphreys*

When Tom Gilmartin waltzed back into town in the late-1980s, after 50 years working in the UK, little did he know he was returning to something out of the Wild West. He had 'shadowy figures' trying to hold him to ransom, and 'strange' hoops to jump through to get business done. But nothing compared to the 'liar' and 'hustler' he first met one Tuesday in May at the Deadman's Inn in Palmerstown.

'He came up along the bar. The bar was between the door and the table where I was sitting. This gentleman arrived and he introduced himself as Liam Lawlor.'

So began Mr Gilmartin's account of his dealings with the former Fianna Fáil TD who would become his nemesis in a game of high stakes that has yet to conclude. 'He said he was a TD,' Mr Gilmartin recalled with disbelief, 'and he knew every piece of land in the area.'

The tenderfoot wanted to talk about Quarryvale, the west Dublin wasteland that he hoped to pan for gold. But Mr Lawlor had his sights set on other riches – a planned development in the city, backed by a publicity-shy British outfit Arlington.

'He wanted to meet Arlington,' Mr Gilmartin recalled. 'I said I would have to ask Arlington.' Two days later, Mr Lawlor turned up unannounced at an Arlington meeting in London, and Mr Gilmartin realised what exactly he had on his hands. 'The man is a f★★★★★★ hustler,' the Sligo-born businessman told a colleague at the meeting when Mr Lawlor demanded 'in' on the project.

Mr Gilmartin then, as now, got on his high-horse and rode out of the meeting to avoid the scenario of 'two Paddies in a room going to start an argument'. He only got as far as the tea-rooms of the Buckingham Gate Hotel, however, before Mr Lawlor tracked him down, demanding a slice of Mr Gilmartin's piece of the action. 'I said, "You know what you can do mate".' Only he said it, 'a bit more strongly'.

So, at least, runs Mr Gilmartin's side of the story.

Mr Lawlor was not at Dublin Castle yesterday to renew the showdown.

**SATURDAY, 6 MARCH 2004**

# Forgetting About the Joneses

*Tony Clayton Lea*

Katie Melua is not jazz, and she's definitely not the next Norah Jones.

Jazz? We don't think so. Now that anything associated with that word has more cachet than any canny marketing executive can dream of, along comes 19-year-old Katie Melua to dispel the notion that anyone who sounds remotely like Norah Jones can sell a bucket load of CDs and provide a never-ending selection of soundtrack smoothies to Starbucks clientele.

Melua has little time for the Norah Jones comparisons, anyway. 'It's a bit difficult to live up to,' she says on a frosty Dublin morning several days ago. 'It's flattering', she concedes, 'but we're so different. The industry has a tendency to place people in boxes, but we all know it's just a way of referencing tastes. Ultimately she's Norah Jones and I'm Katie Melua.' Melua is all ringlets and curls, and is – literally – made up for the day.

She's extra petite, has a face that Helen of Troy would be envious of and is the type of instantly famous person one might think would be a nightmare to talk to.

She was born in Georgia, in the former USSR, in 1984; her family lived in Moscow for a few years, subsequently residing in the seaside town of

*Westlife fans Hayley Thorpe (right) and Emma Coffill, both from Buckinghamshire in England, console each other in Dublin after Bryan McFadden announced his departure from the boy band. Photograph: Bryan O'Brien.*

Batumi until Melua was nine, when her father's work as a heart surgeon eventually took the family to Belfast. She remained in the North until she was 13, which is when her father's work contract ran out – 'he applied for a job in England and when he got that we left'. Her memories of Belfast are fond if a tad too much raked-over for her liking. She played there last Sunday.

'It was great going back because it has always felt like I'm returning to my second home. I love Belfast so much, and I missed it so much when I left. All my relatives are back in Georgia in Eastern Europe, but I have so many friends in Belfast, people I met in schools, all my mum's friends.'

South-East London, 1997, was the next location for the Melua family and it's from this time onwards that her very slow rise to fame commenced.

She won the television talent contest, Stars Up Their Nose – singing Mariah Carey's Without You – which garnered a place in the BRIT School for Performing Arts. Amidst all the swapping of CDs and general getting to know the music business, the BRIT School organised for a few of its singers to back Westlife on the Smash Hit Awards 2000 tour.

'I was backing miming!' she reveals with a swivel of her eyebrows, allowing her aversion to manufactured pop to break through. 'I was 16 and it was great fun. Their music? I haven't got their albums, so I can't really comment.'

It was hearing one singer in particular, however, that drove Melua to new heights of aspiration. 'My main influences came about when I went to music school. I grew up a bit then, and heard and discovered real music and musicians. A lot of it was word of mouth, which is the best way to find out about music, I think. People such as The Beatles, Led Zeppelin, Queen, Ella Fitzgerald and Bob Dylan were great, but perhaps the biggest influence of all was Eva Cassidy. Someone like her gets you right in the heart and it's amazing. That's the beauty of music, isn't it – whatever form it takes, you will always find something universal about it, that jumps over the language barrier, something that can capture people's hearts.'

Certainly, Melua has captured the hearts of the UK. In the past six months, her début album, *Call Off The Search*, has climbed to the top of the charts on the back of word of mouth and radio/ television support from the likes of Terry Wogan and Michael Parkinson. She signed a five-album record deal with the Dramatico record label (owned by her producer/mentor/former Womble Mike Batt, who also wrote six of 12 tracks on *Call Off The Search*; Melua wrote two, while the remainder are divided between the likes of Randy Newman and John Mayall). She differs from the Pop Idol wannabes in areas of taste, class and work ethic. She comes across as a person with a genuine sense of what she wants and where she wants to go.

But how much of *Call Off The Search* is actually Melua? Both the title track and the hit single, *The Closest Thing to Crazy*, are Batt compositions. 'All of it,' she says slightly proprietorially, her ringlets bobbing in mild annoyance. 'It's an interesting project for me because I regard it as my singing album; yes, there are a couple of songs I've written but essentially it's a vehicle for my voice. People who sing and not write songs these days are viewed in a dismissive way – anyone can sing, seems to be the criticism, but I think that's an unfair judgment.

'Singing my own songs comes quite naturally to me, because I don't have to try to make the song my own – it is already. When you sing a cover, it's much harder work, and it takes a lot of skill to make it your own. I don't know if I've succeeded, but I liked the challenge of it.'

She copes with her new-found success by partly denying it exists. 'I haven't really changed to be honest; I don't get recognised in the street too much, which is great and I hope it stays like that. I concentrate on the music and the thing at hand. Someone should write a book about the psychological state people go through from being unknown to so-called famous. Not about the speed of it but the actual phenomenon. To be honest, I think I've managed to stay pretty okay about everything, but you do wonder sometimes about the people that aren't okay with it. Is it voluntary madness or is it something that happens without you'r knowing?'

If it's the latter, Melua ponders, then it's quite scary. She sometimes gets scared, she admits, but only insofar as watching carefully the things she says in interviews (hence her diplomatic silence about Westlife).

'You're almost being much nicer than if you weren't successful. It's not really about putting on anything close to airs and graces. It's more about

*Katie Melua. Photograph: Matt Kavanagh.*

being appreciative of what's happened to you and being thankful for it, which I totally am.'

She's a grounded person, too. The way she looks at life is this: what she's doing doesn't matter at all. It is, she remarks, a tiny speck in the grand scheme of things. 'I mean, what are we all doing here in a posh hotel getting my hair and make-up done at 11 in the morning? It doesn't make any sense, does it?'

But she also realises there are people who have listened to her record and come to her gigs who are affected by what they hear. 'That's the most important aspect of what I do and that's why I love what I'm doing. The money doesn't matter, but the magic does.'

Jazz? Once again, we don't think so.

'You can't really care about things like that. I'm not a jazz artist and neither is someone like Norah Jones. It's just about music, melodies and lyrics in simple form. I find it hard to define exactly what style I am – it doesn't really matter, does it?' She says she's in it for the long haul, which is only to be expected – who'd ever want to be a one-hit wonder? While her songwriting skills have yet to be truly put to the test, longevity might arrive in the shape of well-chosen cover versions (which is, presumably, where the experience of industry veteran Batt enters the picture).

'I always wanted to sing songs,' Melua says, 'but I never imagined it being attached to fame. Fame is incidental.'

**TUESDAY, 9 MARCH 2004**

# 'So Where is my Baby in All of This? I Can't Find Him. He's Lost. …'

*Mary Murphy*

*(Editor's note: In all the thousands of words journalists wrote about the Brian Murphy case, none captured the trauma his family suffered with the power and eloquence of the words spoken by his mother when she read her victim's impact statement in court to Judge Michael White. This is what she said.)*

I am here for Brian. This is the most nerve-wracking thing I have ever done. I'm doing it also for myself because I have been forced to keep silent for so long. But my real motivation in taking the stand here today comes from my deep love for my son.

The love that one has for one's child is primal. It's the type of love where you would put your own safety at risk. It is the only comparison I have for the love that God has for us.

I wasn't there when Brian was savagely kicked and beaten to death. If I had been there you would not have succeeded in your quest to attack my baby because you would have had to kill me first.

I spent a lot of my time over the past week preparing a text for this impact statement. It contained details and a description of how I felt in the immediate aftermath of Brian's death, how we were told not to touch his body in case we would destroy evidence. There were details I wanted to share about Brian's wake, his funeral and his burial. When I read it over in preparation for today, it sounded so hollow. When I asked myself why did I feel this way the feeling came that apart from the judge and my own close family and friends the rest of those listening to me probably didn't want to know. When I thought about that I realised how much I have felt under attack in this courtroom over the past seven weeks.

I will try and outline why I have felt this way.

Firstly, when I woke up the next morning still thinking about this, I noticed as I lay in the bed that I had my two arms tightly over my face and that there was huge tension in my whole body.

In a strange way I felt that there was an uncanny resemblance between Brian's predicament in his final moments and my feelings of being surrounded by people whom I felt didn't want to know about our tragedy.

Just thinking about our family's seating position in Court 23 helps me to further enhance what I'm talking about. In front of us were seated the prosecution barristers, and solicitor. Beside them were the defence barristers and their solicitors. The media and the accused were also present. All of these people had a voice. Brian and our family, I felt, had no voice. That was why I felt surrounded and under attack.

I would like to describe how I felt about these various parties.

First of all we heard the prosecution, who don't represent Brian, but who act on behalf of the people of Ireland and therefore represent the State. I felt the rules governing how they were allowed to argue the case to be so restrictive. To me the evidence of some witnesses was confusing and contradictory, yet the prosecution was not able to recall these witnesses for clarification.

Then we have the defence teams. The main effect that the defence had on me was that I felt I was being brainwashed into thinking that what happened to Brian was somehow his own fault. The repetition of evidence over and over again somehow desensitises everyone to the reality of what happened to Brian.

The summing up of the defence tried to paint all the defendants in such a wonderful light, that it was a tragedy for them to have to be sitting here as defendants at all. Are you allowed, in summing up, to blatantly contradict a scientific witness, such as Dr Harbison, who stated that Brian consumed less than twice the legal limit of alcohol permitted

*Brian Murphy*

*Mary Murphy. Photograph: Dara Mac Dónaill.*

when driving a car? This means that Brian consumed between three and four pints on the night in question. In the summing up there was a suggestion that he consumed twice that amount.

Then there is the media. I think the message abroad from the media is that the tragedy of our family and those of the accused is in some way comparable. The opinion of the general public seems to suggest that any of their children could have been involved in a similar attack. It was a tragedy for these guys. The headline in one Sunday broadsheet epitomises what I'm saying, where Brian is described as 'The Luckless Murphy'. This suggests that poor Brian was just unfortunate to be in the wrong place at the wrong time.

The biggest fault I have become aware of as I have read some media is that they are quoting as fact something that has been alleged, and are using

that to back up their own agenda. This has the cumulative effect for me of diminishing Brian as a human being. I would just like to clarify that I have felt that direct evidence quoted by the reporters which speak directly about the evidence as presented before the jury has been, in my opinion, for the most part accurate. But remember, this is only evidence. People who swear before God to tell the truth, the whole truth and nothing but the truth don't necessarily do that.

And, finally, you have those convicted of their part in Brian's killing, who have attempted to deny and minimise their part in Brian's death.

So, maybe now you can understand why I could not share my innermost feelings about my beautiful darling son to a listenership such as this.

So, I don't intend to go into any great detail about how it felt to watch Brian, as he lay dead on a hospital bed with his two front teeth smashed; or about the long wait before his body was brought back home in a coffin to us; what it was like to watch my child lie in a coffin with my rosary beads wrapped around his hands and Brona's private letter to him lying on top of his body.

I have an abiding memory of so many candles lighting all day and all night in the room with him. I am not going to tell you about the prayers of forgiveness, which we composed ourselves, and which we brought before God at Brian's funeral Mass. I won't attempt to describe the devastation I felt at Mount Jerome crematorium, as the curtain went across Brian's coffin to the music of Brian's favourite song, November Rain, or about the box of ashes I carried to his grave.

I was going to describe the emptiness in my heart and in my home, about the weeks and months afterwards when I prayed that I would die too, about the anger I felt towards God because I felt He could have stopped this. The delay in the trial process added hugely to our pain.

So where is my baby in all of this? I can't find him. He's lost. I'm lost. All my family and friends are lost too.

Where is my pride and joy, my full of confidence child, my crazy, exuberant, full of cheer, larger than life child? My naïve, far from perfect child, who did some silly things and some fabulous things.

On the basis that the judge does want to know who Brian was I will attempt to introduce you to this dehumanised, by the trial process, Brian Murphy. Actions speak louder than words. Anyone who saw the video of Brian interacting with his little brother on TV should be able to see the vitality, the warmth that was in him as he rubbed the top of Robert's head after he kissed him and used the words 'I love you too, Baby.'

Here is my humble attempt to describe Brian. Anyone who knew him would say that he was a free spirit who was larger than life. He had a special charm that drew people to him. He was 18, remember. He had still a lot of maturing to do both physically, emotionally and mentally. He was highly intelligent. His exuberant personality refused to be quashed.

As a person, Brian had time for everyone. He labelled no one. He had so many friends from all schools and our local soccer club. His friends came from every walk of life and every background. He was not an adopted Clongownian. He liked people for who they were and nothing else. What schools people attended was irrelevant to him.

He was a brilliant listener. He made you feel you were important to him. He was so open. There was no pretence, what you saw and heard was the real him, warts and all. He was an individual, with his own views. He was a leader. His sense of humour was second to none. To remember him is to smile. He would introduce humour into the everyday, the banal. The spirit that was Brian was manifested in his appreciation of the finer things of life.

At his funeral Mass a young lady told a story about Brian from the altar. How he brought her into the National Gallery to show her, in his own words, the best painting ever. It was a painting

*Brian Murphy's father, Denis, with his wife, Mary, and their son, Robert. Photograph: Dara Mac Dónaill.*

called *The Opening of the Sixth Seal*, the theme of which was taken from the Book of Revelations in the Bible. It was painted with a black background, with a red sun, and orange and red flashes of lightning. He was fascinated by it.

He loved poetry. I vividly remember the days prior to his Leaving Cert. English exam of him showing off how he could recite every poem on the course, even though this wasn't necessary for the exam.

He loved mountains. His favourite holiday was one we spent camping in the Alps. We have put a picture of Mount Fuji on his memorial book mark because that is a place he longed to visit. In a book where he had read about Mount Fuji, called the *Natural Wonders of the World*, Mount Fuji is described as a place of pilgrimage and a sacred

*Seán Mackey. Photograph: Ronan Quinlan.*

place, the reason being that its coned peak goes above the clouds, and there is an air of heaven and earth coming together at its peak.

Dr Harbison said that Brian had a slightly enlarged heart. Clare said to me afterwards that was a good description of Brian; that is that he had such a big heart. Stories of Brian's big heart abound. The one which sticks in my mind happened during the summer before Brian's death.

He came with me and Robert to visit my mother, who was suffering from Alzheimer's disease. She was in a nursing home in Bray. We walked to the sea front with her with Brian holding her hand. We sat on a bench at the sea front with her. Brian gave her a cigarette, and we laughed as she tapped the ash in the way she would have prior to her illness.

Brian put his arm around her and said, 'Gran, I'm sorry I haven't been to see you in a while,' and he started to cry. She did not understand a word he was saying. He then went to the sea shore with Robert to show him how to skim stones on water.

He was delighted at Robert's success in doing this and gave me the thumbs up from the water's edge. Robert remembers this day also.

There is a story of him bringing home, unbeknownst to me, a man who was down on his luck to our home and Brian cooking one of his specialities for him.

To me he was my best mate. I had completed first year as a mature student in UCD in the faculty of social science. I found studying for the exams really tough. Brian was there for me with his encouragement to keep at it. To his delight I passed my exams. During that summer, I worked as a social care worker with a young girl who was a heroin addict. I found the work emotionally draining and Brian was a ready listener when I described to him what life was like for this young girl.

What I really miss most of all about Brian is the fun we had together. My best memory of this is our day together on his 18th birthday. We went into town and bought his present, having travelled to every shop in town. I will never forget the camaraderie there was between us as we chatted over lunch in a restaurant chosen by him.

He told one of his friends, speaking of me, 'Mary understands me'. I am so glad that he said this as it gives me huge consolation.

How do I convey how Brian's death has affected me? The pain I felt was physical. I could not shed a single tear, which would have been an outlet for some of the pain. The pain was one of shock, numbness and grief which had no outlet because I could not cry. In time, with the feeling of anger came the tears which at least gave some release to the pain.

I have and will continue to have great difficulty letting myself feel the sadness. Devastation is more the word to describe it. I have to blank that out. This will never go away and it is something I have to try to accept.

*Dermot Laide. Photograph: Garrett White/Collins.*

*Desmond Ryan. Photograph: Ronan Quinlan.*

Then I think of what it was like for Brian and his final moments. What was the horror and terror like for him? He must have been pleading in his mind, 'Will somebody help me.'

This talk about Brian's group. What group? If Brian was with a group he would still be alive because they would have come to his defence. The boasting and cheering are scary, like we have gone back to the dark ages. Words like manslaughter and violent disorder make killing sound respectable. This I find nauseating.

I wonder what legal jargon would be used if Brian hadn't died but was left brain-damaged with the suffering that would have been for him and us. Denis and I have lost our beautiful son's future – his maturing, his becoming more sensible as he got older. But the biggest thing we have lost out on is his sense of fun.

Robert was six years old when his big brother, whom he loved, was snatched from him. Robert started to play matches for his football club a year after Brian died. Brian would have been his Number One supporter on the sideline, offering all sorts of advice to his little brother. Denis said just after Robert was born that he was looking forward to the day when Brian, Robert and himself would attend matches together. This never happened. I imagine the slagging there would have been between them over premiership results, Brian being a Spurs supporter and Robert a Liverpool supporter. All Robert has left of Brian is his picture which he has pasted to his bedside locker, a teddy Brian gave him, and an old Spurs shirt of Brian's, which Robert sleeps on at night when he is feeling particularly sad. Robert goes through phases of sadness. It usually happens at night when he cries and says 'I miss Brian'. I hate this loss for Robert more than anything.

Brona told me of an evening when he arrived home, when she was babysitting Robert and he walked in and said to her, 'Brona, you know I love you.' This coming from an 18-year-old boy to his 14-year-old sister shows what a special person he was. There are 16 months between Clare and Brian. They were like peas in a pod, doing everything together.

What effect has the trial had on me? I'm back to when Brian died. That we should be forced to revisit it after three years is inhuman. The shock, the anger, the sadness are back and along with these is fear which must be present as a result of hearing the details of what happened to Brian. I wonder will I ever feel safe again, because the way the justice system works makes me think that we live in a very unsafe society.

I wanted questions answered by coming to this trial every day. The way I see it, there was no fight when Brian was killed. There was a concerted savage attack, where he was surrounded and kicked to death.

I feel brutalised by this trial process. The quest for the truth becomes a battle between two sides caught in a game, each side trying to win points. Brian gets lost. Brian becomes the object in the red shirt. There are some phrases that are ingrained in my mind and will be with me for the rest of my life.

'We got him good.'

Other witnesses used another version of this which I prefer not to repeat.

'This is great craic.'

'Behaving like animals.' As a lover of animals I find that remark insulting to animals.

'He fell flat on his face with no arms to save him.'

'I started all this.'

'The wave of feet.'

'I couldn't put faces with feet,' by witnesses who knew the accused.

The new shoes kicking him. The big-headed guy who walked from the group kicking Brian.

'I heard his head snap, crack and I felt it go soft.'

I used to think that whoever did this will have to live with it for the rest of their lives, which is why I prayed for them and their families at Brian's funeral and at subsequent anniversary Masses.

After attending this trial and hearing what I have heard, I don't think that any more. They just want to get off.

If they had a conscience and if they were really sorry for what they have done, they would tell the whole truth about what has happened, own up and take the consequences.

Truth is lost here. Brian is lost here. I am lost here. I have agonised over forgiveness over these past years since Brian's death, how I couldn't find it in my heart to forgive. I wasn't going to pretend to forgive, it had to come from my heart.

From the way this whole case has gone I am clear on one thing. I cannot contemplate forgiveness until I know the truth and those responsible for Brian's death have acknowledged their part in it and make known the part others played in his killing.

The anger I felt mounting as the trial progressed was all about what I have just said, that nobody was owning up. The way I see it, that is the only way of getting on with the rest of your lives. There is no way of hiding from the truth. It demands to be seen and heard.

On considering this issue for myself, I was reminded of the account in the Bible of the crucifixion of Jesus, where the two criminals were on crosses on each side of him. One said to Jesus, 'If you are a king, you save us.' The one on his other side said, 'Leave him alone, he has done no wrong. We deserve to be here, he doesn't.' Jesus said to this criminal, 'You will be with me today in paradise.' He did not say it to the other one. The man who told the truth won the favour of Jesus.

To conclude, we as a family have to go from here to try and get on with our lives. I know that in time and with God's help, as I move through all the pain that is ahead of me, that I will survive as Brian has survived. I know for Brian that life has changed, not ended. I am not afraid of death any more. I look forward to running into Brian's outstretched arms as he enfolds me in his warm, joyful embrace.

I have a memory which convinces me of Brian's state. Some months after he died I was coming out of a deep sleep when I heard his voice in my head, which just said, 'sorry'.

He had come back to say this word to me. It was a word which I was used to when he was alive. Whenever we had words, which mothers of teenagers often do, he would be heading out afterwards and he'd shout, 'I'll see you, Mum.' Then he'd have qualms of conscience about what had been said and he'd arrive back and say, 'Sorry, Mum,' about whatever the disagreement had been about. I'd say, 'It's okay, Brian,' and he'd head off much happier. The fact that Brian came back and said this word to me is a sign to me that he is still alive.

I am so thankful for the support I get from my husband Denis and my three other children. I hope I can support them also. I am so thankful for the support of the rest of my extended family and for the support of our good, honest, trustworthy, faithful and loving friends.

Can I make an appeal to the media? Please don't misquote me, or quote me out of context. Please, please respect my integrity. It is so hurtful to see yourself misquoted, or the wrong slant put on what you say. If you care in any way about me or Brian and my family please take the time to understand what I'm saying. I feel that the lives of those convicted in connection with Brian's death are not ruined, as some media have said about them. They are not ruined if they can summon up the huge courage that is needed to face the truth.

The truth will set you free.

*(On March 15, Judge White sentenced Dermot Laide to four years imprisonment for manslaughter and two years for violent disorder. He gave Seán Mackey two years for violent disorder and Desmond Ryan nine months for violent disorder. The other accused, Andrew Frame, was acquitted at an earlier point in the trial.)*

# White Town Hides from Reality of a Rainbow State

*Declan Walsh, in Orania, South Africa*

It could be anywhere in small-town South Africa. A sleepy attendant mans a single-pump petrol station. Barefoot children shelter from the heat of the sun on a rickety porch. A tractor rumbles by, ruddy-faced labourers hanging off the trailer.

Except that, in Orania, there is one striking difference: no blacks. Only conservative, God-fearing Afrikaners live in this dusty town on the edge of the Karoo desert. They speak Afrikaans, fly the Boer flag and do all their own work. A large sign by the grocery store heralds their aspiration. It reads 'Orania – Afrikanertuiste', which means 'Afrikaner homeland'.

'This is a laboratory,' said Prof. Carel Boshoff, a former university lecturer and one of the town's founding fathers. Orania, named after the nearby Orange River, is the last redoubt of a people under siege, he says.

The new, democratic South Africa threatens to swamp Afrikaner tongue and traditions. So since 1991 he has led the retreat to this small racial corral, halfway between Johannesburg and Cape Town, where the colours of the 'rainbow nation' bleach into one, freckle-speckled, white.

'It is necessary to protect our culture, our language, our religion. Otherwise it will be assimilated and die,' he said. His many critics say otherwise. Whites make up 4.3 million of South Africa's 45 million people, of which about 60 per cent are Afrikaners. The tiny community of 600 Oranians is at best an affront to the national spirit of reconciliation, they say; at worst it is a racist holdout from the separationist past.

*Farm workers at a melon plantation in Orania, Northern Cape Province, South Africa. Photograph: Tienes Martines.*

Dr John Strydom, a chatty, moustachioed man is Orania's official tour guide. He sells a jumble of herbs, leather shoes and key rings with the slogan 'Orania: Live the Dream' from his 'winkel', or provisions store.

He easily anticipates the obvious questions. 'A lot of people think this is a refugee camp for people who can't live under a black government, or who yearn for the apartheid years,' he said. 'But it's not.' The town is run on an ethos of strict morals and self-sufficiency, he says.

A six-person committee vets potential residents – who come from across the country – for religious and moral beliefs. Cohabiting couples are forbidden, and attendance at the Calvinist churches is encouraged. Excessive drinking and premarital sex are frowned upon, he says.

Farmers grow melons for export to Europe, pecan nuts and some olives. Light industry includes a coffin manufacturer, whose clients are mainly the families of Aids victims in the nearest town, 40 kilometres away.

Eco-friendly innovations are common – some residents shun artificial fertilisers and pesticides; one woman turns the soil in her garden using chickens instead of a plough. The private school has its own curriculum.

And unlike elsewhere in South Africa, there are no maids, gardeners, drivers or cooks. Instead, former army officers and university professors mow their own lawns, cook dinner and scrub toilets. 'In a certain sense we are liberating the blacks,' said Dr Strydom. But that's not how the neighbours see it.

Orania refuses to come under the local authority, and residents boycotted the last municipal elections in 2000. Black delivery men from nearby Hope Town need written permission to enter a residential area. 'They are just racists,' said Peter Demas of Thembehle municipality. 'We thought we had abolished apartheid, but it is still there.'

Tensions were heightened some years back when a group of young white men opened fire on a passing bus late at night, wounding a black passenger. The case went to court but there were no convictions.

The looming presence of Hendrik Verwoerd, the 'architect of apartheid', bolsters the charges of racism. A diminutive statue of the former prime minister, who was assassinated by a deranged messenger in 1966, stands on a rocky hill over the town. His last suit, complete with stab marks, is on display in the Verwoerd museum. Sculptures and busts litter the garden, hastily donated by public buildings in the post-apartheid clean-out. 'They are trying to get rid of these things as quickly as we can say thank you,' lamented Dr Strydom.

Verwoerd's widow, Betsie, lived in Orania until her death three years ago. In a famous gesture of reconciliation, Nelson Mandela once visited, quipping at the Verwoerd statue: 'I didn't know he was so small'. Her daughter, Anna, is married to Prof. Boshoff and manages the local school. She remembers her father as a good man. 'We only know that he did his best for this country,' she said.

Although small and isolated, Orania reflects a broader crisis in Afrikaner identity. Torn between the loss of power and their tainted apartheid dominance, many feel marginalised and lost in what they wryly call 'the new dispensation'.

Elsewhere, extremists such as the Boremag group have made farcical attempts to overthrow the ANC government. Oranians prefer comparison with the Voortrekkers, their hardy forebears who fled English domination on cattle wagons in the nineteenth century.

Boer independence was once an international cause, they like to remind visitors, pointing to a monument commemorating Irish volunteers who fought on their side in the 1899-1902 Anglo-Boer war. Today the English language is the enemy.

'We must keep Afrikaans alive for the next generation,' said Roelof Stols, a 17-year-old schoolboy, in faltering English.

For many, however, the attraction is less philosophical – the prospect of safety and quiet, far from the violent crime and security fences of the big cities. And some are clearly drawn for reasons of naked racism.

As we leave the Verwoerd museum, an elderly couple pulls up. From out of town, they look like a sweet old pair on a Sunday drive. 'It's wonderful here, but how do you manage to have no blacks?' the grey-haired man marvels to Dr Strydom. 'I thought you would need guards to keep them out.'

'He has no idea about Orania. He thinks it is an all-white town,' said Dr Strydom afterwards. But is that not exactly what it is? 'Incidentally, yes,' he retorts testily. 'Just as almost all Germans are white and all Zimbabweans are black.'

The 10 young men working at the melon farm come from poor white city backgrounds. The pay is poor – just 50 rand (€6) a day – and the conservative Oranians complain they drink too much, but it is better than the outside world, they say. Tienes Martines (17) came in response to a newspaper advert. He dropped out of school in Newcastle, a mining town in Natal province, because 'the blacks were taking over,' he said.

Asked if he had any black friends, he replied: 'No. A kaffir's a kaffir, isn't he? It's a dirty thing.' But most Oranians are at pains to stress they are not racists. They argue that Afrikaners need their own patch of land to consider home, just as Zulus and Xhosas have theirs. Prof. Boshoff dreams of a new 'volkstaat', stretching across the arid Northern Cape plains to the Atlantic Ocean.

Willem Botha, a jolly 70-year-old former weapons engineer, sat over a glass of wine in his living room. 'I have excellent relations with blacks, and I'm no racist. But I favour race differentiation.' Next month the town will introduce its own currency, swapping rand for local vouchers, in an attempt to keep money in the local economy. But it may be no easier than forcing the people to remain. The town has a high turnover of residents. Some leave because of the lonely rural life, others for the strict moral code or simply the hard work involved.

For Antje Kroc, an award-winning Afrikaans novelist and poet, Orania represents a futile attempt to fossilise a living, breathing culture. 'In 50 years time it will be a marvellous museum to visit,' she said from her home in Cape Town. 'But things change all the time, and that's the way it should be. And if a culture is incapable of adapting, it will die.'

**SATURDAY, 13 MARCH 2004**

# United in Grief

*Lynne O'Donnell, in Madrid*

Red candles and yellow flowers, the colours of the Spanish flag, began to appear outside the entrance to the Atocha railway terminus in central Madrid yesterday, creating a tiny point of focus for the overwhelming grief that has descended on this city.

Slowly, people gathered in a hushed semi-circle around the impromptu altar, reading handwritten notes that had been dropped among the daisies, praying silently and crossing themselves, wiping away tears.

Just metres away, on the tracks that fan out from Atocha station to every point of Madrid, workmen with their faces covered against the stench of death trained their blowtorches on the twisted wreckage of the carriages that were ripped apart by Thursday's bombs – planted by whom and

for what purpose, no one yet really knows.

One man, standing at the base of the escalator beneath the Atocha atrium, handed out small strips of black grosgrain and offered pins from a round plastic container that mourners used to attach the ribbon, in a bow, to their chests. That black bow of mourning has become a poignant symbol of Madrid's sudden and profound sense of loss.

Across the city, balconies fly the Spanish flag, or sometimes a plain white one, with the black bow attached to the centre, a spontaneous expression of the entire country's shock, anger, confusion, grief.

The enormous nineteenth-century colonnaded Metropolis building that dominates the sprawling intersection of Calle de Alcalá now wears an enormous black bow, attached to the yellow mesh that covers its renovation scaffold.

As Spain began three days of mourning, marked at midday when the nation came to a standstill and millions of people raised an open hand to signal *basta* – enough – to terrorism, a steady drizzle fell on the usually jovial capital.

Renowned throughout the world as a sunny weekend city that never sleeps, Madrid has, since the fall of Generalissimo Francisco Franco three decades ago, rediscovered the joy of its history, culture, music, art and food. The shock felt throughout Europe after the bombings was in no small part due to the place Spain in general, and Madrid in particular, enjoys in millions of hearts.

But there were no smiles in Madrid yesterday. The carefree bustle of the teeming city had been engulfed by a sense of trauma. People moved as if through treacle. On every corner, it seemed, stood a man or a woman staring into space, or at the ground, frozen in contemplation of the horror that has hit their home.

At bus stops, waiting commuters could be seen brushing away tears. While the city put on a show of getting on with the business of doing business, most shops were shuttered, most bars and restaurants were closed, most people wore black. Even the notoriously choked roads were relatively clear

*Hundreds of thousands of people gathered in Madrid's Plaza Colon on 12 March to protest in silence at the murder of 199 people and wounding of 1,463 others in the Madrid bombings. Photograph: Sergio Perez/Reuters.*

— and what traffic there was came to a standstill at midday when drivers stood beside their vehicles to join the national minute's silence. Taxi drivers taped black crosses to their cars and tied the black bow to their aerials.

The extent of the terror felt by the innocents aboard the Atocha train that was first struck at 7.30 a.m. on Thursday — and then again three more times before the horror gave way to silence — was brought home when an FM radio station replayed a tape-recorded call to the police emergency line.

In the space of just a few seconds, two loud explosions can be heard. After the first, a woman's panic-stricken voice screams: 'I think there's been a bomb. We're in Atocha station.'

Another explosion is heard and, after a split-second, the line goes dead.

A middle-aged man with a huge handlebar moustache pressed the moisture from his eyes as he listened to the broadcast.

Mila Hidalgo (27), a film student who studied English in Belfast six years ago, took her hand-held video camera to Atocha station. She didn't really know why and she struggled to describe what it was that compelled her to record the day. As she tucked the tiny camera inside her thick woollen jacket, she said: 'I brought the camera because I thought it was something I must do, to film what I am seeing and what we are living through.

'I feel confused and empty. I was recording

*The scene outside Madrid's Atocha station on the morning of 11 March. Photograph: Pablo Torres/Reuters.*

and I was feeling and realising that Madrid today is not as noisy as usual. People look depressed. It will take people a long time to recover, especially those who haven't found their friends and family.'

Given the enormous toll of the bombing – 199 dead by late Friday afternoon, more than 1,450 injured, a seven-month-old girl among the latest fatalities – Hidalgo said: 'Everyone in Madrid has been affected by this. One of my friends from school called me last night; he was crying because a friend of his, at 11 o'clock at night, they still didn't know where he was.

'I have a new telephone number at home, so someone had it before me. I've had a lot of calls from people asking for people I don't know, people who had the number before me. I couldn't say to them that everything is OK because I don't know. They were looking for friends and relatives.'

As she spoke, Hidalgo's black wavy hair was framed by the green windows of the college behind the station, which, like other schools across Spain, was closed as a mark of respect for the dead.

Inside the station, an elderly couple dressed up

for a trip to Pamplona, famed for its annual running of the bulls, peered, a little dazed, over balustrades at the departure terminals below. 'Awful, yes,' said the man of the bombings that a day earlier had shaken the ground he now stood on. 'But yes, I will travel today. What else can I do?'

Cassandra Sandovar (21), from Colorado, caught a train to Madrid from Salamanca with two friends, American students like herself, living with Spanish families while studying the language for a year. All were shaken by the similarities between Thursday's atrocity and the attacks on New York and Washington exactly two and a half years earlier.

'It's scary,' Sandovar said. 'Especially that it happened on the 11th. The family I'm staying with were really upset, my señora was yelling at the TV. We felt like we were a part of it – but not. When 9/11 happened it was a little different because we are from the country. But here we are outsiders.

'We don't know if it's ETA or al-Qaeda, and if it turns out that it's al-Qaeda it will make our stay here more uncomfortable, as maybe some Spanish people will think that because of their government's support for our country it was our fault.

'Before this happened, there was already some animosity. If we went to a bar or a nightclub and people realised we were American, they'd say "I hate Bush", as if we all supported him. I just say I'm Venezuelan.'

Sandovar attributes such hostility to the lack of support among Spaniards for prime minister José María Aznar's wholehearted backing of the Washington-led war in Iraq. Aznar, leader of the People's Party (PP), stood shoulder to shoulder with George Bush and Tony Blair throughout last year's build-up to the war and then dispatched a contingent of troops to Iraq. Yesterday he was the focus of some of the anger that came to the surface in the Spanish capital.

Black lettering scrawled on a piece of A4-sized paper and stuck to an escalator at the station spelled out: 'Al-Qaeda = PP. No hay derecho' ('it's not right'). This was an indication, said a middle-aged woman who paused for vigil by the candles nearby, that some people blamed the policies of the government for bringing international terrorism to Spain. As she pulled her thick blue coat close and shuffled away, two men, workers in jeans and denim jackets, pinned black ribbons to each other's lapels.

The confusion about just who is responsible for the bombings was reflected in other hastily made messages of revulsion that could be seen on the streets of Madrid: multi-striped Pace flags flapping from balconies around the Plaza del Campillo Mundo Nuevo; huge black-and-white signs screaming 'ETA No!' on the Avenida Ciudad and 'ETA: Asesina merder' outside Atocha's broad entrance; 'Basta Ya' on the Calle Gran Vía; and simple black swatches on the Calle de Ibiza.

Arturo Azcorra Salona, director of an Internet company, flew home from Hong Kong to attend last night's mass rally, which was expected to draw an estimated two million people on to the city's streets despite the relentless rain. 'It's important to be here, to show unity, for us as Spaniards to demonstrate that we will not tolerate this type of atrocity,' he said.

Again echoing the confusion about who is to blame, Salona reeled off a list of recent offences suggesting that, despite its denials, ETA, the Basque separatist group, was behind the blasts.

'They tried to bring explosives into Madrid a couple of weeks ago and this is before the election, which is their normal pattern,' he said, adding details about a thwarted attempt to blow up a train on Christmas Eve last year, and a series of bombings last June that injured more than a dozen people.

'They could be working with al-Qaeda,' he conceded. 'Because some of the younger people, those who have not been arrested, could be drawn into these methods, killing many people to make their point.'

As a sea of umbrellas moved slowly through central Madrid to the 6 p.m. chime of church bells, ETA issued its most emphatic denial yet that it was involved in the bombings. And as evidence seemed to grow that forces outside ETA were involved – with the identification late yesterday of copper detonators, unlike any ETA has used in the past – doubts about the organisation's guilt appeared to infiltrate Aznar's administration too.

Aznar is insisting that tomorrow's general election must go ahead, to prove that Spain's democratic institutions cannot be undermined by its enemies. A victim himself of an ETA assassination attempt, Aznar has made the fight against terrorism, at home and abroad, a central plank of his tenure.

His campaign of extra-judicial arrests of ETA leaders, both in Spain and at their base of exile in France, was thought to have routed the militant leadership that had brought the organisation a high profile in the 1970s and 1980s. In the hours immediately after Thursday's attacks, Aznar was given credit for his determination to rid his country of the scourge of home-grown terrorism, and to take that fight outside his own borders if necessary.

But for many in last night's crowd, the memory of the carnage still fresh, it made little difference if their protest was aimed at al-Qaeda or ETA.

'For me, this is against violence; it doesn't matter if it is ETA or al-Qaeda. That is not the question. It is a question of the suffering of the people,' said one man in his 30s. 'If it's ETA, it is what they've been doing for many years. We're a democratic country; they don't need to express their views with violence.'

If, however, the perpetrators do prove to be linked to the al-Qaeda network of Osama bin Laden, who has promised to eradicate 'crusaders' from what he believes is soil that rightly belongs to Islam, Aznar's position could begin to look misguided or, worse, reckless. Criticism of his role in the worst atrocity in Spanish history – compared in yesterday's newspapers with the worst of Franco's regime or even Napoleon – could begin to hit home.

**MONDAY, 15 MARCH 2004**

# Green Party Seeking to Broaden its Appeal and Get Into Government

*Mark Brennock*

They want to be in Government. They said it at their convention in Galway all weekend. Trevor Sargent devoted the opening passage of his party leader's speech to it. Party chairman John Gormley titled his speech: 'Preparing for Government.'

The co-leader of the German Green Party came over to talk about what it's like, to tell delegates frankly about the compromises that must be made and the achievements that can be gained through becoming a government party rather than simply an external pressure group. For a party whose members are used to the luxury of taking clear principled positions, the compromises involved in being in government can come as a shock.

The party leadership clearly needs no convincing. 'Most of us got into politics to make a difference, to effect real change,' said Mr Gormley. 'It's not simply a case anymore of greening the political agenda, it's a case of implementing the Green political agenda, and that has to happen sooner rather than later.'

Mr Sargent pointed to Germany, New Zealand and Sweden as countries where the Greens were in government. The first ever Green prime minister was elected last week, he said – in Latvia.

Coupled with the stated desire to be in government comes a significant move to redefine the party's position on key issues, most notably on Europe. The Green Party became very uncomfortable during the second Nice referendum campaign when its opposition to the Nice Treaty associated in the public mind with other opponents such as Justin Barrett's No To Nice campaign and Sinn Féin. A substantial part of the party's current support base consists of urban, middle-class younger liberals – many of whom feel little hostility to the EU but considerable hostility to many of those who lined up on the anti-EU side.

So, since last year the party has been conducting an internal debate on Europe, which may lead to a recasting of their position. The impression the leadership wants to give is clear. For the first time the EU flag hung beside the Irish flag on the speakers' podium throughout the weekend.

Several key speakers sought to position the party's traditional criticisms of aspects of the EU within a position of overall support for the Union.

'Our task as Greens is not to isolate ourselves in Europe,' said deputy leader Mary White, the party's European Parliament candidate in the East constituency. While criticising the Union's 'inflexibility and remoteness', she said these were things they should campaign to change, rather than reasons simply to oppose the EU.

Outgoing Leinster MEP Ms Nuala Ahern was

the most direct, challenging her party to be more positive towards the EU. 'It is unrealistic to demand that the European Commission takes action on the nitrate directive, for example, while denying that it needs to act effectively through a new constitution,' she said.

Ms Patricia McKenna MEP raised her concerns about the militarisation of the EU. But she too portrayed the Greens' role as campaigning within the EU 'to try to limit this mad drive towards militarisation'.

The Green Party may end up opposing the next EU treaty should it be agreed. But first it is to have a special party convention on the matter. Some senior party sources suggested at the week-

end that the leadership would stand back from the debate, allowing members to make the decision.

The party's broad ideological message outlined at the weekend marries elements of traditional Green thinking with left thinking. Throughout the weekend, speakers criticised the Government's overt focus on promoting the needs of business.

Trevor Sargent returned to the theme in his keynote speech on Saturday night: 'For this Government the promotion of the interests of big business is sacred,' he said. 'Markets and market-led language are creeping into every facet of our lives and into our debates on key public services, including education.

'It is the language – not of citizens – but of

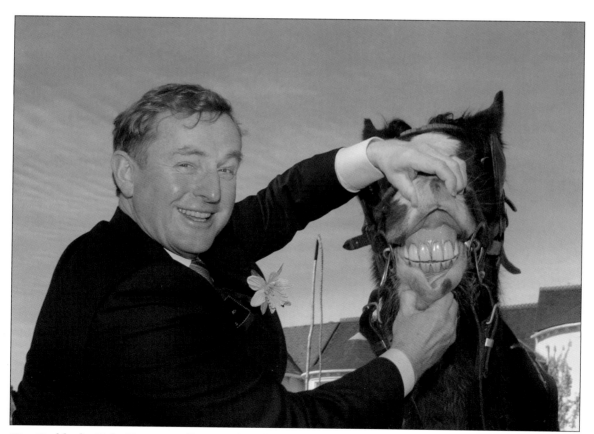

*Fine Gael leader Enda Kenny in Killarney to launch his party's local elections campaign. Photograph: Eamonn Keogh/MacMonagle Killarney.*

consumers and clients. It is the language of the internal market, choice, customers, and privatisation. The sad new world envisaged by the Fianna Fáil/PD Government is a hostile world of solitary individuals competing endlessly to outdo their neighbour in every field from higher education to the shopping centre. 'Economic growth at any cost and the survival of the fittest replaces our traditional culture of watching out for each other.'

It was this passage of his speech that received the most spontaneous applause. He spoke of the rise in Ireland of 'the anxious class'. Even those who have done relatively well economically are still faced with a host of challenges and threats to true quality of life, he said. It was a message that will appeal to many who are relatively well off.

Most interestingly, his remarks would appeal to a substantial section of those who vote for Fine Gael. Three of the four new seats won by the Greens in the last General Election came from Fine Gael.

The fourth had been a Fine Gael target. The Green Party has joined the PDs in targeting Fine Gael supporters and hopes to reap dividends in local and European elections in June. Yet they face the contradiction of needing Fine Gael to do well in order to realise their ambitions.

In denouncing Fianna Fáil and the PDs and insisting they must be removed from government, Trevor Sargent appeared to tie his party's prospects of going into government to the prospects of a Fine Gael/Labour/Green coalition being able to gain an overall Dáil majority.

It is the same position Labour has taken under Pat Rabbitte. If Fine Gael is not significantly strengthened but further weakened, this will be impossible.

Such calculations are on hold, at least until after June's elections. They are hoping that a good performance, with potential Dáil candidates winning local authority seats, will bring them closer to the day when, as Nuala Ahern said, the party will be 'not simply Green protesters but also the movers and shakers, the decision makers'.

WEDNESDAY, 24 MARCH 2004

# A Curtain is Drawn Back to Give a Glimpse

*Colm Keena*

Yesterday at the Moriarty tribunal was one of those days where you felt the curtain had been pulled back a bit to give a glimpse of the true nature of the relationship between government and big business.

The glimpse that emerged was not reassuring.

By the end of the day's proceedings Mr John Bruton had made it clear he felt his 1994-1997 Rainbow Coalition government was punished with negative coverage in the Independent Newspaper group because it had failed to satisfy commercial demands made by the group and its chairman, Sir Anthony O'Reilly.

Oddly enough – perhaps – it seemed as if Mr Bruton's true feelings as to what had happened between his government and the Independent group were revealed with reluctance.

It was only during questioning by counsel for Mr Michael Lowry, Mr Rossa Fanning, near the end of the day's proceedings, that matters began to be stated bluntly.

The background to the fraught relationship between the powerful newspaper group and Mr Bruton includes Independent's investment in 1989 in MMDS licences for the distribution of TV signals. (The investment was to eventually cost the group €100 million.)

Illegal deflector groups were taking business away from the MMDS company, and Independent was annoyed that the government was failing to act against these groups. However, the matter had become a political one and the government was loath to act.

In May 1996 Sir Anthony O'Reilly, chairman of Independent News & Media, told that company's a.g.m. that it had lost more than €26 million as a result of the government's failure to enforce the

*Former Taoiseach John Bruton at the Moriarty Tribunal: Photograph: Bryan O'Brien.*

law. Representations to the minister for communications, Mr Michael Lowry, had not led to government action on the issue.

There followed a meeting in Glandore, Co. Cork, in late July 1996. It seems Mr Bruton knew a meeting was likely and had sought background briefings on the issues likely to be raised. He was already concerned about the coverage he, his party and his government were receiving in Independent group newspapers.

Mr Bruton met Sir Anthony alone in Sir Anthony's west Cork home and listened to what the former taoiseach agreed were the businessman's 'gripes'. In order to end the meeting on as amicable a note as possible, he said he would have his senior adviser, Mr Seán Donlon, meet Sir Anthony's representatives.

A letter sent by Sir Anthony, who is a former president and chief executive of the Heinz group, to Mr Bruton two days after the Cork meeting outlined a number of business areas in which he had an interest. They were: Heinz; Independent Newspapers; Fitzwilton; Waterford Wedgwood; Arcon; and a number of luxury hotels.

Mr Bruton, in a note faxed to Mr Donlon on the night of the Cork meeting, listed four issues of concern mentioned by Sir Anthony at the short, informal meeting. These were: the MMDS issue; a

*Young people playing in the Luminarium at Merrion Square in Dublin, part of the city's St Patrick's Festival 2004 celebrations. Photograph: David Sleator.*

grant for a Heinz factory in the Louth region; access to a mine in the midlands; and the fact that Mr Denis O'Brien had won the second mobile phone licence competition despite international bidders. Sir Anthony was associated with one of the failed bidders, Irish Cellular Telephones Ltd.

Mr Donlon, a former Irish ambassador to the US, met representatives of the Independent group in September 1996. He has told the tribunal in a statement of intended evidence: 'In spite of the relaxed mood I was left in no doubt about the newspapers' hostility to the government parties if outstanding issues were not resolved to their satisfaction.'

Mr Bruton couldn't recall Mr Donlon reporting back to him in this manner but said he was 'well aware that these newspapers didn't love us particularly'.

Mr Fanning said Mr Lowry will say he recalls being told by Mr Donlon that the Independent executives had said the government would lose Independent newspapers as friends if its 'demands' were not met.

Mr Bruton said he thought Independent's view would be 'conveyed in a more subtle way', but such a message being conveyed to the government by Independent would not surprise him, he said.

He agreed with Mr Fanning that it could be said that the Independent group had threatened him and his government. Subsequent to these events the Independent group newspapers did take a negative view of him and his government, he said.

On the day of the 1997 general election the *Irish Independent* carried a front-page editorial 'urging people not to vote for a government that had succeeded in getting a 9 per cent annual growth rate during its term of office'. It indicated a 'certain perversity of political opinion', he said.

MONDAY, 29 MARCH 2004

# Jewel-studded Crown

*Gerry Thornley*

Ireland 37 Scotland 16

Whatever else, the class of 2004 will always have a Triple Crown. A dedicated, well-organised, well-backed group of Irish athletes studded with as rare a collection of jewels as Irish rugby has had in two decades, they deserved an overdue, if mythical, reward.

This being only Ireland's seventh Triple Crown, history has taught Irish rugby that after long barren periods, success such as this tends to come along in pairs (1894 and 1899; 1948 and 1949; 1982 and 1985), and the hope must be that this vintage crop can eclipse that two-crowns-a-decade haul in the first decade of the new millennium.

Why not? For the time being, Eddie O'Sullivan – true to his word in raising the bar – can bask in the glow of a little piece of history. The lap of honour to the sound of U2's 'Beautiful Day' will no doubt be chided by some, but it seemed utterly justified at the time and O'Sullivan and Brian O'Driscoll were

*Irish flanker David Wallace gets Ireland's crucial third try in their 37/16 Triple Crown win over Scotland at Lansdowne Road. Photograph: Shaun Botterill/Getty.*

entitled to lead it. Only then were the crowd relaxed enough to vent their delight, and only then did we see the forest of green placards.

Up until the preceding half hour or so, the Lansdowne Road air had been heavy with expectation, which assuredly contributed to a less-than-foot-perfect opening 50 minutes. But if this team is to go on and challenge for more and bigger honours, then days such as this are a necessary part of the growing pains toward greatness. It will stand to them. Coping with expectancy and hype goes with the territory.

Nerves? 'Of course there was. We're only human,' admitted O'Driscoll. 'If we'd lost against England it would have been a bit of a nothing game. I'm sure Scotland would have been striving to avoid the wooden spoon and we might have been pushing for second place but there was an element of pressure, particularly with the huge amount of hype about the 1985 team. I thought we came through it extremely well.'

The 25-year-old, 50-cap veteran can list many fine days in his career, Ireland's under-19 World Cup win in France five years ago among them, but rates this the best yet. 'I would probably say that was the greatest achievement, because it's so special not only playing for your country but managing to achieve something special as well. We're going to enjoy it now for the next couple of days anyway,' he added with an impish smile.

If one other player typifies this squad's desire to leave an even more lasting imprint on the record books it was O'Driscoll's stand-in as captain for the opener in Paris, Paul O'Connell, and he struck what must have been one of the night's few sober notes. While he saw it as a vindication of how good the team is, O'Connell added: 'We've a long way to go. We need to start beating teams from the Southern Hemisphere now, we need to start beating France more often.'

Mindful that this team has 'let ourselves down' on big days in the past, such as last season's Grand Slam shoot-out with England and the World Cup

quarter-final, O'Connell added: 'People might be running away with themselves a bit because if you analyse it coldly enough, I think we've only really beaten England away at Twickenham. That's the only big one in there. While it was great to beat a resurgent Wales, we would expect to beat them on our form of the last few years, and we would expect to beat Scotland too, especially at home. People shouldn't get carried away but we're definitely going in the right direction.'

With a real shot at cementing their place amongst the world's elite in South Africa in June, and with England and France due in Dublin next season, this team is entitled to be ambitious.

By the time the 2007 World Cup arrives, and that seems almost the chosen place for O'Driscoll to lead the charge, this squad will be largely still intact, in their prime and have a further truckload of caps under their belts.

But all these considerations and others were tempered by the news of John McCall's death, which cast a terrible pall over the Irish dressing-room and the day. David Humphreys and Simon Best were the first to hear the news, and they relayed it to Declan Kidney.

'I can't find the words,' admitted Kidney. 'When you get into coaching, particularly at under-age, you always have fears, even though you know it keeps kids off the streets. For something like this to happen is beyond belief.'

As someone who has coached and taught at schools level extensively, Kidney would have a particular empathy with McCall's family and the Irish squad in South Africa. 'My heart and my thoughts would be with them now, trying to cope and to deal with everything there. They're in a situation where they are staying with a lot of other teams. We talk about the ups and downs of the game, and this really shows that that's all it is.'

On a day that should have been about unbridled celebration, young McCall's passing seemed cruel beyond words.

**THURSDAY, 1 APRIL 2004**

# Mob Mayhem as Bodies are Dragged Through Streets

*Lara Marlowe, in Baghdad*

The scenes of bodies being pulled from the flames, kicked, battered and dismembered were deemed too gruesome to be shown on television in Europe. Only the Arab satellite station Al-Jazeera showed a close-up of one of at least four Western civilians murdered in Fallujah, 50 km from Baghdad, yesterday.

Five US soldiers from the First Infantry Division were also killed yesterday morning in the same area when a bomb exploded beneath their vehicle. It was the worst day for US occupation forces since 8 January, when a US military helicopter was shot down near Fallujah, killing nine men.

Iraqi cameramen working for Reuters and AP television news filmed the aftermath of the particularly brutal attack on two four-wheel drive vehicles, one red, one white, on the main boulevard through Fallujah not far from the town hall.

'The mujaheddin attacked the cars,' a young man says on the APTN tape. 'They threw two hand grenades at each car and dragged the occupants out. Four of them were Americans.'

A US military spokesman confirmed that four civilian contractors employed by the Coalition Provisional Authority were killed.

Eye witnesses in Fallujah told an Iraqi source there that six men and two women were riding in

*Margaret Morris at work in A1 Grooming Service for pets in Glasnevin, Co. Dublin. Photograph: Dara Mac Dónaill.*

the two vehicles. Some reports mentioned a third vehicle in the convoy which evacuated other dead or wounded.

The videotape shows a man lying on the asphalt, a white shirt raised above his stomach, his charred arms held in an arc, as if trying to protect himself or begging for mercy. Another body is pulled out in front of the camera and beaten with pipes. A man kicks the head, which detaches from the corpse. The bodies are hacked with shovels.

A frenzied crowd shouted 'Allahu Akbar' (God is great), 'Down with the occupation, down with America,' 'Long live Islam,' and 'Fallujah is ours.'

Some of the young men covered their faces so they could not be identified. 'Fallujah will be the cemetery of the Americans,' predicted one man with a hidden face.

Men in the mob wrapped their own hands in cloth to avoid touching the burned flesh, then trussed up the charred corpses with yellow tape, attached them to the backs of cars and dragged them through the streets of Iraq's most rebellious town.

The videos also show a man holding up what appears to be a set of military 'dog tags'. A flak jacket and a blue US passport lie on the ground beside a body.

Two bodies, presumably the same two which were filmed, were later attached to the criss-crossed girders of a British-built former railway bridge across the Euphrates, on the edge of Fallujah.

The bodies were hung upside down. One was headless, and neither had hands or feet. While traffic continued across the bridge, an AFP correspondent saw locals throwing stones at the corpses.

An Iraqi-American photographer who arrived at the bridge after the bodies were cut down saw children stabbing the carbonised bodies with knives.

A local resident who had witnessed the killings told the photographer that two men were dragged from the vehicles pleading for their lives, but were doused with petrol and set alight.

A hand and a leg were strung from an electrical pole on the main street.

In recent weeks US missionaries were murdered in northern Iraq, and Finnish contractors were killed. The strategy appears to be based on the assumption that all Westerners are somehow connected with the occupation, and that attacking them will ensure that Iraq remains ungovernable.

Commenting on the murders at a press conference in Baghdad, Gen. Mark Kimmitt, the second-in-command in Iraq, said, 'Fallujah remains one of those cities in Iraq that just doesn't get it. It's a former Baathist stronghold.'

**SATURDAY, 10 APRIL 2004**

# With Warmth and Comic Genius, She was Marked Early on for the Stage

*Maureen Potter, Obituary*

Maureen Potter, the actress, comedian, singer and dancer who died on 7 April, was for many years Ireland's best-loved popular entertainer, both with the public and with her fellow-professionals.

Born in 1925, a fifth-generation Dubliner, she was the daughter of James Benedict Potter, a commercial traveller who died when she was only seven, and of Elizabeth Carr.

Marked for the stage from an early age, she would say that she only agreed to go to St Mary's National School in Philipsburgh Avenue in Fairview, the street where she lived, on condition that she could attend dancing classes.

Enrolled in the dancing school run by Jewel Byrne in the local CYMS hall, she showed a precocious talent that made her All-Ireland junior dancing champion two years later, at the age of seven. From there she went to the classes run by Connie Ryan, in the city centre, which were the

*The remains of Maureen Potter being carried by her sons Hugh and John into Clontarf Cemetery, Co. Dublin. Photograph: Cyril Byrne.*

seedbed for Connie Ryan's Kiddies, a troupe of juvenile dancers who performed in pantomimes and variety shows in all the major theatres of Dublin.

Of all her many talents, dancing was the one she claimed to love best, and years later she was particularly pleased when she danced in one of her shows with Brian O'Connor, the champion traditional Irish dancer.

Maureen Potter started to perform in variety shows and pantomimes shortly thereafter and was to recall: 'My first professional engagement was when I was nine in the Queen's Theatre, where I was paid the princely sum of seven shillings and sixpence. I remember making my Confirmation and rushing to the Queen's for the first matinee.'

In 1935 she appeared as a fairy in a pantomime with Jimmy O'Dea, then Ireland's foremost

comedian, and performed a sketch that brought the house down in which she mimicked Alfie Byrne, the popular lord mayor of Dublin.

She was spotted performing by English impresario and dance-band leader Jack Hylton on one of his visits to Ireland, and invited to do a number in his show. Billed as 'the Pocket Mimic' because of her tiny stature (she was just under five feet), she was subsequently invited to join his troupe in its tour of England, Scotland and Wales.

Although she was only 12 years of age and too young to be allowed work legally, she pretended to be 14, using a birth certificate she had borrowed from a friend. That was the end of her formal schooling, but she was a highly intelligent person, always well read and well informed.

Of her lack of education, she said: 'Education, perhaps, is something I missed by going on stage so

*Maureen Potter in the Gaiety Theatre, Dublin, getting ready for the Panto in 1977.*

early, but there is little else I really missed. I think I had a better childhood than many kids today who appear so confused with our modern society.'

Her work with Hylton took her all over the variety theatres of Britain, and on one occasion to Nazi Germany, when she played before Hitler, Goering and Goebbels. Hitler did not come back-stage after the show, but the other two leaders did, 'with their fat wives' as she said. The cast were each given a wreath in commemoration of the visit, which her mother, who did not approve, threw in the bin when Maureen brought it home.

The outbreak of the second World War brought her back to Ireland, where she resumed working for Jimmy O'Dea and his company. The shows toured all over Ireland, and she described how the actors, who travelled in the back of an open lorry, would get down outside the towns in which they were to appear and brush the dust off their clothes. Then they would stroll into town, as if they had just got off the train, that being regarded as more respectable.

O'Dea, himself a master comedian, became her mentor. 'I loved working with Jimmy O'Dea,' she said, 'and I had a unique relationship on the stage with him. He taught me my business. He's the one who taught me to be funny, he was the master of timing.'

When she started she was one of the 'feeds' who set up his jokes, but as time went on she became more of a partner to him, playing among many other parts the daughter of his celebrated Biddy Mulligan character and one of two comical Dublin 'wans', Dolores and Rose.

She met her future husband, Jack O'Leary, an army officer, in 1943, and he would hear her lines when she was rehearsing. Gradually he began suggesting improvements and eventually became her main scriptwriter, writing her many solo items including the famous 'Christy' numbers in which she played the ambitious mother of a naughty Dublin child. O'Leary also wrote her popular, long-running radio series *The Maureen Potter Show*.

They married in 1959 and, living in Clontarf, were to have two sons, John and Hugh. Although her work kept her busy, she enjoyed family life greatly after her long years of touring, being particularly fond of watching sport, mainly football and cricket.

Her career with Jimmy O'Dea was to continue until his death in 1965, and she appeared in his last show, the musical *Finian's Rainbow*. After that she took the lead in the annual pantomimes at the Gaiety Theatre and also in a series of summer revues, *Gaels of Laughter*, produced by Fred O'Donovan and directed by Ursula Doyle, Jimmy O'Dea's widow.

The shows packed the theatre for 15 years and featured most of the major comedians and popular singers in the country at that time, including Milo O'Shea, Danny Cummins, David Kelly, John Molloy, Patricia Cahill, Rosaleen Linehan, Hal Roach, Vernon Hayden, Des Keogh and Val Fitzpatrick.

Although best known for revue and pantomime, Maureen Potter made several notable appearances on the legitimate stage, in films and on television. The plays in which she appeared included a Hilton Edwards-Michael MacLiammoir production of *The Informer*, Shaw's *Androcles And The Lion* with Cyril Cusack, *Arsenic And Old Lace*, in which she co-starred with Siobhán McKenna, Sheridan's *School For Scandal* and Hugh Leonard's *Moving* and *Da*.

In 1986 she took the part of Maisie Madigan in Joe Dowling's production of O'Casey's *Juno and the Paycock*, which after opening at the Gate Theatre toured to Jerusalem and New York to great acclaim. She also appeared in the musical *Annie* at the Gaiety.

Although, like many actors of her generation, she preferred working on the stage to the screen, she appeared in several films and television shows. They included *Ulysses* and *A Portrait Of The Artist As A Young Man*, two versions of Joyce's novels, directed by Joseph Strick, and two John Ford films, *Gideon's Day* and *The Rising Of The Moon*.

On television she did a situation comedy series, *Me And My Friend*, with Rosaleen Linehan, and *The Maureen Potter Show* on television, which topped the TAM ratings in 1973. Almost her final public appearance was when she made an appearance on *The Late Late Show* last January, celebrating 100 years of the Abbey Theatre.

Towards the end of her career she suffered greatly from aggravated arthritis in her hips and knees, probably brought on by her highly energetic dancing. As a result of this, she had to give up pantomime in 1987. However, she worked on for several seasons in a very successful cabaret show at Clontarf Castle.

Maureen Potter received many awards and honours in her long career. In 1984 she was granted the freedom of the city of Dublin. Dublin University conferred an honorary degree on her in 1988, and in the same year she received an honorary Harvey's Irish Theatre Award for her services to Irish theatre.

She appeared at the Gaiety in 1996 to take part in a concert for the stage director Mai McFall, and in 1999 a special celebration of her life was staged in the same theatre, attended by the President, Mrs McAleese, who paid a tribute to her from the stage, and virtually all the luminaries of the Irish theatrical profession. In 2001 she was the first person to place her handprints in the walk of fame that was established outside the theatre with which her name will always be associated.

The quintessential Dubliner, Maureen Potter was loved not only for her warmth and comic genius, but also for her generosity. Without ever letting it be known she helped many a person down on their luck and, on stage, was always ready to share her great experience with younger performers.

Her final line in her shows was always: 'If you liked the show tell your friends, and if you didn't, keep your breath to cool your porridge.'

Maureen Potter: born 1925; died 7 April 2004

*(Obituaries in* The Irish Times *are published unsigned.)*

**FRIDAY, 16 APRIL 2004**

# Blood and Guts

*Rosita Boland*

'We need more blood,' says Andrew Bennett distractedly as he emerges from the messy business of murdering Banquo, lying prone in a glass-faced room at the back of the stage. 'And we need it to be the glistening kind of blood,' he says firmly.

It's the day before Pan Pan's production of *Mac-Beth 7* starts previewing, and the absence of blood bags is just another item in a long list that the crew is making in this stop-start technical rehearsal.

*Macbeth* is one of the most regularly performed of Shakespeare's plays, which has both advantages and disadvantages. The audience's familiarity with a text and the shape of a play is always useful, but it also carries a potential disclaimer: if you've seen one *Macbeth*, well, you've seen a thousand. The challenge of making something new out of a text that has been around for centuries does not automatically make an interesting production. Also, any text that has had a life on a school curriculum stands a fair chance of being avoided ever after by those who studied it.

Pan Pan's production of *Macbeth* is in fact defined and inspired by its place as part of the educational canon: the play is set in a classroom, complete with textbooks, uniforms and schoolbags. 'We were trying to come up with a strong setting and came up with the idea of the schoolroom environment,' says Gavin Quinn, the play's director and Pan Pan's joint artistic director. The company first started working on the show 16 months ago.

'We wanted to give the idea of people wondering about Shakespeare, enjoying the lines, holding the sweets in your mouth that are lines from Shakespeare. We didn't want to perform this play as a museum piece. While having full respect for the text, we wanted to engage a modern audience.'

The first scene the audience sees, as traditional, has the witches in the 'open place' of the stage directions. The three women who slink silently out between the curtains are dressed in school uniform, with hooded coats, and clearly on the mitch. One is smoking. They huddle together silently, eventually spitting out their lines with the disdain particular to angst-ridden teenage girls. The hoods of their duffel coats echo the shape of witches' hats. One actress, Emma McIvor, is seven months pregnant, which makes the scene even more surreal. The sulky, huddled demeanour of the uniformed trio is eerily effective as the coven with their portents of doom.

Two rows of desks frame the stage, males on one side and females the other; the textbook open on each desk is *Macbeth*. The bell that rings to summon Macbeth to Banquo's chamber is the classic brass and wooden-handled school handbell. For the banquet scene, where Banquo's ghost appears, the desks are moved to form a long central bank of tables; the banquet is composed of Tupperware lunch boxes of juice and sandwiches. As a device, the schoolroom setting proves itself to be both imaginative and clever.

Although the play was not chosen with a potential school audience in mind, the show would be a terrific introduction to Shakespeare for any audience of school-going age. After its run at the Project arts centre, in Dublin, Pan Pan hopes to

*Eugene Ginty and Nicola Sharkey in* **Mac-Beth** *7. Photograph: Patrick Redmond.*

tour the show, possibly next year, to festivals and venues abroad, before taking it around Ireland.

A technical rehearsal is just that: functional and technical. Every few minutes comes a pause to make lighting notes, costume notes, notes about pacing, cues, props, even the tempo at which the curtain is closed for the end of the first act. It's not a true reflection of the finished show. Even from a technical rehearsal, however, it's clear that Pan Pan's production of *Macbeth* has an element of the three-ring circus to it: there is something happening on stage everywhere you look.

The glass-sided room at the back of the stage is effectively another performance space. Even when the curtains are closed the audience can see what's happening inside via a digital camera that feeds into one of six screens banked up, tower-like, at the side of the stage. The other screens constantly change, telling five visual stories, their cameras

focused on different desks where the actors are constantly placing objects under the cameras. Thus we see wiggling worms, bugs in container, scraps of text, scribbled writing, splayed hands.

When Banquo is murdered we see compasses being jabbed into hands, blood-stained bandages, the claws of dead birds. You could spend the entire show just watching the silent story being told on the bank of screens. It's ambitious and risky to have so much going on: with such a busy space there is a fine line between engaging and distracting the audience.

It's not unusual for actors to perform several roles within a play, but it is uncommon to see different actors taking turns at playing the same part. Macbeth, for instance, is played by four actors: Bennett, Ned Dennehy, Eugene Ginty and Dylan Tighe. 'I think it makes the journey more interesting,' Quinn says. 'It gives you different interpretations of the role at different times. It's much more interesting to try things out, to experiment. And the actors learn from each other. It gives them an objectivity to the role when they see how other people play it in the same production.'

The cast also includes the opera singer Nicola Sharkey – key parts of the text are sung – the dancer Katherine O'Malley and an eight-year-old girl, Drew Barnes, who is on stage throughout, drawing pictures. 'The show is about the total poetic experience,' Quinn says. 'Music, imagery, movement, words: the total effect. Music can bring you somewhere spiritually that spoken words can't, to another level. We're trying to look at other forms of communication to tell the story. To tell the story in a surprising way. Pan Pan has been around for 11 years now and this production is a culmination of all our work as a company. You could say it is our flagship show.'

Quinn sees Pan Pan's production as telling the story of *Macbeth* in two different and separate ways: visually and verbally. It could be argued that all theatrical productions aim for a layered examination of a text in which the interpretations fuse together into a whole. The difference is that Pan Pan, which has always approached its productions in a challenging way, seems literally to see its show as composed of different, quite specific components: shows within shows.

'The show is a piece of performance art by Gavin Quinn and we are all raw material,' says Bennett during a break in rehearsal. 'I've seen Gavin's productions before and liked them but never necessarily understood them,' he adds, grinning. What marks *Mac-Beth 7* out as a Pan Pan production? Bennett doesn't pause to think before replying: 'General insanity.'

Tighe adds: 'One constant of all the shows is

*Natasha Byram wearing an 'interpretation' of a dress worn at the Hollywood Oscars by actress Jamie Lee Curtis from Audrey Taylor of Sandycove, Co. Dublin. Photograph: Eric Luke.*

*Dog's Bay in Connemara. Photograph: Brian Lynch/Fáilte Ireland.*

Gavin's approach to acting. At no point are we hiding the fact that we're just being ourselves. The authenticity of delivery is less to do with acting and more to do with the audience believing what we're saying.' He draws a deep breath, then says: 'It's brave and it's ambitious.'

**SATURDAY, 17 APRIL 2004**

# The Battle for the Beach

*Lorna Siggins, in Galway*

It was one of those memorable, final moments in Gabriel Byrne's film *Into the West* – Papa Riley setting fire to his Traveller caravan and releasing his late wife's spirit as the white horse, Tír na nÓg, appeared before Riley's young sons, Tito and Ossie. But when Byrne, alias Riley,

lit that match on Trá Garbh, he did so with a special permit. For the beach is part of a unique commonage arrangement involving a group of tenant farmers. It is also at the heart of a committed community battle against coastal erosion.

Now, some eight years after the first fences were put up and marram grass planted, the tenant farmers of Gurteen and Dog's Bay are winning their war against the Atlantic. For James Conneely, Joe Rafferty and Pat Mullen, it is particularly satisfying – although they realise that this will always be 'work in progress', Conneely, a school bus driver and sheep farmer, Rafferty, a retired sheep farmer and Mullen, caravan park owner, joke about the fact that they aren't 'your typical environmentalists'.

Rafferty remembers the visiting doctor who first alerted them to the challenge. 'She would notice the changes every year, how the sands and grass were being eaten away by the prevailing westerlies and the tide,' Rafferty says. 'She told us we were going to lose our beaches to the sea, and it took us a while to realise that she was right.'

The spectacular Gurteen Bay/Dog's Bay landscape is characterised by a tombolo – where beaches are formed when sediment is deposited in the slack water between an island and the mainland. There are no more than half a dozen examples of this in the 32 counties, according to scientists familiar with the area, such as Dr J.M. van Groenendael of the University of Nijmegen in the Netherlands.

The pure calcareous material which makes up the tombolo provides two 'back-to-back' and almost 'pure white' beaches, and the ridge connects to a large machair covered by grass sward. The area is a designated special area of conservation (SAC) under the EU Habitats Directive.

'Machairs themselves form a unique feature, with no more than a few dozen examples, many of which suffer from overgrazing and blow-outs once the sward gets destroyed,' Dr van Groenendael notes. A large shingle spit, a lake surrounded by a brackish marsh full of orchids, and the visible origin of the Murvey fault which runs across Roundstone Bog to Clifden give the area some 'unique flushes full of rare and characteristic plants', he says.

Among these are the blue green sea holly (*Eryngium Maritimus*), the Ladies Tresses (*Spiranthes Spiralis*), and many species of indigenous grass. The calcareous sands of Gurteen Bay and Dog's Bay are also famous for their *foraminifera* – tiny shells of single-cell organisms living on the sea floor.

Since about 1975, the Dutch academic and others have witnessed a continuous degradation of the tombolo ridge, with parts of it overblown, parts of it eroded into cliffs and parts of it 'blown out'. In 1999, he was pleasantly surprised to see a change.

Marram grass had been planted, vulnerable parts had been fenced off, and there were fewer livestock grazing, while there was a one-metre increase in dune height. By then, the trio –

Conneely, Rafferty and Mullen – were already at work, in co-operation with Galway County Council. The Roundstone Beaches Environmental Project was in action.

Initially, their project was 'rudderless', says Rafferty. 'We talked, we consulted, we went down a few wrong paths.' A former local councillor, John Mannion, gave them valuable support when they eventually presented a proposal to the local authority.

The first work began on October 1995, and the rest, Rafferty says, is 'environmental history'. The proposal involved a number of remedies, but overgrazing was never going to be one of them. The 16 tenants using the commonage, including James Conneely, had inherited a grazing pattern developed by their forefathers. Their first task was to identify the vulnerable areas, such as rabbit burrows which had become 'sand blow-outs' through the prevailing winds.

'We checked from south Donegal to Clare then for a source of marram grass, which would help to hold the sand in place, and we found one outside Belmullet, Co. Mayo, on property owned by the Land Commission,' Rafferty recalls. 'It can't be grown from seed, has very long roots, and the season for planting is October to March. Also, it has to be replanted within 24 hours, which put us under a lot of pressure.'

The team went up with trucks and fish boxes to transport the marram. 'We had to have trenches ready, at times we had to work through the night, but we were delighted with the effect,' Rafferty says. 'The beauty of marram is that it grows even better in areas where the sand is more exposed to the wind, and therefore more agitated.'

Rafferty's granddaughter browsed the Internet to find out more information on marram. 'And we discovered one of the world's experts, Alan Lees, living down the road from us in Moycullen!' Teagasc and Dúchas were also consulted, and fencing of fragile dune areas was carried out by Galway County Council. Gates were constructed

*Six-year-old Eoin Gavin with members of the Galway Youth Theatre at NUI Galway for the opening of the Cúirt International Festival of Literature. Photograph: Joe O'Shaughnessy.*

to allow for visitor access on to the beaches. 'We still found people trying to break holes in the fence, use posts for firewood, and even tear up marram grass,' Rafferty notes.

A type of mulch, using seaweed and several stages of rye grass, was developed to spread over disued rabbit burrows, and brushwood was spread to trap sand in the short term. Gabions, or flexible steel-mesh boxes filled with stones, were erected in very vulnerable spots. Teagasc also advised that a boardwalk should be constructed above ground

level to protect grass from visitors and to allow other vegetation to become established.

The graveyard headland at Gurteen, in which Bulmer Hobson and Maurice McGonigal are buried, represents one of the most exposed areas on which the beach project now wishes to focus. It intends to fence it and plant with marram, while also spreading mulch. It also plans to make a land bridge over the stream at 'small Gurteen', one of the most popular beaches, and install walkways here as part of its five-year strategy.

'Yes, our main aim was to save the common-age, but also to keep this area for our tourists and for generations to come,' Rafferty says. 'When you take the population of the two caravan parks here, it reaches about 3,000 in summer – which is the size of a fairly large village. This can have a significant impact on the environment, but a positive one if we handle it right.'

Rafferty and Conneely are anxious to pay tribute to the local authority, which has recently given the project another grant to fund information brochures. 'We were the motivators, agitators, rejuvenators, but thanks to Galway County Council we have been able to carry this through.'

**TUESDAY, 20 APRIL 2004**

# An Irishman's Diary

*Kevin Myers*

Last Wednesday night, as I watched President Bush giving his full backing to the permanent maintenance of Israeli settlements on the West Bank, I finally changed my mind. The man is mad. Only someone who has lost his senses would have torn up the road map so carefully produced just a year ago, and made himself an unconditional ally of prime minister Sharon's policies. Insanity; utter insanity.

A Palestinian acceptance of armed Israeli settlements on the West Bank could possibly be one (though improbable) outcome of negotiations between the Palestinians and the Israelis. And the Israelis could reasonably demand a Palestinian acceptance of those settlements, if only as a tough opening stance in secret talks. But for President Bush to megaphone-endorse the Israeli settler policy as a feature of a permanent agreement, and then to expect the Palestinians to enter discussions on how to achieve it, suggests the man has had a frontal lobotomy, without anaesthetic.

No doubt some codicilled small print might just possibly allow for the ultimate dismantling of the settlements; but small print is for courts of law, not the bar of popular opinion. Israeli and Palestinian alike believe the US government has backed the permanent settlement option. Many Israelis – foolishly – are jubilant. Moderate Palestinians despair, for no Palestinian leader could undertake to steer his people to such an objective and survive, politically or even literally.

For it would be difficult even for a nation of Pollyannas to accept the permanent presence of an armed and hostile host such as the Israeli settlers in their midst; but for a people who have produced Hamas, Islamic Jihad, the Martyrs' Brigade, and God knows what else, it is quite inconceivable. It cannot happen, and no force in the world can make the Palestinians freely submit to such an outcome. Only a madman would think otherwise.

There's more. I supported the war in Iraq a year ago, in part because I believed President Bush's assurances that Iraq had weapons of mass destruction. Moreover, Saddam was such an evil savage that the world would be – and is – a far better place now he has been overthrown, and his unspeakable sons killed. Even without the WMD, he was a permanent threat to peace, and the war was morally and politically justified. But it should have been executed with proper resources, for it is axiomatic in such operations that overpowering force is used to ensure peace, pending the reorganisation of the country's own security forces.

Instead President Bush opted for economy of effort, naïvely hoping that the popularity of regime change would ensure a smooth transition of power. Instead, the allies have been presented with a murderously ruthless and entirely predictable terrorist insurgency campaign. To compensate for the lack of rifles on the ground, the US has had to resort to technology: hence the helicopters and artillery firing chain-guns into densely populated suburbs. Lesson one, page one in the terrorist handbook: Provoke your stronger enemy into over-reacting, thereby turning hitherto unsympathetic neighbours into your allies. Done.

Moreover, there is an immutable integrity to events in the region. The world has been here before. After a previous regime change in Iraq at the end of the first World War, in the summer of 1921, the British army lost 2,000 casualties to an insurgency campaign. Twenty years later, in 1941, another regime change, and another insurrection, led by an old adversary, Fawzi Qawukji, whom the British had met before in a previous Arab Rising. Where? Iraq? No. Palestine, three years earlier. In this part of the world, borders are on maps, not in hearts. The US cannot hope to bring peace to Iraq while simultaneously seeming to shaft the Palestinians.

Bush's insane endorsement of Sharon's policy of making the larger West Bank Jewish settlements permanent means that the US has now effectively become – in Arab eyes – both the bankroller and the instrument of Israeli policy-makers. The US has written a moral, political and financial blank cheque for Israel. It has thereby forfeited any possible role as a fair and disinterested arbiter between the two sides.

Even if Gaza is successfully evacuated of settlers, which I very much doubt will happen, countless Palestinian suicide bombers will still yearn to perform their own mini–Holocausts. They see no future for their people.

A recent report by international military observers concluded: 'The Israeli army is pursuing a deliberate policy of mass repression and collective punishment, similar in many respects to the tactics the French pursued in Algeria. It routinely flies in the face of international humanitarian and legal

*Ariel Sharon and George Bush at the White House when the US President declared his support for the Israeli prime minister's unilateral pull-out from the Gaza Strip. Photograph: Pablo Martinez Monsivias/AP.*

norms, and is contrary to all civilised post-war counter-insurgency doctrine.'

Israel's neighbours, meanwhile, are backward, despotic, incompetent. The combined GDP of the resource-rich Arab League, in area the size of the US, is less than that of Spain. With almost no growth in the region, another 50 million Arabs will be looking for jobs by 2010. Anti-Semitic mantras are the standard opiate of the Arab poor and élite alike, and are the almost universal substitute for political discourse: blame the Jews and the US for everything, as al-Qaeda recruiting sergeants dole out Osama's shillings.

So the Zionists' arable dream has become an Arabic nightmare, a vigil of a thousand and one sleepless nights spent gazing from the ramparts at a growing array of enemy campfires stretching over the twin horizons of land and time, like a vast starlit sky. An Israeli missile strikes a campfire, a dot of light vanishes, and a half-dozen new stars flare into existence on the ink-black sands.

**SATURDAY, 24 APRIL 2004**

# Still a Contender, So No Messing

*Donald Clarke*

After our interview David Carradine, the 67-year-old star of Quentin Tarantino's smashing *Kill Bill Volume 2*, leans forward and urges me not to write the kind of article he has been reading about himself for the last three decades. He was tempted not to answer the questions I asked about the wilder times in his life but felt – and this is a very *Kill Bill* thing to say – that he detected something 'honourable' about me. I'll do what I can.

The period that Carradine is most concerned about is the early 1970s, when he and actress Barbara Hershey became the signature couple of the counter-culture. I can imagine that it must be more than a little tedious to still be making excuses for

your patchouli-scented adventures more than 30 years down the line.

There is, after all, plenty else of interest in his life: his complicated childhood for a start. The man who, in the vintage TV series *Kung Fu*, would inspire a million schoolboys to inject artistry into their playground brawls, grew up thinking that his father, the splendidly cadaverous actor John Carradine, was a sea captain.

'He had a 54-foot schooner and he always dressed in his yachting cap,' Carradine says, as we stroll out of Dublin's Clarence Hotel to enable him to suck down a cigarette. 'It was the most amazing sort of childhood: thinking your dad was a sea captain and then later seeing him on stage in Shakespeare.'

This rather takes me aback. I had read that Carradine had a pretty wretched time of it as a youth. Following the break-up of his parents' marriage, he was shuffled from foster home to boarding school and, after a period of truancy, ended up in reform school. 'My father thought that would teach me a lesson, and it worked,' he says.

There was even a story that he attempted suicide while still a toddler. 'Yeah, that's funny, isn't it,' he ruminates in his chocolatey drawl. 'I was about five. It is hard to explain. I think I might have been unaware that it would hurt and that it would be irretrievable.'

Carradine, who had been deeply disturbed by his mother's attempt to separate him from his half-brother, Bruce, flung a rope over a beam and attempted to hang himself. 'Miraculously, my father just came round the corner at that moment,' Carradine says. 'I don't know how he knew that his firstborn son was about to cease to be.'

These are just the sort of childhood traumas that are supposed to poison adult lives. But Carradine seems a fairly mellow chap. Thin and taut, his face elegantly crinkled by the years, he looks like the kind of fellow you would expect to meet leaning against an empty water tower in the dustbowl.

Only those terrifying American teeth – as solid and regular as the tombstones in a military cemetery – speak of a life in the entertainment industry. So, does he still carry any scars from that difficult upbringing? He laughs. 'I'm not really sure that could happen to an Irishman. Psychology means nothing to the Irish,' he says. He is proud of his Irish heritage and has pinned a sort of Celtic brooch to his tweed jacket to advertise the fact.

But he has a thimbleful of Cherokee blood to thank for much of his success. When he threw himself into acting in the mid-1960s, his vaguely exotic features enabled him to play characters from a bewildering array of racial groups. But to the generation now in its late 30s and early 40s he remains best known as Caine, the philosophical Chinese nomad with the deadly fists, from *Kung Fu*. The series, which ran from 1972 until 1975, combined slow-motion brawling with fortune-cookie aphorisms to charming effect and still has many fans throughout the world.

I wonder whether he ever resents the fact that so many people still identify him with that one role. 'No, because firstly I am not like William Shatner, who is only allowed to play that one part,' he says. 'I have been in 102 theatrical movies, aside from all the TV. Every part has been different. I have worn a dress. I've played heroes and villains. I've played idiots. But also fans don't just come up to me and just say: "Boy, I sure liked that series." They say: "Your series changed my life." Or they even say sometimes: "Your series saved my life." I don't see how you can feel bad about that. This little Chinese hobo has had that effect on people, and that's really great.'

He delivered a superb performance as Woody Guthrie in Hal Ashby's *Bound for Glory* and, alongside his half-brothers, Keith and Bobby, was one of several reasons to savour Walter Hill's fine western, *The Long Riders*. But real movie stardom eluded him. I wonder whether he was the victim of the snobbery Hollywood then felt towards actors who had come to fame on TV (stars such as Bruce Willis

*Actor David Carradine, who plays Bill in* **Kill Bill 2**, *and his partner Annie Bierman, at the opening of the film in the Savoy Cinema in Dublin. Photograph: Dara Mac Dónaill.*

and George Clooney have softened those attitudes in recent decades).

'Well, no. Stardom was possible,' Carradine says. 'I was definitely in the running. And after I made *Bound for Glory* the president of United Artists said: "I want to build you." I said I wanted to do a dancing movie. It had to be about this guy who actually is a dancer – we don't want the music to start out of nowhere – and it has to be modern music. He said: "What?"'

The chiefs wanted Carradine for Karel Reisz's post-Vietnam drama *Who'll Stop the Rain?*. Then Ingmar Bergman called and asked him to appear in the bizarre highbrow potboiler, *The Serpent's Egg*.

'So I had to turn United Artists down,' he says. 'They said: "You can't." I said: "I have to do this. This is a once-in-a-lifetime – once-in-an-eternity –chance." As a result the studio head cast Michael Moriarty and Nick Nolte and the next time I saw him he had his arm around John Travolta and was talking about making a dance movie. That is what happened. I took the artistic rather than the commercial choice.'

Somehow I can't see Carradine – who would by then have been more than 40 – in *Saturday Night Fever*, but let's allow him that fantasy. Others have suggested that his wild living and devotion to alternative lifestyles proved a barrier to mainstream success. At the height of his fame, during the *Kung Fu* years, he and Barbara Hershey were deeply into the hippie experience. They named their son Free and, following an unfortunate impact between her car and a seabird, Hershey became, briefly, Barbara Seagull.

'That is what we were. We were very public about it,' he says. 'I have never kept secrets. I am very open. That is why I have a reputation for this and that. I just sat there and told *People* magazine flat out. *People* magazine, in particular, has always liked to trash me. They printed this cover which said "David Carradine has taken 500 acid trips".'

And was that accurate? Are the tales of his drink 'n' drugs hell exaggerated? 'The psychedelic experimentation we did a lot of. And we smoked a lot of pot,' he says. 'Liquor was not something we did. We looked down on alcohol and smoking tobacco in those days.'

But it has been reported that he took to booze in a big way in the decades that followed. 'I didn't get into drinking till I was in my 40s and by that time I had stepped away from the rest of drugs,' he says. 'There was only a period of a few years when I was drinking too much. I had a friend who was a mentor and he suddenly said: "I've never seen you abuse a substance before." I said: "Am I doing that now?" And I was. That was spring of 1996. I like to think that I stopped drinking on St Patrick's Day, but it was actually a month later.'

For whatever reason, the years after *Kung Fu* saw him appearing in a huge number of low-end exploitation features – some as good as *Death Race 2000* and *Q – The Winged Serpent*, most as grim as *Safari 3000* and *The Mad Bunch* – while his name began to slip out of A-list agents' Rolodexes. He did manage to direct the decent, if neglected, film *Americana*, in 1981 and reappeared as Caine in the TV series *Kung Fu: The Legend Continues*, in 1993. But his profile was still far lower than he would have wished.

'But I knew that at a certain point I'd come back to the centre again,' he says. 'I also knew that it would take somebody with enormous courage, like Quentin [Tarantino], to do it.'

The world of the exploitation picture is, of course, Tarantino's hinterland, the place from where he draws many of his ideas and (re-)discovers many of his actors. It was therefore utterly appropriate that he should cast Carradine as Bill, the grizzled samurai master, against whom Uma Thurman directs a rampage of bloody revenge in the second part of his violent epic.

'Within a few moments of me returning Quentin's phone call I got a call from [*Lethal Weapon* director] Richard Donner and one from Tom Cruise wanting to know if I could speak Japanese,' he says. 'It is just one of those moments that can fix things. It was a vortex of a moment and things cluster around those moments.'

Though Bill was originally written with Warren Beatty in mind, Carradine makes the part his own. Husky-voiced, gimlet-eyed and leathery, he rekindles memories of Lee Van Cleef and Jack Palance, while investing the role with something approaching humanity. He must have had mixed feelings when the director told him he was cutting the picture in two and that he would not appear in part one.

'I did think it might be a marketing mistake, because I do have a lot of fans,' he says. 'About 200 million people watch *Kung Fu* even now. But I knew that even if I wasn't in the first movie I

*At the launch of Sky television's Irish news service were (from left) Lisa Burke, a weather presenter with the station, Gráinne Seoige, news anchorwoman, and Eibhlín Ní Chonghaile, West of Ireland correspondent. The service began broadcasting on May 10. Photograph: Bryan O'Brien.*

would be in the first scene of the second and I would dominate it. I realised that rather than dominate the second half of a movie I would dominate an entire movie.'

After 102 mostly forgotten pictures, four failed marriages and a fair amount of antagonistic press coverage, Carradine deserves a break. Is he now getting the respect he feels he is due?

'Well, it is funny,' he says. 'Ever since *Kill Bill* came out the press hasn't wanted to bend my words any more. They actually want to use the good quotes.'

Wait till he sees what I intend to do to him. His eyes narrow. 'Well, just remember: I know where you live,' he says.

And, of course, he has been studying Kung Fu for decades. 'Yeah,' he says. 'I know Kung Fu. I also know a lot of Kung Fu masters and some very big guys and I know a lot of Hell's Angels. So, I wouldn't f★★k around with me.'

I think he's joking, but I wouldn't like to put it to the test.

SATURDAY, 24 APRIL 2004

# Judiciary Must Have Credibility

*Carol Coulter*

Judge Brian Curtin is innocent of the charge of possessing child pornography. His acquittal yesterday, by direction of Judge Carroll Moran, means that there is no accusation outstanding against him, and he should be able to resume his life.

But is this a realistic prospect? The accusation made against him is of such a heinous nature, and arouses such revulsion in many people, that, despite the acquittal, he may be tainted by it in the eyes of many.

For many people, this would be a difficult, but essentially private, matter. For Brian Curtin, it is more than that. As a judge of the Circuit Court, sworn to uphold the law, handing down verdicts and sentences to those who violate it every day of his working life, he must be, like Caesar's wife, above suspicion. Otherwise, the credibility of the whole judiciary is in question.

However, there is no provision in law or in the terms of employment of judges for their removal on the grounds of suspicion. Indeed, this would fly in the face of natural justice.

Had he been convicted, he could have been impeached by both Houses of the Oireachtas for 'stated misbehaviour', and removed in that way. But this did not happen.

It is difficult to see how the Oireachtas can proceed to impeachment in the absence of a criminal conviction. However, the seminal authority on the Irish Constitution, known colloquially as 'Kelly on the Constitution', speculates that 'stated misbehaviour' could include a situation where a judge was charged with a serious criminal offence but was acquitted on a technicality relating to proofs.

In the absence of impeachment, it will be up to the judiciary itself to deal with the thorny issue of how to protect its own credibility within the procedures available to it.

Those procedures are very limited, as proposals for a mechanism to deal with judicial ethics, made by the Chief Justice three years ago, have not yet found their way into legislation.

For routine matters, each member of the judiciary is subject, in his or her administrative day-to-day work (but not, of course, his or her judicial determinations), to the president of the court to which he or she is assigned. Therefore, District Justices work under the President of the District Court, Judge Peter Smithwick, and those of the Circuit Court under its President, Judge Esmond Smyth. The High Court is under the rule of Mr Justice Joe Finnegan and the Supreme Court – and ultimately all members of the judiciary – is presided over by the Chief Justice, Mr Justice Keane.

Usually, the presidents decide which judges hear what cases. In the District Courts, where there are more than 60, this cannot be done in a detailed way for practical reasons, as most of them are outside Dublin. To a lesser extent, this is also the case in the Circuit Court, although in Dublin the president is quite directly involved.

The presidents can, therefore, decide that there may be reasons why certain judges cannot hear certain cases. If a judge had displayed stress-related health problems, for example, it is likely that the president of that court would not assign him or her highly-stressful cases.

If he returned to the bench, it is possible that Judge Curtin might find himself with few cases sent to him to hear. If that happened, his position could soon become untenable.

Before the case went forward to trial, his solicitor told Tralee District Court that his client had suffered severely from the strain of the case and had even been hospitalised as a result. His health had been undermined, he said. It could well have been undermined to such an extent that he will be unable to return to the bench and take up the stressful duties of a Circuit Court judge.

*Judge Brian Curtin (centre) leaving Tralee Court House in Co Kerry after his acquittal on charges of possessing child pornography. Photograph: Eric Luke.*

Legal experts agreed on only one thing when contacted about this yesterday – there is no law or procedure out there to deal with a judge who has been charged with a serious criminal offence but has been acquitted.

**MONDAY, 26 APRIL 2004**

# Poor L'viv is Ukraine's Window onto Europe

*Bridget Hourican, in L'viv*

Lines of cars queue at the Polish–Ukrainian border. Most of them, like ours, have Polish number plates. We've been here an hour. Poles, unlike Western Europeans, don't need visas to get into Ukraine, which explains the delay: the border guards are asking the questions normally reserved to the consulate.

We offer a guard $40 and he moves us into a faster line. An hour later we're still there, but closer to the top. We joke that it's like the Mexican border, but admittedly none of us has ever been to Mexico. In another hour we're through.

This will be Europe's Eastern border from May 1st. We drive the 70 km to L'viv, formerly Lvov, Lwow or Lemburg. In Poland you hear a lot about Lwow, at least from the older generation, who wax nostalgic over its beauty and cultural vibrancy.

L'viv has been tossed around by emperors since its foundation, but for over half of its 800-year history it was Polish, and was, with Krakow, the pride of Poland, a university town whose buildings run from thirteenth century to Renaissance, to

Polish Roccoco, to neo-classicism. The Austrians took it after the partition of Poland in 1772 and ran it in their haphazard Hapsburg fashion until Poland regained it after the first World War.

L'viv is in Galicia, one of the centres of Ukrainian nationalism, so ownership of the city was always going to be in dispute, but the question wasn't decided by Poles or Ukrainians, but by Stalin. In 1939 he moved in and in 1945 refused to move out again.

At Yalta, Roosevelt pleaded for L'viv's return to Poland but he was in no position to refuse the Russians. Stalin solved any future ethnic problems by ruthless population exchanges across the border. L'viv was incorporated into Ukraine which was incorporated into the USSR until, in 1991, it gained independence.

*L'viv — so near to the European ... and so far.*
*Photograph: Bridget Hourican.*

This is the city we're approaching — cut off from Poland by 60 years, 70 km, one hour time difference, three hours border wait, $40 in bribes and, soon, by Schengen. At night, by the very dim lights strung from wires over the roads, it looks like another Eastern European glory, like Budapest, Krakow, or Prague.

By daylight it looks more like an illustration for 'poverty in grandeur'. All of Eastern Europe is poorer than the West, but L'viv isn't Eastern European poor, it's Russian poor. Crowds of babushkas (grandmothers) line the lovely cobbled streets, patiently selling bags of apples or bunches of flowers. Every second building houses an exchange office, all offering identical rates.

The magnificent buildings are crumbling where they stand. Open drains release waste water onto the streets. Legs and noses have crumbled off statues. Columns have fallen off buildings. A coat of dirt covers everything.

In one sense, however, it's miraculously well-preserved. Nothing has been torn down, no Soviet blocks put up. The only sign of the USSR is a few statues in the brute realist style. Moscow ignored L'viv. If the Party had held onto it much longer neglect would have finished it off. As it is, there's nothing a massive injection of cash couldn't resolve.

Cash, however, is the problem. I walk the streets with Andrey Salynk, head of an NGO for the preservation of L'viv's heritage. He is gallant as a cavalier in the face of imminent ruin and given to sudden paroxysms of mirth. 'There are 1,000 concerned citizens in L'viv' (pause) 'out of 800,000' (explosive laughter). 'I have $6,200 for Boims chapel.' (pause) 'I need half a million dollars' (explosive laughter).

The Ukrainian government has earmarked $5 million for L'viv in this year's budget, which is enough to restore three buildings. Salynk estimates $3 billion would halt the process of decay. That figure doesn't include renovation.

The EU is the Ukraine's biggest donor and has given €1.2 billion in aid over the past 10 years but this money is for technical assistance, administrative reform and nuclear safety. Ukraine has poverty and Chernobyl. There isn't money for buildings.

L'viv has the surreal, glazed look of a city which has changed hands too often. Outside our hotel is a nineteenth-century statue to the Polish poet Adam Mickiewicz. To the Poles, Mickiewicz is a kind of Moore, Yeats and Joyce rolled into one but in L'viv the people I ask have only the vaguest idea of him. In the adjacent square is a massive recent black statue to the Ukrainian poet Taras Shevchenko.

Today, unsurprisingly, L'viv is putting out Ukrainian colours. Of the seven main museums, three are devoted to Ukrainian peasant art and ethnography. I look for the Scottish café, where in the inter-war Polish years, L'viv's mathematicians, including Stanislaw Ulam, who later helped invent the atom bomb, hung out and drew equations on the marble-topped table. I can't find it. The tourist office says it's a bank; the internet says it's a bar.

Jewish L'viv was obliterated by the Nazis. The city used to have the third largest Jewish community in Poland. Now only stones of the sixteenth-century synagogue remain. There was a concentration camp here, called Janowska. In Poland I'm told the camp is now a prison, but the tourist office disputes this. They say it's been 'absorbed' into other buildings. In any case it can't be visited, but there is a plaque.

Austrian L'viv survives in the buildings. The authorities are resisting erecting a statue to Leopold Sacher-Masoch, L'vivian author of *Venus in Furs* and inventor of masochism. Maybe his just isn't an image they want for their city.

Polish-Austrian-Jewish-Ukrainian. What every- one agrees is that it's a European city. Ukraine, despite having cities, whose names – Odessa, Yalta – are familiar to Western readers through Chekhov and whose inhabitants only speak Russian, has distanced itself from Russia and applied for EU membership. The EU is being coy about this application. Agnes Schubert of the EU delegation in Kiev says 'we support Ukraine's

strategy for entry' but 'integration isn't on the agenda yet'. The Ukrainian press has noted bitterly that the EU always uses words like 'rapprochement' for the Ukraine, never 'integration'. The latest EU term is 'Neighbourhood Policy'.

Says Schubert: 'The Neighbourhood policy means Ukraine, and other countries, like Belarus and Moldova, could have access to the internal market but not yet to the EU institutions'.

Ukraine isn't joining any time soon. In the meantime, its borders are being regulated. On 1 May it will border three EU countries, Poland, Slovakia and Hungary. All three are currently implementing the necessary visa restrictions.

Ukraine's Polish minority are indignantly flooding their consulate but they're insignificant in numbers – about 5,000 in L'viv.

Ukraine's ex-foreign minister Anatolii Zlenko has called the borders a 'Schengen Wall' but says Schubert: 'The EU doesn't want dividing lines between Ukraine and its neighbours.' It's financing lots of cross-border initiatives to smooth things over. These include a bridge into Poland.

In Auden's 1930s line, 'where Poland draws its Eastern bow' was where Europe began. This is still the case. Its bow is just being drawn further west. L'viv is Ukraine's window onto Europe.

---

SATURDAY, I MAY 2004

# Guest and Gestapo

*Róisín Ingle*

Coming home from work after a hard day there are a few things you just do not want to find on your dining room table. A used cotton bud, fresh from the ear of your long-term house guest, has to score very highly in this department. But there it was. An unappetising combination of cotton wool, plastic and earwax resting innocently on the table. You

*A participant in a reclaim the streets demonstration in Dublin jokes with gardaí. Photograph: Bryan O'Brien.*

should have thought about this before you agreed to let him stay for five months, it seemed to mock.

I know I am not easy to live with. Every one who has ever lived with me knows I am not easy to live with. That includes an ex-husband, a family, a mother and a boyfriend who every day has to bite his lip and marvel at how difficult to live with I am. However, even I never left used cotton buds on the table. Half empty flagons of cider maybe. The odd dirty sock. I like to think I have some standards.

It all seemed like such a good idea at the time. Can I stay in your house, when I come over? he asked. Course you can, I said. We planned his visit. He would bring all his Indian spices and cooking instruments and herbal toothpaste and pictures of the holy mountain. We got a room ready for him,

a chest of drawers, a table and a chair. I looked forward to us meditating together, cooking sumptuous Indian banquets, enjoying deep conversations deep into the night. Five months? Why not make it 12? He'd bring a little bit of India to Dublin 3 and all I had to give him was a roof over his head.

May Day! May Day! It's not quite working out like that. Forget Cottonbudgate, it was Carpetgate that really made me question my decision to let him stay.

You see, he likes his baths. And the fact that I had asked him to please make sure and let the man in when he came to lay the carpet didn't deter him from his daily ablutions. The boyfriend and I were up at six that morning clearing out the room for the carpet. All my long-term house guest needed to do was let him in.

I rang him at 11 a.m. And at noon. No sign of the carpet man, said he. So I rang the carpet people, who told me their man had been banging on my door for 15 minutes, calling through an open window if you wouldn't be minding. But answer came there none. The houseguest was in the bath with the radio blaring. The carpet men moved on to another house. Two weeks later I'm still getting over it.

There have been a million other incidents that may sound insignificant to you but have rocked my otherwise steady domestic life. These include: him not turning off the hot water switch after he has a shower. Him dumping all his stuff (anything from Zen cards to incense) on the table instead of putting them away. Him putting coffee grounds down the plughole and questioning me about it when I ask him not to. Him using the tumble dryer without asking. Him breathing. Himmmmm.

I'm beginning to feel like the Gestapo in my own home. Snooping around for signs that he has been breaking the rules. Ve haf vays of making you put ze tea bags in ze bin instead of ze sink. That kind of thing.

Then there are the lectures. Since his arrival, our domestic habits have come under scrutiny. He is, after all, a doctor and knows a thing or three about health. He won't use our cheap saucepans, for example, because he says the aluminium on them will give him Alzheimer's. He thinks we are mad using regular toothpaste because, hellooo, fluoride is mega-toxic. Friends are jealous because my houseguest is also a yoga teacher who happens to be extremely generous with his time, but with all the inner turmoil I'm experiencing I just can't bring myself to get on the mat.

Worst of all, if I'm really honest I don't think any of this is actually his fault except perhaps the bit about the carpet and the used cotton bud. His stay has turned me into a bit of a monster, and I'm constantly on high alert for his next dodgy move.

It has got to the stage where if he just sat meekly in his room, listening to gentle water music

*Taking the sun at Palmer's Rock in Salthill, Galway. Photograph: Joe O'Shaughnessy.*

*A giant portrait of Hungarian model Anita Korsos hangs from the columns of the Elizabeth Bridge in Budapest to mark Hungary's accession to the European Union. Photograph: Barnabas Honeczy/AP/MTI.*

and praying for world peace I'd be up there ranting at him like a woman possessed.

There have been chinks of light in this dark tale. The other night I had a dinner party, during which he played the guitar and sang and read his Zen cards for the guests. It was a joyful night that reminded me why I wanted him in my house in the first place. The next day I got home from work, cleared his stuff from the table, turned off the shower switch and fished out a teabag from the sink. He ain't heavy, he's my brother. I just have to keep telling myself that.

# The Lights Go Up All Over a New Europe

*Denis Staunton, in Brussels*

From the west coast of Ireland to the eastern borders of Poland, Europeans were last night celebrating the EU's biggest expansion to date and political reunification of a continent divided for half a century by the Cold War.

Fireworks exploded and church bells rang out across the 25 countries of the enlarged EU, which has moved its borders 1,000 kilometres to the east and increased its population to more than 450 million people.

The biggest celebrations planned for last night were in the 10 new member-states, with Malta – now the EU's smallest state – planning the largest fireworks display.

In Budapest, the Hungarian Prime Minister, Mr Peter Medgyessy, was due to set a giant hour-glass in motion to symbolise the beginning of a new era. Lithuania's government called on citizens to use lamps, candles and fireworks to make their country the brightest spot in Europe.

In a statement published at midnight, the European Commission President, Mr Romano Prodi, praised the courage and determination of the new member-states and the generosity and vision of older member-states in making enlargement possible.

'United in diversity, we will be stronger and better equipped to find solutions to common problems. United in diversity, we can work more effectively for safety and prosperity for all. I urge all Europeans to join in the celebrations of our astonishing achievement. Welcome to the New Europe,' he said.

Mr Prodi will be in Dublin today, along with the leaders of all 25 member-states and the President of the European Parliament, Mr Pat Cox, for a ceremony at Áras an Úachtaráin to celebrate enlargement. The leaders will dine together this evening at Farmleigh House, but officials said that the dinner would be strictly social, with no discussion of political issues, such as the proposed EU constitutional treaty due to be agreed next month.

The biggest celebrations last night were in the new member-states, eight of which lay behind the Iron Curtain for almost 50 years. The Commissioner responsible for enlargement, Mr Günther Verheugen, said yesterday that the accession of the new states represented the symbolic end to Europe's division. 'It is Europe's response to the end of the Cold War and an opportunity to heal the wounds of the past, wounds of war and dictatorship,' he said.

Mr Lech Walesa, who led the Solidarity trade union that overturned Poland's communist system in 1989, agreed. 'Poland's entrance into the European Union fulfils my dreams and lifetime work,' he said.

Germany's President, Mr Johannes Rau, addressed the Polish parliament in Warsaw yesterday, urging Europeans in east and west to overcome their fears and embrace a common destiny. 'Without Poland, Europe would not be Europe,' he said.

Cyprus will stage two days of celebrations to mark its accession to the EU, although the country's President, Mr Tassos Papadopolous, can expect an icy reception from other EU leaders in Dublin today. EU governments are angry at his role in persuading Greek Cypriots to vote against a plan to unify Cyprus.

*Fireworks explode during a display on Sandymount Strand in Dublin to mark EU Accession Day. Photograph: Ian Waldie/Getty.*

*All-Ireland Sheep Shearing Champions David Kingston from Cork and Tom Kennedy from Athenry in Galway with two animals they sheared in a Dublin city centre hotel as part of the launch of the Clik All-Ireland Sheep Shearing Championships to be held at Milford, Co. Donegal. Photograph: Bryan O'Brien.*

**MONDAY, 3 MAY 2004**

# Bertie Presides Over the Enlargement Like Tense Father of the Bride

*Frank McNally*

Bertie Ahern paced the doorway at Farmleigh like a nervous father at a wedding. Not even his recent experiences in the latter role could have fully prepared him for the Day of Welcomes, as 27 prime ministers and two EU delegations swept up his driveway at short intervals. (The Bulgarian, Romanian and Turkish prime ministers were invited, as well as the leaders of the EU states.)

Between arrivals, he walked back and forth, head down, as if rehearsing his speech. He could at least relax in the knowledge that his place was looking well.

Jacques Chirac was clearly impressed as he climbed out of the car, gesturing at the house and gardens and the Phoenix Park, and saying 'beautiful' over and over. 'And only two miles from Dublin?' he asked, eyebrows raised, as his host led him inside.

Farmleigh has its own grounds, of course. But with the whole Phoenix Park cordoned off like a crime scene, Mr Chirac could have been forgiven for thinking the house had the largest private garden in Europe. Versailles paled by comparison.

The balmy conditions, and the fact that Dublin was deserted apart from policemen, created the eerie atmosphere of a Central American city after a coup. But the ceremony over at Áras an Uachtaráin was undeniably touching, with the presentation of the 25 flags by schoolchildren, and the raising of the colours to the sound of the RTÉ Philharmonic Choir singing *Ode to Joy*.

Then it was back to Farmleigh where guests enjoyed a simple-sounding dinner of salmon, duck and 'wild berries in a tuile basket', with wines representing the new and old Europes. The white was from Slovenia, and the red from the great French vineyard of Chateau Lynch Bages – a deliberate nod to the memory of the Taoiseach who brought Ireland into the then EEC in 1973.

After dinner, the prime ministers were entertained by musicians, including Altan. 'Please come closer to us,' appealed Mairéad Ní Mhaoinigh, as guests hung back in the Farmleigh marquee. But when Gerhard Schröder starting clapping to the music and danced the distant relative of a jig, everyone looked a bit nervous.

The disturbances at the Phoenix Park's Ashtown Gate had no chance of reaching the ears of the guests.

The Office of Public Works said yesterday a 200-year-old sycamore tree near Farmleigh House was cut down because it was rotting and not to provide TV cameras with a better view of the State mansion. The OPW said the tree suffered from a root-decaying fungus called ganoderma, and was chopped down in recent weeks for safety reasons. 'The tree was in an area off to the left of the house, and it wouldn't have mattered (for television images) whether it was there or not.'

*Michael McDowell (left) tries out a cell at the new garda station in Templemore, Co. Tipperary, as Supt Jim Mulligan looks on. Photograph: Eric Luke.*

*Beverely Flynn at Leinster House on the day of her expulsion from the Fianna Fáil parliamentary party. Photograph: Cyril Byrne.*

**WEDNESDAY, 5 MAY 2004**

# Sackable Offence in Fianna Fáil

*Editorial*

The gradual metamorphosis of Ms Beverley Flynn from active predator into hapless victim has been a sight to behold. It is hard to reconcile the character who went before her Fianna Fáil parliamentary colleagues yesterday and pleaded she was being scapegoated because of her actions as an official at National Irish Bank and the TD who, full of righteous indignation, instituted libel proceedings against RTÉ five years ago for daring to suggest she had engaged in those same activities.

Had Ms Flynn won her case, she would be significantly better off financially. But she lost. And she is now looking for understanding and forgiveness.

Some members of the Fianna Fáil parliamentary party had sympathy for Ms Flynn. And they gave her a hearing, just as they had done three years ago, before they voted for the second time to remove the whip from her. The Taoiseach, Mr Ahern, was the opening speaker to the disciplinary motion. And there never was any question about the outcome. With a Cabinet reshuffle due to take place after the local and European Parliament elections in June, members of the Dáil and Seanad were on their best behaviour.

Discipline may not be so tight when the national executive of Fianna Fáil meets on Friday to consider the more drastic action to expel Ms Flynn from the organisation. The constituency organisation in Mayo supported her. And members of the national executive have been lobbied in her favour. But the expulsion motion is still likely to be carried by the required two-thirds majority.

The Taoiseach appears determined to make a clean cut. With elections pending, he does not want ethical and taxation issues to dominate the headlines. Mr Ahern's own uncertain performance before the Mahon tribunal was something of a shambles. And so he has apparently opted to show vigorous and decisive leadership. On the last occasion, Ms Flynn was allowed to retain Fianna Fáil membership and she secured nomination as a party candidate before being accepted back into the parliamentary party. This time, the back door is being bricked up. Evading tax, or facilitating tax evasion, is in the process of becoming a sackable offence in Fianna Fáil. And about time too.

Many of the arguments put forward by Ms Flynn in her defence are risible. As an adult citizen, she was responsible for her actions, no matter what tax culture existed within National Irish Bank.

But her treatment is harsher than that previously meted out to other party members, such as Mr Denis Foley and Mr Ray Burke. In that regard, Mr Michael Collins TD was found to have evaded tax and to have made a voluntary settlement with the Revenue Commissioners last year. He is still a member of Fianna Fáil, though he resigned from the parliamentary party.

If the Taoiseach is to be consistent in his treatment of such offences, Mr Collins must also lose his party membership.

**SATURDAY, 8 MAY 2004**

# The Shaming of America

*Conor O'Clery, in New York*

The shaming of America this week had its beginnings in an exchange of a CD in January between two army buddies, both reservists serving at Abu Ghraib prison outside Baghdad. When Specialist Joseph Darby, a young man with shaggy brown hair from the coalmining hills of south-west Pennsylvania, slid the CD into his laptop, he was horrified by the images that came up.

There was Corp. Charles Graner, a bespectacled prison guard from Pennsylvania, arm-in-arm with a woman reservist, grinning and giving a thumbs-up sign behind a pile of seven naked Iraqi prisoners. In another image, Graner, who has a history of violent spousal abuse, stood smirking as the woman, Lynndie England, formerly a chicken processing worker in West Virginia, bent her head laughing towards the anus of a naked Iraqi.

Joseph Darby, who was brought up 'respectful' according to a neighbour in his home town of Jenners, was so upset by what he saw that he slipped an anonymous note under the door of a superior, and later came forward to tell the officer he 'felt very bad about it and thought it was very wrong'.

The military in Baghdad reacted swiftly. Lieut. Gen. Ricardo Sanchez, the senior commander in Iraq, quietly suspended the general in charge of prisons, Janis Karpinski, and asked Maj. Gen. Antonio Taguba to conduct an investigation. On 16 January the Pentagon issued a press release about an inquiry into possible abuse in Iraq, without specifying the prison. Some days later – the White House cannot give the exact date – President Bush was told by Defence Secretary Donald Rumsfeld during a regular briefing that abuse charges had been made. But Rumsfeld said nothing about pictures. The Pentagon received Gen. Taguba's 53-page report on 3 March. It was devastating.

It found that between October and December of 2003 there were numerous instances of 'sadistic, blatant, and wanton criminal abuses' at Abu Ghraib, the notorious prison now run by the US army, where Saddam Hussein had his opponents tortured. Soldiers of the 372nd Military Police Company and intelligence agencies, aided by

*A hooded Iraqi prisoner is made to stand on a box by US captors, his hands connected to wires in an apparent attempt to frighten him by making him think he might be electrocuted. Photograph:* **The New Yorker/AP.**

civilian contractors, had committed atrocities on some prisoners.

They included: 'breaking chemical lights and pouring the phosphoric liquid on detainees; pouring cold water on naked detainees; beating detainees with a broom handle and a chair; threatening male detainees with rape; sodomising a detainee with a chemical light and perhaps a broom stick, and using military working dogs to frighten and intimidate detainees with threats of attack, and in one instance actually biting a detainee'.

A military policewoman asserted in the report that in one instance a hooded prisoner was kept awake by placing him on a box with wires attached to his fingers, toes, and penis. The report cited

gross sexual abuse, with male detainees forced to simulate oral sex. It said there were graphic photographs of these indignities, making Muslim detainees involuntary bit players in a series of hundreds of pornographic pictures.

Whether or not senior Pentagon officials were fully aware of the possibility of a looming catastrophe that could do incalculable damage to America's image should the pictures ever be published, the media were alert to the brewing scandal. CNN reported in January of an inquiry into abuse and the possible existence of photographs of torture in Abu Ghraib. It wasn't until mid-April, however, that CBS 60 Minutes contacted the Defence Department in Washington to say it had pictures of flagrant abuse at Abu Ghraib prison and was planning to broadcast them.

Gen. Richard Myers, who, as joint chiefs of staff chairman represents the armed services in the White House, asked the network to hold off, pleading it could inflame the insurgencies against the US occupation that had flared across Iraq. CBS producers agreed, but two weeks later came back to tell Gen. Myers that it was going ahead with the broadcast on 28 April as the pictures had started to circulate on the Internet.

In Baghdad, Brig. Gen. Mark Kimmitt told reporters hours in advance what was coming, saying it was the work of a few wrongdoers, who would be punished. That day, after Brig. Gen. Kimmitt's briefing, Rumsfeld again met the president in the White House for a routine briefing. Astonishingly, he said nothing about the pictures, nor gave any indication of the storm that was about to break.

The first Bush knew about the photographs, according to White House officials, was when he saw them on television later that evening. Last weekend, as the pictures evoked horror throughout the US, and presented the world with an enduring image of the occupation, another bombshell exploded on the Internet edition of the *New Yorker* magazine. Investigative reporter Seymour

Hersh, who had first reported on the Mai Lai massacre by US soldiers during the Vietnam War, had got Taguba's report. The pictures now had a context.

Far from being an aberration they were clearly part of a pattern. That evening, the president and the defence secretary were in a jolly mood at the White House correspondents' dinner where Bush poked fun at himself for never admitting he was wrong. But as the international furore beat down on the White House the next day, the mood soured.

First, Gen. Myers on Sunday and then Donald Rumsfeld on Monday strained credibility by claiming they had not seen the two-month-old Pentagon report, even though Hersh had already published its main findings. On Tuesday, as questions swirled about who knew what and when, Bush summoned Rumsfeld into his office. For the first time in his presidency, he publicly chided a senior official by revealing later what he told Rumsfeld: 'I said I should have known about the pictures and the report,' he snapped to reporters.

It was a huge embarrassment to admit being out of the loop, but it may have been a strategic move, designed to distance the president from the scandal and show he was sharing the nation's outrage at photographs that 'sickened my stomach'. But many commentators were quick to point out that presidents historically took the blame when things went wrong. In 1961, John F. Kennedy accepted full responsibility for the Bay of Pigs disaster; in 1980 Jimmy Carter took the blame for the failed rescue mission of US hostages in Iran; and in 1987 Ronald Reagan admitted to the nation after the Iran-contra arms for hostages scandal, 'I was stubborn in my pursuit of a policy that went astray.' Bill Clinton also said, often, that his relationship with Monica Lewinsky 'was wrong'.

In contrast, neither the president nor anyone in the Bush administration has accepted any culpability for anything that has gone wrong concerning Iraq, from the false intelligence about weapons of mass destruction, to the debacle of the post-

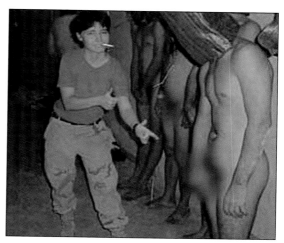

*US Army Reserve Pfc Lynndie England humiliates naked and hooded Iraqi prisoners held by US forces in Abu Ghraib prison in Baghdad. Photograph:* **The New Yorker/**Reuters.

invasion planning, to the failure to provide proper armour for soldiers, to the blunders that led to Falluja and Najaf.

As the full force of the Iraq crisis bore down, the administration, which had been noted for its public cohesion, began to come apart at the seams. The relationship between the State Department and the Pentagon, already strained, turned poisonous. A senior State Department official pointedly told the *Washington Post* that Rumsfeld and the Pentagon had resisted appeals by Secretary of State Colin Powell, at several White House meetings over the last few months, to release Iraqi detainees quickly and to see those in custody were properly treated. Paul Bremer, the US proconsul in Iraq, had also warned about the consequences, officials said.

Bob Woodward's book, *Plan of Attack*, recently revealed the depth of the animosity between Powell and the Rumsfeld team of neo-conservatives, including Paul Wolfowitz, Richard Perle, and Douglas Feith – about whom Gen. Tommy Franks said, according to Woodward: 'I have to deal with the f★★king stupidist guy on the face of the earth almost every day.'

*US Army Spc Sabrina Harman of the 372nd Military Police Company and Sgt Charles Graner of the 372nd Military Police Company pose with a pyramid of naked and hooded Iraqi prisoners. Photograph: The New Yorker/Reuters.*

Even before the Abu Ghraib scandal broke, Powell was putting the word out through his friends that he was just about finished with the administration.

Several spoke frankly to GQ magazine about how Powell was bitter, uncomfortable with the president's agenda and exhausted from his battles with the Pentagon. Powell's closest buddy, Deputy Secretary of State Richard Armitage, told GQ's Wil Hylton that Powell's disastrous speech at the UN last year was 'a source of great distress for the secretary [Secretary of State]'.

His chief of staff, Larry Wilkerson, said Powell was tired 'mentally and physically', doing damage control and apologising for some 'less-than-graceful actions' by other cabinet members. Wilkerson assailed the Pentagon neo-conservatives in a memorable phrase: 'I don't care whether Utopians are Vladimir Lenin on a sealed train to Moscow or Paul Wolfowitz,' he said. 'Utopians, I don't like. You're never going to bring Utopia, and you're going to hurt a lot of people in the process of trying to do it.'

As the US was convulsed with embarrassment over the photographs, the focus turned to the Bush administration's attitude to human rights since 9/11. The *New York Times* highlighted cases of innocent Muslims picked up in New York and beaten and held without charge in a Brooklyn prison for months before being thrown out of the country. The *Washington Post* charged Rumsfeld with setting the foundations for Abu Ghraib in January 2002 when he instituted a system of holding detainees incommunicado, declaring they did not have any rights under the Geneva conventions.

This meant their treatment became an arbitrary matter for government agencies not subject to any normal legal restraints. This week, the Pentagon admitted 25 prisoners have died in Afghanistan and Iraq with almost no accountability. The anger at the scandal now stretches across the political spectrum.

*New York Times* columnist Thomas Friedman commented: 'We are in danger of losing America as an instrument of moral authority and inspiration.' There is now ebbing support for a mission which claimed the moral right to regime change. President Bush still takes credit in his stump re-election speech for shutting down Saddam Hussein's torture chambers, but the boast rings somewhat hollow today.

Americans, already disillusioned by seeing the marines turn to one of Saddam Hussein's Revolutionary Guard commanders who led pogroms against Kurds and Shiites, to get them out of Falluja, are turning against the war, according to new polls this weekend. As for the military police in the digital pictures that have tainted the image of America – perhaps for a generation – they are back in the US. Charles Graner is again working as a guard on death row in Maryland.

Lynndie England is in Fort Bragg, North Carolina, where she is expecting a baby by Graner. Her mother told the *New York Times*: 'Everything she did, she did because someone higher up told her to.'

# Unregistered, Struck-off Doctor Still Treating Cancer

*Eithne Donnellan, Health Correspondent*

There are no direction signs to Dr William Porter's clinic. His name isn't even on the plaque outside the door of 29 Marine Village or the house next door in Ballina, Co. Tipperary, across the Shannon from Killaloe, Co. Clare. But it is in these bungalows overlooking scenic Lough Derg that Dr Porter is providing what he describes as a breakthrough treatment for cancer patients. And it doesn't come cheap at €20,000 a shot.

Dr Porter, who was struck off for gross negligence in California, moved his light therapy practice from Killaloe to Ballina during the past year after parting company with local GP Dr Paschal Carmody. Dr Carmody was himself finally struck off the medical register in recent weeks for professional misconduct, after several encounters with the Medical Council.

These run-ins were over a host of complaints relating to the manufacture and supply of unauthorised medicines, over record-keeping and sending patient samples for analysis, charging large fees, and over his treatment of deep-seated cancers with photodynamic therapy (PDT).

It is a form of PDT therapy that Dr Porter, who is not registered here, is now providing to patients from all over the world. He calls it cytoluminescent therapy or CLT.

There are no scientific studies on the efficacy of CLT. One review published in a US medical journal found 17 of 48 patients treated with CLT by Dr Porter in Killaloe were dead within six months.

Dr Porter continued to insist this week that his therapy is amazing and beneficial to virtually every type of cancer. He also claims it is beneficial for HIV and AIDS.

When a young woman showed me to the front room of his house/clinic he was alone, relaxing in an armchair. We had just exchanged niceties when men in suits began to file into the room. One was a professor, another a doctor, another a barrister and another a biochemist, I was told.

The barrister, who happens to be former Fine Gael TD Mr Liam Skelly, says he is chairman of the company promoting CLT and that Dr Porter will give me a power point presentation on the therapy. Then I'm told the meeting is being recorded.

The presentation includes pictures of women with breast cancer before and after treatment. The patients are given 'an agent' called PhotoFlora derived from microscopic chlorophyll containing plants and developed in Killaloe. It is given orally and the patients are then subjected to light therapy in something resembling a sunbed.

According to Dr Porter the agent collects in cancer tissues and is activated by the light therapy and destroys cancer cells.

I express surprise that PhotoFlora is being given to patients without having been tested on animals. Dr Tom Cleary, a registered doctor whose nameplate is on the door outside, says it's perfectly all right to do so under some EU directive.

The biochemist in the room, who also happens to be a Russian Olympic marathon runner, is dispatched to get me a copy of directive 2001/83/EC. Dr Cleary has taken over from Dr Carmody as the 'attending physician' when CLT is administered.

Susan's (not her real name) husband, a man in his late 40s, had parts of his liver, stomach, spleen and pancreas removed by the time he heard of Drs Porter and Carmody. Susan says Dr Carmody told her that, not alone would he keep her husband's cancer at bay, he would destroy it. Dr Carmody was not at the East Clinic when *The Irish Times* called to discuss the case. I put it to Dr Porter that he told Susan her husband, who is now dead, would be cured by his light treatment for which they paid over €17,000. He denies it.

Susan says that after her husband underwent the light treatment, Dr Porter asked her to look at an ultrasound. He said he could see her husband's tumours dispersing. When she asked where would they disperse to, she claims he told her about a man who had a tumour in his oesophagus and who, after one treatment, 'coughed it up'. Dr Porter says he would never have said such a thing. Looking back Susan is embarrassed at having believed such a story, but says she completely believed this man as he was a doctor.

A few weeks later when her husband went for a hospital scan it emerged his condition was worse than ever. She rang Dr Porter and accused him of being a fraud. He hung up on her, she says.

Asked about this, Dr Porter says her husband was 'in dreadful shape' when he arrived at the clinic. He had undergone chemotherapy and had lost lots of weight. 'The clothes were falling off him,' he claims. He says he told her husband he couldn't guarantee anything. 'In anybody's book he was a failure from surgery.'

Dr Porter says 'the scandal' is not that he is providing CLT, but that cancer specialists are not offering it to patients and instead subjecting patients to surgery and chemotherapy. He says there are many references in medical literature to how brilliant PDT is. I point out that he is providing CLT, for which there are no references. He agrees but says the difference between PDT and CLT is 'just semantics'. But then he claims CLT is much better than PDT.

I point out that one of the few references to CLT in the literature is a review by Dr Ralph Moss, who documented the outcome for the 48 patients mentioned earlier. Dr Porter claims the Moss review asked people to report negative reactions and was thus biased, something denied by Dr Moss.

Furthermore, he points out that Dr Moss is not a medical doctor. But he acknowledges several patients died within a short time of treatment and that many suffered after-effects. But he says they were all people with advanced cancers.

Dr Moss's review says it was not possible 'to categorically attribute any deaths to CLT'. But he says the treatment of this group with CLT was 'a qualified failure with a high incidence of after-effects'.

Based on the findings of the Dr Moss review, the Medical Council has asked the gardaí to investigate Dr Porter. 'We have never been investigated by the gardaí for anything,' Mr Skelly says. When asked by *The Irish Times*, a spokesman at the Garda press office said he could not comment on individual cases.

Why is the company charging so much for CLT? I ask. These are vulnerable patients who would pay anything to save a loved one, I suggest. Mr Skelly explains this is a new treatment and costs money to develop. It's not expensive compared to the cost of hospital-based cancer treatments, he asserts, and as it becomes more widely available, he claims, the cost will come down.

Asked was he concerned that a review showed many patients suffered after-effects of his treatment and some believed it had made their tumours increase, Dr Porter says he always does the best he can with 'the technologies available' at any given time. He says the treatment has improved since the Moss review and patients are given no guarantees about whether it will work or not. Patients say differently.

Susan kept some of the many tablets which Dr Carmody's East Clinic gave her late husband. The Midland Health Board sent them to a Western Health Board laboratory for examination after being requested to do so by a Department official. In its report of March 2003, the lab said it did not have the resources to analyse them all.

But it made a number of observations. Its report said many of them were labelled as containing vitamins or mineral supplements. The amount of vitamin A on the label of one product exceeded the recommended daily dose.

Susan and a number of other women are now seeking a meeting with the Minister for Health, Mr Martin, to discuss how their relatives were treated by the two doctors. Callers to RTÉ's *Liveline* programme this week said they should be investigated for fraud.

The Medical Council president, Dr John Hillery, admitted the stories of people attended to by these doctors were distressing. He said specialist treatments needed to be supervised by medical specialists 'in appropriate settings'.

Those who want to meet the Minister are questioning why he hasn't acted earlier to prevent an unregistered doctor operating in the country.

They are also asking if the Medical Council acted quickly enough in relation to Dr Carmody. The council claims it went to the High Court as soon as it got complaints about his treatment of patients with PDT.

The roles of other bodies should also be looked at, former patients say. Tipperary North County Council acted in recent weeks by serving an enforcement notice on Dr Porter, ordering him to cease using both of his bungalows for commercial purposes.

*'Dr' Bill Porter with his 'light therapy' sun bed that he claims helps destroy cancer cells. Photograph: David Sleator.*

**THURSDAY, 13 MAY 2004**

# 'I Would be Unconscious After Beating'

*Kitty Holland*

Maria Alexi (18) says she 'fell in love' when she was 15 with a man who promised her 'many things and a great future' in Ireland.

But within a few months of being brought into the country illegally, she found herself living in fear of the man who arranged for her to travel, being held captive and forced to have sex with men in flats in the city.

When she first came to Ireland in January 2001, she worked for a few months in a kebab shop run by a friend of this man as well as packing vegetables in a warehouse. Within months, however, the man who had helped her come to Ireland started bringing men home and telling her she had to have sex with them.

'They said "He is the boss. If you don't perform sex he will kill you." I think I had sex with maybe 200 men since I came here.'

Last Tuesday afternoon, sitting on her single bed in a tiny, dingy bed-sit near the Phoenix Park,

*Ginger (right) feeling the heat in Dublin's Merrion Square. Photograph: Bryan O'Brien.*

this diminutive, sallow-skinned girl with wide deep brown eyes, tells how she first met the man in her home town, Bistrita, in the Transylvania region of northern Romania.

He, she explains, is Romanian, aged about 30, and has residency here on the basis of having an Irish-born child. She says he is married to a Romanian, and has been living in Dublin with two children.

In Romania her parents did not get along. 'My father hit my mother and she died and I was living with my grandmother.' Speaking though an interpreter, she says her financial situation there was not good; there could be days when she did not eat. Then she was out with a friend one evening and met the man, and she says she 'believed his compliments'.

'He told me I was beautiful, that I had a great body and said he could give me a great life in Ireland.' He arranged that she travel by bus to Spain, where she was met by 'his friend' who had arranged a false Italian passport and false Italian driving licence. She flew to Dublin where the man met her and brought her to another Romanian man's house.

'I was very happy working for a few months. He used to bring me out to clubs in the beginning. I had no Irish friends but I was happy. After a few months he came home and told me I had to perform sex with some friends of his because we need money. I cried, I said "I no want", but he said he was the boss.' She was just 15.

'First I work with two men from Romania. It took about half an hour each. Then also men from Bulgaria and China.' She could be forced to have sex with up to six men a night. It was a source of contention between her and the man that she refused to perform oral sex or take part in anal sex.

She said she would, in the first months, tell the men she didn't want to have sex with them but they told her he would kill her, and she believed them because he used to threaten her with a knife. Lifting her jumper she now reveals a long gashing scar extending from between her breasts and down her torso. 'After he cut me I really believe he was capable of killing me.'

Asked how often he would bring men back she says it would depend – 'two or three days break, then he would bring more clients for another few days. They pay him – nothing for me.'

One Romanian man, whom she was told last summer to accompany to a disco in Phibsboro and have sex with, gave her €100, but she gave it to the man. 'He was waiting outside.' At no point, she says, did she ever have money of her own. He bought her food and clothes. 'He take the clothes back if he thought I looked too good in them.'

Throughout her time here she says he 'kept' her in a number of flats until settling on one in Portland Row some time last summer. She was moved again from there about a month ago.

*Staff at Chatsworth House in England line the driveway to bid farewell to the Duke of Devonshire as the hearse carrying the coffin passes them en route to his funeral. Photograph: John Giles/PA.*

He locked her in if he wasn't staying with her. Otherwise she would be in the company of another Romanian man, whose name she gives, and who was 'running' another Romanian girl, Oana (20) who escaped, and, she thinks, went to England. This girl had a badly scarred face, having been beaten with a heavy ash-tray.

She thought of running away herself but with almost no English and threats from the man who had helped her come to Ireland that he would kill her if she did, she says she was too frightened.

Another girl, Yolanda (21), also from Romania, was similarly brought to Ireland by another man with promises of a great future. 'But she is back in Romania now. She was deported.'

In the flat in Portland Row she had good neighbours, who used to intervene when she was being beaten, telling him she was only a girl and to stop. They thought she worked as a stripper, says Maria. Six months ago she became pregnant by the man. Though he insisted clients use condoms, he would not.

'He told me he didn't like having sex with the protection. He told me that if I was having a baby it wouldn't be a problem. When I become pregnant I was desperate. He brought me to a private clinic and ask for medication to make me lose the baby. He told the doctor I was too young to have a baby. The doctor refused.'

The man told her he 'didn't give a f..k' about the baby and started beating her, she says, 'very badly, three or four times a week'. He punched and kicked her in the stomach, as well as breaking her lips and mouth.

'Sometimes I would be unconscious after being beaten and he would throw water in my face to wake me up. I would have big pain in my stomach. Sometimes I cried so much at night I thought I would lose five kilos.'

The last time he beat her, was about two weeks ago. She was six months pregnant. He called to the flat and let himself in. After talking to her a bit he made to leave. However, he instead locked the door and turned to slap her to the floor.

'After I was down he took this towel on the bed and put it around his hand and started punching me very hard in the stomach. I was feeling I was wetting myself and I started crying and screaming. Blood was coming out down here,' she says, pointing at her vagina. 'I was all blood. He brought me to the toilet. I felt something coming out of my body. He pulled the chain and he left me here,' she says, gesturing to the floor. He told her if she went to the gardaí he would 'paralyse' her.

However, a neighbour called an ambulance and the gardaí, and she was brought first to the Mater Hospital and then to the Rotunda. She had lost the baby. She developed an infection in her uterus which required attention and she was kept in hospital for a few nights.

Until this point, smoking continuously, she seems almost disconnected from the horrors she reveals. But speaking of her lost pregnancy she gets tearful, and clearly finds it difficult to speak. 'I used to feel him move after I ate things,' she says quietly, stroking her belly. 'I wanted to have my child.'

On Monday night she made a full statement to the gardaí in Fitzgibbon Street, and she was taken into garda protection yesterday.

FRIDAY, 21 MAY 2004

# More Demolitions as Rafah Residents Bury Their Dead

*Nuala Haughey, in Rafah*

The group of women, all dressed in black, came scurrying down Rafah's deserted main street yesterday afternoon, clutching plastic bags full of clothing.

*Labour Party leader Pat Rabbitte (left) and Michael D Higgins TD in the Great Southern Hotel in Galway for the launch of their campaign for a No vote in the citizenship referendum. Photograph: Joe O'Shaughnessy.*

*A Palestinian man carries a dead boy killed when Israeli forces opened fire on a protest march at the Rafah refugee camp in southern Gaza Strip. Photograph: Mohammed Salem/Reuters.*

Their house, they said, had been freshly demolished by Israeli army bulldozers as part of the intensification of the siege of this southern Gaza town and adjacent refugee camp.

'They demolished our house half-an-hour ago,' said Aziza Abu Ubed, a rosy-cheeked 21-year-old who escaped on foot from the scene with her sisters and other female relatives.

'They [the Israeli army] said "We want young men. Where are the young men?" But we told them there were no young men in our house, only an old man. So they got us out of the house and they told us "Don't come back".'

As they were talking, the hum of an Israeli Apache helicopter stirred them, and they took off down the dusty street, their dark overcoats flapping behind them as they ran to safety in a local United Nations school.

Israel's Operation Rainbow entered its third day yesterday, and the Palestinian death toll crept up to an estimated 39, men and children, militants and innocents. The count over the past three days includes 10 people killed in an Israeli army strike on a peaceful demonstration on Wednesday.

In the wake of this incident, the Israeli army continues demolishing more homes and advancing its armoured tanks into more neighbourhoods in what it says is a hunt for militants and tunnels used to smuggle weapons from Egypt.

Locals again reported that the Israeli army continued to attempt to round up men aged up to 45, demanding through loudspeaker announcements that they leave their houses.

Sporadic cracks of gunfire could be heard throughout the day yesterday in many parts of Rafah, including the Tel Sultan district, which is completely isolated from the rest of the town, its residents under curfew since the early hours of Tuesday. Local officials warned yesterday of a looming humanitarian crisis there unless electricity and water supplies were restored. Rafah's mayor, Mr Saeed Zuroub, said the Israelis allowed them yesterday to distribute two small cars full of food and bread to Tel Sultan's 27,000 besieged residents, but this was far from sufficient.

The streets of Rafah town were largely deserted yesterday, most of its shops closed. The Israeli army denied reports that it had destroyed the town's small zoo, one of the few amusement amenities in this impoverished area, but there were local reports that some animals had escaped, including an ostrich and a parrot.

At lunchtime a flag-waving crowd set off for the funeral procession of five people killed in Wednesday's attack. 'By our blood and souls we redeem you martyrs,' they chanted.

At 4.30 p.m. several UN lorries rumbled into the centre, bringing bedding, food and water for the latest batch of displaced residents seeking shelter in the UNWRA-run Rafah Elementary Girls' School.

Families gathered round the school's central courtyard yesterday, distressed at the loss of their homes but relieved to have found refuge, at least for now. Most of the displaced families originally sought refuge here in 1949 when they were uprooted by Israel's war of independence. This week thousands have found themselves homeless again.

Sabrine Abdulal (23) sat in the shade outside one of the rooms with a group of other women and her husband, her nine-month-old baby Dima in her lap. 'The Israeli tanks rolled into our area at about 2 a.m.,' she said. 'The bulldozers started demolishing some homes just in front of us. We felt them getting closer and closer to us, especially when they destroyed a family meeting hall 30 metres away. We waited until the tanks pulled a bit back and then we left the house at around five.'

She said the Israelis called for men under 45 to go to an area near one stadium and men under 45 to go to another. None did.

As darkness fell last night, the gunfire once more intensified around Rafah, and Apache helicopters could be heard in the sky. And so, for the fourth night in succession, the 147,000 residents of Rafah town and refugee camp once again braced themselves for what Operation Rainbow would deliver.

**THURSDAY, 27 MAY 2004**

# Easy Listener Mary Lou Keen to Make Hard Sell

*Kathy Sheridan*

There's something about Mary Lou. To anyone stalking the big beasts of the campaign jungle, this petite, smiley prey in the soft blue linen jacket and well-worn tan suede boots is a bit of an enigma.

While the big beasts thump their chests on the streets, then scuttle back to the cave when threatened with a question or two, Mary Lou gets stuck into that old-fashioned thing called door-to-door canvassing.

Some observers might put this down to a Sinn Féin reluctance to be exposed to potentially explosive confrontations in big public places like shopping centres, but the truth is that angry folk are more likely to open fire – so to speak – in the privacy of their own doorsteps. And anyway, she does both.

In Ballymun shopping centre on Monday, the few openly angry shoppers confined themselves to striding stonily through the candidates. When this reporter asked a couple of women to explain their stoniness – the McCabe case? IRA organised crime? – they were thunder-struck.

'They don't interest me. None o' them. Right?' snarled the first, returning to her holiday snaps. 'They'd annoy the arse off ya, the way they get in your face,' explained her eye-rolling friend. And that was it really.

But the thing about Mary Lou is she doesn't get in your face. This is partly because she prides herself on her listening skills ('the most undervalued skill of all'), but it could also be down to a tactical conundrum here.

How to convince the electorate of a disaffected, working class redoubt like Ballymun that this Rathgar-born, highly-educated, former Fianna Fáiler might have useful insights into their concerns? Simple. You team her up with a local

election candidate, known as 'Sparky', who refers repeatedly and mockingly to his uncustomary suit as the 'tin o' fruit' or 'the Communion suit', prides himself on being 'a mouth', and whose battle cry is 'more consultation'.

Ray 'Sparky' Corcoran has street cred. He's been involved in voluntary work since he was 15. 'Ray is why I'm a mechanic,' says a passing youth, asked why he has such a welcome for Sparky.

On this sunny Monday afternoon, there's just the three Sinn Féiners, Sparky, Mary Lou and her campaign manager, plus one big Mary Lou-

*Mary Lou McDonald. Photograph: Haydn West/PA.*

*Fine Gael European Parliament candidate in Leinster Mairéad McGuinness looking surprised during a visit to the Meath Community Workshop and Training Centre in Navan. Photograph: Cyril Byrne.*

emblazoned bus prominently parked. She stands back, allowing the local candidate his place in the sun. But the ambling, relaxed demeanour can be deceptive. When Sparky says he has to contact a named man before they start into the shopping centre, her response is quiet but sharp: 'I thought this was cleared?' and suddenly you got an insight into the Mary Lou whose regular job is 'co-ordinating the work of the party's elected representatives across the island'.

'So what are you going to do for us?' asks a woman in the Welfare Rights centre. 'Oh loads', she says wryly. Perched on the edge of a desk, she listens first before her twin campaign mantras emerge. Community involvement and getting the vote out. No politician can get things done alone, she says. A hangdog chap in the same office block greets their presence with an old joke – 'Don't

vote, it'll only encourage them'. Mary Lou laughs dutifully. 'But this is the big plague – apathy,' she sighs later, 'and from the most rational, intelligent, sensible people …'

But it's not only about apathy. Confusion is rife. 'There's another girl going for Sinn Féin', wails a woman helplessly at them, 'which one am I voting for?' Well, Mary Lou is going for Europe, someone begins … 'Jazus', mutters a temporary hanger-on, 'what'll they be like when they're handed the third paper in the polling station?'

That night when Mary Lou hits Cabra, veteran party member Ann Speed nails the big question for Sinn Féin: 'Is there a swing away from Fianna Fáil – and if there is, is it a swing to go out to vote or to stay at home?' Some 30 to 40 canvassers meet up at St Finbarr's GAA club at 7.30 sharp. Teams of up to 14 have been out two

*European Parliament candidate in Munster Kathy Sinnott seeking the vote of a Limerick taxi driver. Photograph: Matt Kavanagh.*

to three times a week since January. The local candidates here are bricklayer and outgoing councillor, Nicky Kehoe and Áine Ní Gabhann, a fervent Gaelgeoir and equality worker whose nephew scored for Meath last Sunday.

If the doorsteps are to be believed, there's a staggeringly healthy *Questions & Answers* viewership around Cabra. Image-wise, Mary Lou's appearance on it – even news of her appearance on it – is a coup. Nicky Kehoe makes a point of asking: 'Did you see her on *Questions & Answers?*'

'Ah yeah, all gangin' up on her,' agrees a fan, who may or may not have seen it, 'don't mind those Fianna Fáil assholes.'

Decentralisation comes up twice, the first time from a woman using very un-civil servant type language to describe how she's set to be decen-

tralised three times in 25 years: 'The first when f***ing McSharry f**ked us off to Sligo, the second when Reynolds f**ked us down to Longford and the third when that stupid, silly bitch in Donegal … I'm not going to f***king Buncrana.'

'Buncrana'd be good in the summer,' quips Nicky.

Further down, another civil servant points to his upstairs window, declaring, 'I was born in the front room up there, and I'm NOT going anywhere … You're looking at 20,000 votes for someone who speaks out about it.'

Even so, Mary Lou won't lie. 'The problem is that most of us are in favour of decentralisation provided it's done in a planned way, and not about political opportunism … We can get the responses from our TDs in the House and get them to you — would that be an idea?' she asks, turning hopefully to the troops. 'Take a note,' she says, mildly but meaningfully, to no great fluttering of notebooks (except from the journalists). Bit more 'co-ordination' required here.

Further on, to the soundtrack of the Wolfe Tones blasting out an IRA ditty nearby, a Sinn Féin voter is very exercised about the citizenship referendum. 'I'm not too pleased with the way Sinn Féin is going on that. I live in the real world. That only came into law with the Good Friday agreement to facilitate the nationalists of the North, not for people from Nigeria or Kosovo or anything like that.'

Mary Lou won't lie about that either. 'We are going to be seeing more and more people from the new communities and that's not going to change. We asked the Government to show us the figures to explain the need for this referendum and when they did, they were minuscule. What is very, very clear is that we haven't had enough time to debate it.'

'We're in Europe now … the buzzword,' adds Nicky.

The man looks at him. 'I'm going to give you a bit of friendly advice. Nicky, you keep your mouth shut about that.' He's even less impressed with Mary Lou's contention that two babies born in the same ward would end up unequal as a result of the vote. 'The men of '16 didn't die for that.'

'They'd die for equality for everyone though,' says Mary Lou, uncowed. And so it ended at around 9 p.m., outside Nicky's sister's house for a hug and chat about Mary Lou's 11-month-old daughter, Iseult.

Not a word in nine hours about Garda McCabe, or the peace process or Europe or even about the MEP gravy train.

For the record, if elected, she would take 'just above the industrial wage' from her salary. As with all elected Sinn Féin members, the remainder would be 'reinvested in constituency services'. Is

there any point to this relentless, exhausting tramp across Dublin? 'People want to have a look at you,' she says with a weary grin.

---

WEDNESDAY, 2 JUNE 2004

# Ahern Fails to Look on Bright Side of 'Monty Python' Banking

*Dáil Sketch: Michael O'Regan*

The president of Europe stared downwards at his brief on the Taoiseach's bench, and listened as a possible explanation for the current bank controversies was put forward.

The Socialist Party deputy, Joe Higgins, believed that it might all have to do with a song from the Dubliners' ballad group and the miracle of immaculate conception.

He suggested that the air of injured innocence of the most senior people involved might have come from a Monty Python script. 'A chief executive, who had €40,000 invested for him with magnificently generous returns, is giving the impression that the closest he ever came to hearing a word like "Faldor", might be a Dubliners' song containing the words "with me right fal-de-o".'

The same chief executive, said Mr Higgins, had claimed he was an unknowing beneficiary of this structure, resulting in 'the generation of unexpected tax liability', while another senior executive had €33,000 invested in 1989, and, inexplicably, a few short years later it had grown to a massive €81,000, at which he professed amazement. 'This must be the banking sector's very own phenomenon of immaculate conception — amazing things happen but nobody knows quite how.'

Still staring at his brief, and refusing to look Mr Higgins in the eye, Mr Ahern seemed like a man

*Fianna Fáil's director of elections, John O'Donoghue, at the RDS count centre in Dublin contemplating his party's poor results in the European and local elections. Photograph: Bryan O'Brien.*

who would prefer to be dealing with the arcane subject of an EU constitution. But there was no stopping Mr Higgins.

While the banks were defrauding taxes, speculators were bribing top Fianna Fáil politicians and getting rotten rich on consequent rezoning, said Mr Higgins. Meanwhile, he added, at the time, 'the Taoiseach was writing blank cheques for Charvet shirts.'

Mr Higgins wondered if the Minister for Justice, Michael McDowell, was ordering a wing of Wheatfield prison to be cleared to make way for senior banking executives suspected of serious tax evasion as he did around May Day for young persons suspected of stealing a garda's cap.

'Perhaps he is sending water-cannon into the bank's boardrooms to flush out the truth about those who organised all this racketeering?' The president of Europe remained unimpressed. 'I have already stated the powers that exist,' he said, sharply. 'These issues should not be treated in a light-hearted manner. The result of doing so is that they are not taken seriously. These are very serious matters.'

Mr Higgins was philosophical. 'When all else fails, one must resort to humour.'

Earlier, the president of Europe revealed that he will be in France, Britain, the Netherlands, Belgium, Luxembourg, Germany and Denmark this week. Presumably, there will be a stopover in Drumcondra.

WEDNESDAY, 2 JUNE 2004

# Long Walk to a Real Retirement Ends

*Declan Walsh*

Even living legends have to step down sometime. Adored at home and considered an icon of peace abroad, former South African president Nelson Mandela is pulling back from public life – or, as he termed it, 'retiring from retirement'.

Since leaving politics in 1999 Mandela has been caught up in a frantic whirl of meetings with world leaders, addressing conferences, negotiating peace deals and collecting awards. After giving so much, the 85-year old announced yesterday that he was taking something back – his time.

'Don't call me, I'll call you,' he joked to those thinking of inviting him to future public engagements, during a press conference at one of the three charitable foundations that bear his name.

'I'm turning 86 in a few weeks' time and that is a longer life than most people are granted,' he said. 'I am confident that nobody here present today will accuse me of selfishness if I asked to spend time while I'm still in good health with my family, my friends and also with myself.'

Famous for peacefully shepherding South Africa from the racist rule of apartheid to a black-led democracy, Mandela has become one of the world's most revered – and busy – public figures.

He receives 5,000 appearance requests every year, only a fraction of which he can accept. His engagements involve a punishing schedule of globe-trotting, sometimes flying in a private jet loaned by a Saudi prince.

Last November he organised a pop concert – featuring Bono, Beyonce Knowles and other international stars – to raise funds for his favourite cause, the fight against HIV/Aids.

But apart from his charity work, Mandela has remained an influential international figure, whether leading efforts to mediate an end to the long-running war in Burundi or hectoring George Bush on his plans to invade Iraq. He considers Tony Blair and Fidel Castro as his friends. However, President Bush, stung by this criticism, pointedly ignored him during a visit to South Africa last year.

At home, Mandela criticised the confused Aids policies of his successor, Thabo Mbeki, and expressed regret at not doing more during his own term of office.

In recent months, aides worried about the heavy toll Mandela's schedule was taking, but denied press reports that his health was failing.

Last month, for example, Mandela travelled to the Caribbean to bolster South Africa's bid to host the 2010 soccer World Cup. After flying home briefly to bury his first wife, Evelyn, he continued to the World Cup meeting in Zurich, where his appearance is believed to have helped swing the decision South Africa's way.

'When I told one of my advisers a few months ago that I wanted to retire, he growled at me: "You are retired." If that is really the case then I should say I now announce that I am retiring from retirement,' he said yesterday.

Known affectionately in South Africa by his clan name Madiba, Mandela said he wanted to work on the second volume of his autobiography – the first was titled *The Long Walk to Freedom* – and to have more time for 'quiet reflection'.

'I do not intend to hide away from the public, but henceforth I want to be in the position of calling you to ask whether I would be welcome, rather than being called upon to do things and participate in events,' he said.

A natural leader and a consummate politician, Mandela was born into a royal family in the Transkei region in 1918. After training as a lawyer, he shot to national prominence as an anti-apartheid activist in the 1950s, alongside his law partner, Oliver Tambo.

In 1964 he was found guilty of attempting to

overthrow the government, and sentenced to life imprisonment, 18 years of which he spent on Robben Island prison near Cape Town.

The long, solitary sentence informed the thinking that transformed South Africa on his release in 1990, but was, nonetheless, difficult. He once said: 'In prison, you come face to face with time. There is nothing more terrifying.'

After his release, Mandela was rarely out of the spotlight, although he was uncomfortable with the quasi-saintly adulation he received. 'The impression you are a demi-god worries me. I wanted to be regarded just like an ordinary human being with virtues and vices,' he told the BBC's David

Dimbleby in a recent interview. Yesterday his friends, many of them former liberation struggle comrades, reacted to the news of his 'second retirement' with a combination of regret and relief. 'I have such mixed feelings about this. It is almost like the end of an era,' said Housing Minister Lindiwe Sisulu.

Mac Maharaj, who spent 12 years with Mandela in Robben Island, said he believed Mandela had a genuine desire to sit back and reflect, if only the public would let him. 'We're all very sympathetic and really wish that he had the time,' he told Reuters. 'But at the same time all of us want a piece of him even now.'

*Nelson Mandela at his office in Johannesburg announcing his retirement. Photograph: Mike Hutchings/Reuters.*

WEDNESDAY, 2 JUNE 2004

# Where's CAB When You Need It?

*Vincent Browne*

In 1996 in the wake of the hysteria caused by the murder of Veronica Guerin, the Oireachtas passed a piece of legislation about which there has been much self-congratulation on the part of its initiators: the Criminal Assets Bureau Act, 1996.

Part of Section 4 of that Act provides that the objectives of the bureau shall be '(a) the identification of the assets, wherever situated, of persons which derive or are suspected to derive, directly or indirectly, from criminal activity, (b) the taking of appropriate action under the law to deprive or to deny those persons of the assets or the benefit of such assets, in whole or in part, as may be appropriate …'

Section 5 of the Act states that the functions of the bureau shall be 'the taking of all necessary actions (a) in accordance with Garda functions, for the purposes of the confiscation, restraint of use, freezing, preservation or seizure of assets identified as deriving, or suspected to derive, directly or indirectly, from criminal activity, (b) under the Revenue Acts or any provision of any other enactment, whether passed before or after the passing of this Act, which relates to revenue, to ensure that the proceeds of criminal activity or suspected criminal activity are subjected to tax and that the Revenue Acts, where appropriate, are fully applied in relation to such proceeds or activities, as the case may be.'

Now we know for a certainty that some of the assets of AIB were derived from criminal activity, those derived from the deliberate and planned fraud over the DIRT tax. We have reason to suspect that further assets were derived from other criminal or dubious activity, those derived from the scam on foreign exchange and the mortgage protection caper. We now know also that AIB remunerated its senior executives in part through a further tax scam, thereby generating assets for itself (one assumes that the beneficiaries of that tax fiddle contributed to the bank's assets in part because of that illegal remuneration).

So where is the Criminal Assets Bureau? If this much vaunted institution, copied, we are asked to believe, in several other jurisdictions, is such an effective instrument in the detection and prevention of crime, why are the sturdy boots of officers of that body not tramping around the plush carpets of the top floors of AIB bank centre this morning?

It's not as though this outfit has been embarrassed by a once-off misdeed. This is part of a long-standing pattern of conduct. It would be excessive to characterise AIB as a criminal conspiracy, but that pattern has been so long-standing and so persistent that one is entitled to suspect that there is criminality in the bank's ethos.

The Irish people are entitled to feel a special anger with AIB and for the following reason.

In 1985, in a state of great anxiety, members of the board of AIB rushed around to Government Buildings to tell the minister for finance, Alan Dukes, and the minister for industry and commerce, John Bruton, that the bank was in crisis because of the collapse of the Insurance Corporation of Ireland (ICI), which it had recklessly purchased and then even more recklessly managed.

Bruton and Dukes in turn rushed around to the sickbed of the taoiseach, Garret FitzGerald, on St Patrick's Day 1985, and, in panic, they agreed the State should take over ICI along with its liabilities, then estimated at between £50 million and £120 million.

It has never been clear why they agreed to do that or why, if it was necessary, they did not demand a shareholding for the State in AIB in return. AIB's profits in 1984 and 1985 were well in excess of the ICI liabilities. So brazen was AIB even in those desperate days that it insisted on paying a substantial dividend to its shareholders in the year of the ICI crisis. John Bruton insisted the State bail-out was the 'responsible' thing for the government to do, even in the face of the dividend pay-out.

Tomás Mac Giolla, then a Workers' Party TD, said: 'I find that when people are being responsible it means that they are standing by the big boys in some place or other.'

Members of that coalition government (1982-87) insist that the banks ultimately funded that bail-out. Not true. Garret FitzGerald's economic adviser, Patrick Honohan, has since shown in an academic paper that the State paid £18 million in 1985 money terms, which is in the region of €80 million nowadays.

In the year after that bail-out, 1986, the deposit interest retention tax (DIRT) was introduced. And in the succeeding several years AIB, which had sought and received a massive bail-out by the State in 1985, cheated the State to the tune of roughly £130 million. The Revenue Commissioners let them get away with it for years.

As time goes by you have to have more and more admiration for Charles Haughey. He was the only one who treated AIB in the way it should be treated. When they demanded repeatedly from 1974 to 1980 that he stop running up a massive overdraft and repay the money he had obtained from them, he told them what to do with themselves. We need a bit more of that kind of leadership nowadays.

**MONDAY, 7 JUNE 2004**

# Reagan Was Always One Step Ahead of the Posse

*Mark Steyn*

All weekend long, across the networks, media grandees who had voted for Carter and Mondale, just like all their friends did, tried to explain the appeal of Ronald Reagan.

He was the 'Great Communicator', he had a wonderful sense of humour, he had a charming smile. All true, but not what matters. Even politics attracts its share of optimistic, likeable men, and most of them leave no trace – like Britain's 'Sunny Jim' Callaghan, a perfect example of the defeatism of western leadership in the 1970s.

It was the era of *détente*, a word barely remembered now, which is just as well, as it reflects poorly on us. The presidents and prime ministers of the free world had decided that the unfree world was not a prison ruled by a murderous ideology which had to be defeated but merely an alternative lifestyle that had to be accommodated. Under cover of *détente*, the Soviets gobbled up more and more real estate across the planet, from Ethiopia to Grenada.

Nonetheless, it was not just the usual suspects who subscribed to this theory – Helmut Schmidt, Pierre Trudeau, François Mitterrand – but most of the so-called 'conservatives', too – Ted Heath, Giscard d'Estaing, Gerald Ford.

Unlike these men, unlike most other senior Republicans, Ronald Reagan saw Soviet Communism for what it was: a great evil. Millions of Europeans across half a continent from Poland to Bulgaria, Slovenia to Latvia live in freedom today because he acknowledged that simple truth when the rest of the political class was tying itself in knots trying to pretend otherwise. That is what counts. He brought down the 'evil empire', and all the rest is fine print.

At the time, the charm and the smile got less credit from the intelligentsia, confirming their belief that he was a dunce who would plunge us into Armageddon. Everything you need to know about the establishment's view of Ronald Reagan can be found on page 624 of *Dutch*, Edmund Morris's weird post-modern biography. The place is Berlin, the time 12 June 1987: 'Mr Gorbachev, tear down this wall!' declaims Dutch, trying hard to look infuriated, but succeeding only in an expression of mild petulance.

*People pay their respects to the memory of former US president Ronald Reagan at the funeral home in Santa Monica, California. Photograph: Carlo Allegri/Getty.*

What a rhetorical opportunity missed. He could have read Robert Frost's poem on the subject, 'Something there is that doesn't love a wall', to simple and shattering effect. Or even Edna St Vincent Millay's lines, which he surely holds in memory. 'Only now for the first time I see this wall is actually a wall, a thing come up between us, shutting me away From you … I do not know you any more.'

Poor old Morris, the plodding, conventional, scholarly writer driven mad by 14 years spent trying to get a grip on Ronald Reagan. Most world leaders would have taken his advice: 'You're at the Berlin Wall, so you have to say something about it, something profound but oblique. Maybe there's a poem on the subject …'

Who cares if Frost's is over-quoted and a tad hard to follow? Who cares that it is, in fact, pro-wall – a poem in praise of walls? Edmund

Morris has described his subject as an 'airhead' and concluded that it is 'like dropping a pebble in a well and hearing no splash'. Morris may not have heard the splash, but he's still all wet. The elites of the world were stupid about Reagan in a way that only clever people can be. Take that cheap crack: If you drop a pebble in a well and you don't hear a splash, it may be because the well is dry, but it's just as likely it's because the well is of surprising depth.

But then I suspect it's a long while since Morris dropped an actual pebble in an actual well. As with walls, his taste runs instinctively to the metaphorical. Reagan looked at the Berlin Wall and saw not a poem-quoting opportunity but prison bars.

I once discussed Irving Berlin, composer of 'God Bless America', with his fellow songwriter, Jule Styne, and Jule put it best: 'It's easy to be clever. But the really clever thing is to be simple.'

At the Berlin Wall on that day it would have been easy to be clever, as all those Seventies *détente* sophisticates would have been. And who would have remembered a word they said? Like Irving Berlin with God Bless America, only Reagan could have stood there and declared without embarrassment: 'Tear down this wall!' And, two years later, the wall was, indeed, torn down.

Reagan said it for everybody – which is why his 'rhetorical opportunity missed' is remembered by millions of grateful Eastern Europeans. The really clever thing is to have the confidence to say it in four monosyllables.

Ronald Reagan was an American archetype, and just the bare bones of his curriculum vitae capture the possibilities of his country: in the Twenties, a lifeguard at a local swimming hole who saved over 70 lives; in the Thirties, a radio sports announcer; in the Forties, a Warner Brothers leading man … and finally one of the two most significant presidents of the American century.

The 'Great Communicator' was effective because what he was saying was self-evident to all but our dessicated elites: 'We are a nation that has a government – not the other way around.' And, at the end of a grim, grey decade – Vietnam, Watergate, energy crises, Iranian hostages – Americans decided that they wanted a president who looked like the nation, not like its failed government. Thanks to his clarity, around the world, governments which had nations have been replaced by nations which have governments. Most of the Warsaw Pact countries are now members of NATO, with free markets and freely-elected parliaments.

One man who understood was Yakob Ravin, a Ukrainian émigré who, in the summer of 1997, happened to be strolling with his grandson in Armand Hammer Park near Reagan's California home. They happened to see the former president, out taking a walk. Mr Ravin went over and asked if he could take a picture of the boy and the president. When they got back home to Ohio, it appeared in the local newspaper, the *Toledo Blade*.

Ronald Reagan was three years into the decade-long twilight of his illness and unable to recognise most of his colleagues from the Washington days. But Mr Ravin wanted to express his appreciation. 'Mr President,' he said, 'thank you for everything you did for the Jewish people, for Soviet people, to destroy the Communist empire.'

And, somewhere deep within, there was a flicker of recognition. 'Yes,' said the old man, 'that is my job.' Yes, that was his job.

**SATURDAY, 12 JUNE 2004**

# Back to the Beaches

*TV Review: Joe Humphreys*

Ireland just doesn't get D-Day commemorations. All those parades in the midday sun. The wreath-laying ceremonies. The 21-gun salutes. The Queen standing throughout, her handbag locked around one elbow in trademark fashion.

Sure, we show some token footage from Normandy and Islandbridge on the evening news. But overall the day largely passes us by – thanks in part to RTÉ and TV3, neither of which found a place in their television schedules for a programme on the Irish contribution – or lack of it – to the start of the end of the second World War 60 years ago last Sunday.

It is not just Irish war veterans who are let down by such indifference. It is all our loss that Ireland can't stop for an afternoon, and simply remember. Where were you, after all, on the 60th anniversary? Shopping? Sunbathing? Watching *Big Brother?* We can hardly blame our 'busy' lifestyles for failing to take time to acknowledge the liberation of Europe from Nazism. Rather, there seems to be an underlying anxiety about facing up to the war – a collective guilt, perhaps, that we weren't there on 6 June 1944. Certainly, D-Day – and the unmistakable righteousness of it – sits awkwardly with Irish neutrality. But that's all the more reason for us to remember it, and remember it in the context of our unique, non-militaristic world view.

In fairness to RTÉ, it did run a series of imported D-Day-related programmes, including some Hollywood movies on the theme and the BBC docudrama D-Day, which was broadcast at the same time in the UK. The two-hour flagship production for the Beeb was as good a way as any of retelling the events of 60 years ago, mixing camera footage from the time with dramatic reconstructions.

Various survivors were interviewed, from one of the first American soldiers to land on Omaha amid 'the smell of hot blood', to one of only two defending gunmen out of a platoon of Germans to live through the day. 'We were praying and killing each other at the same time,' Franz Gockel recalled.

Among the other revealing stories was that of Robert Capa, the *Life* magazine photographer, who joined the initial landing party only to do what anyone else would have done in his situation: turn and flee in a retreating landing craft.

In an earlier mini-drama, we learned of an extraordinary meeting between the German Field Marshal Erwin Rommel and George Lane, a Hungarian-born recruit to the British army's commando wing who had been captured on a reconnaissance mission ahead of D-Day. Rommel had a habit of interrogating imprisoned Allied soldiers to judge the calibre of men he was fighting, and his conversation with Lane had been recorded word for word in German military archives up to and including the point when the Field Marshal blew a gasket at the prisoner's impertinence in mentioning Germany's treatment of the Jews.

The presentation of such events was refreshingly even. Unlike so many historical dramas, D-Day avoided as much as possible faux dialogue, relying instead on recorded conversations, or direct narration by survivors. The only note that jarred

was the reconstructed BBC broadcasts which pompously announced that, throughout the day, Auntie had 'been telling the world that Allied forces have crossed the channel into France'. Even with something as sacred as D-Day, media outlets can't help trying to claim credit for being 'first to the news'.

It is hard to think about D-Day today without asking whether or not it could be done again. Several programmes in the run-up to the anniversary seemed to reply in the negative, among them Destination D-Day, in which raw recruits to the British Army were tested in similar conditions, and generally fell short of what was required. There was also Secret History: D-Day Disaster, which illustrated how difficult it would be to mount a surprise attack on the scale of the Normandy landings in our globalised world of breaking news.

Two months before the invasions, some 749 lives were lost in a disastrous training exercise off the south coast of England, and several hundred were shot dead by their own troops in simulations near Plymouth beach. Soldiers who witnessed the massacre admitted it was the closest thing to a war crime on British soil. Yet it was covered up, and perhaps necessarily so. While Britain didn't have its satellite news channels back then, its tea-rooms were home to a powerful gossip network that threatened to undermine Operation Overlord. Despite heavy censoring of communications, and warnings about loose talk costing lives, some 80 per cent of letters posted in the south of England in 1944 referred to preparations for the invasion.

**MONDAY, 14 JUNE 2004**

# An Alternative Emerges

*Mark Brennock*

Suddenly, there is an alternative government in waiting. Despite the leaching of political support from the established political parties to Sinn Féin and

*A convoy of Defence Force vehicles on the way to Shannon Airport in Co. Clare to provide security during the visit by President Bush. Photograph: Kieran Clancy/PicSure.*

Independents, Fine Gael has gained enough to be able to present itself credibly as the core of an alternative coalition in waiting.

With Labour's first preference in the local elections standing still, Fine Gael's recovery will now help it solidify Enda Kenny's position as leader of that potential alternative government, despite Labour's claims for Pat Rabbitte. The weekend results do not solve all Fine Gael's problems, but at last the party has the momentum it has lacked since 2002.

The political landscape has therefore changed, and not just because of the quantum leap in the size of Sinn Féin's presence. For the Government parties, the days when 'it's the economy stupid' was an adequate election mantra are over. Unemployment, inflation and taxes are low,

economic growth continues to pick up. Yet the Government parties, particularly Fianna Fáil, have been given a savage beating.

Fianna Fáil's worst election result since the 1920s has been matched by a Fine Gael resurgence to around 27 per cent, a five point gain since the 2002 General Election and just one point below its good 1999 local result. Enda Kenny ran himself into the ground over the past month, covering some 12,000 kilometres in a national tour with the energy normally associated with, well, Bertie Ahern.

Bertie Ahern was on his own tour for much of the campaign: Around Europe for final talks on the EU Constitution, and to the US for the G8 Summit. However, it is doubtful whether his presence in Ireland throughout the campaign would have made much difference. Voters have done to Fianna Fáil what opinion polls and canvassers have over the last month predicted they would do.

In contrast, Fine Gael has surpassed all predictions, barring its own. Last night it was on course to achieve in style the four objectives it set for itself at the start of the campaign: to retain four European parliament seats; to increase its first preference vote above the 2002 figure; to retain its local authority seat numbers; and to elect new councillors who will make credible General Election candidates in 2006 or 2007.

The party has pushed its vote up beyond what most observers thought possible. It was set last night to retain its four Euro seats, and to come close to retaining or even surpassing its 277 local government seats won in 1999.

Most importantly, perhaps, it has put in place new councillors with potential to be Dáil candidates in the future. In Dublin, where it was reduced to just three of 42 Dáil seats in 2002, it has elected articulate young councillors such as Brian Gillen and Lucinda Creighton in Dublin South East, Leo Varadkar in Dublin West, Maria Bailey in Ballybrack and others.

Pundits and political opponents said they couldn't do it. They were wrong, and the Fine Gael figures who crowed a little about this yesterday were entitled to do so.

Sinn Féin has made its expected gains. It has won representation around the State in places where it never had it before, and may find itself sharing power in a number of councils, most significantly in Dublin.

Initial indications last night were that working-class urban voters had deserted Fianna Fáil in significant numbers, and that Sinn Féin, the subject of concerted attack and denunciation by the Government in recent months, was the beneficiary.

Sinn Féin won its first seat in Waterford, while the party's Waterford-based Munster Euro candidate David Cullinane now has the profile with which to build towards a Dáil seat. The party's

impressive Euro candidate in the East constituency, John Dwyer, has also made himself a serious contender for the Wexford Constituency, while Donegal North East-based Pearse Doherty was the revelation of the Euro campaign in the North West and will challenge for a Dáil seat at the next General Election.

In Dublin city there are now just three wards where Sinn Féin does not hold a council seat. The party topped the poll in Artane, Ballyfermot, Cabra-Glasnevin, Donaghmede, Finglas and North Inner City. The party still has to perfect candidate strategy – in Artane Sinn Féin's Larry O'Toole won over one-and-a-half quotas but with no running mate to transfer to, his surplus was of great assistance to the Labour Party.

The other components of the potential alternative coalition government had contrasting results. Labour became the largest party on Dublin City Council and won a second European Parliament seat. But last night it looked as if its national first prefrence vote in the local elections was static at 11 per cent, although it may win some extra seats.

The party would have been hoping for better than that. With the parliamentary party acknowledged as having an unacceptably high average age, and at least two sitting deputies expected to retire at the next election with no high profile replacements available, they would have been hoping to elect more prospects for the future. A number of new councillors were elected in different parts. The party will be pleased with its four extra councillors in Carlow/Kilkenny, but disappointed with its failure to win any council seat in Meath.

While Fine Gael is on course for significant Dáil seat gains on the weekend's performance, Labour still has work to do. It also faces an interesting internal debate in the coming days over whether to share power with Sinn Féin in Dublin City Hall.

The Green Party saw just a moderate increase in its vote, but this doesn't compensate for the loss of at least one, and possibly both, European Parliament seats and both of its representatives on Dublin City Council. Party figures yesterday were questioning aspects of their campaign, such as the decision to use substantial numbers of posters containing still-life images of tomatoes and the like, rather than mugshots of their candidates. In an election dominated by talk of giving the Government a kick, the Greens' solid platform concentrating on local issues didn't catch the public imagination.

Independents, standing on a host of different issues, have done well as they tend to do in local government elections. Among the most striking features of these elections was the voter turnout, at 57 per cent up seven points from the equivalent 1999 elections. Party activists speculated at the weekend that this was down to an enthusiasm to give the Government parties a good kick, coupled with an appeal by Sinn Féin to young and working-class sections of the electorate who often don't bother to vote.

The ousting of the two-term coalition is now a real possibility. Of course the handling of the economy didn't feature as an issue in this campaign. In a General Election campaign it will, and the alternative will have to convince voters that it is equipped to manage the economy. But if Fine Gael, Labour and the Green Party continue to move closer together, presenting themselves as a viable alternative and drawing up a joint programme closer to the next General Election, they will pose a major challenge to the Fianna Fáil/PD attempt to win a third term.

However, with Fianna Fáil now at risk of losing Dáil seats and Sinn Féin having a high chance of making major Dáil gains, another arithmetic possibility has come clearly into view: a Fianna Fáil/Sinn Féin coalition. It seems unthinkable that this could happen so soon, with the IRA weapons issue still unresolved, and with the IRA, or elements of it, still involved in illegal activity.

But there are up to three years to go before the

next General Election and there is plenty of time for further development in the peace process. The election results will confirm to Sinn Féin not only that it can become a substantial political force in the Republic, but that it will be a part of Government one day if it manages to convince the other parties that it has irrevocably left its war behind and rid itself of weapons.

So it was a great day out for Sinn Féin and Fine Gael, a mediocre one for Labour, a disappointment for the Green Party and the PDs and, of course, a disaster for Fianna Fáil. The 29th Dáil now moves into a new phase with the prospect of a real choice being on offer to voters at the end of it.

*Sister Carmel (left) and Sister Bridget of the Poor Clare enclosed order of nuns who attended a hearing of An Bord Pleanála in Ballsbridge, Dublin, to object to a proposed €100 million development at the RDS. Photograph: Dara Mac Dónaill.*

SATURDAY, 22 JUNE 2004

# Crowning My Career in a Major Way

*Colin Byrne*

I have caddied for quite a few major champions in the past. Last week I was caddying for the 2004 US Open Champion from start to finish. It was 'my' first major, my boss's second and an experience that crowns a long caddying career.

Walking around Shinnecock Hills early last week I was firstly impressed by the course and secondly pleasantly surprised by how it was set up. You learn never to be over-confident in a fickle game that can leave you down and out as quickly as you were on top of your game. But I felt like the course suited a player like Retief.

Retief is a long hitter, but Shinnecock would not require the driver more than six times in an average round, so length was not vital. This meant he could hit plenty of strategic irons off tees. He shapes his iron shots with ease. Shinnecock required that you 'held' the ball against the wind so that it came down on the greens as softly as possible.

My boss has got a vivid imagination around the greens. With the shaved areas around every green, you needed to use different clubs to chip or run the ball up to the greens. His bunker play is as good as any other top player. Of course he is a very skilful putter. Before last week I always marvelled at his delicate touch on the greens, especially with long putts.

I would observe him as he surveyed a twisting 40 footer, intense and calculating, computing every turn and undulation. Nothing happens by chance.

It was his putting that won Retief his second US Open. It took a deft and fearless touch to hole even a two footer in Shinnecock last Sunday and it took unlimited skill and belief to continue doing so in the final round when you could feel the negative energy hissing over the ropes from the patriotic American spectators.

We all know that a finished product can often be taken for granted. But preparation and honing are the basis of a good outcome. Retief's practice sessions were as calculating and scrupulous as his play during the four rounds.

If you are playing well in a major you will have one early tee-time and three late ones. We played two practice rounds at 3.0 in the afternoon and the third at 8.30 in the morning. Our early tee-time in the event was 8.30. Our lates were 1.30, 2.30 and 3.0. We couldn't predict the weather, but we were fortunate to play our practice rounds in different wind directions which was extremely helpful.

Retief is the type of person who will cautiously prepare himself for the worst possible scenario. So when he was putting to various points on the greens he took the extreme locations, mostly on the precipice of the abyss.

He understands the USGA very well. We had discussions in the practice rounds about where the holes would be cut. As it turned out, I was hopelessly naïve when it came to just how severe the pin placements would be. My boss was not.

Playing in a major tournament is intense. It is the first time that I have been in a leading situation in a major. From the start of the week every simple aspect of the tournament is at a higher level of intensity.

Huge mouthy crowds and hyper-vigilant security. Getting from point A to B can be troublesome. The whole week just seems to take forever, getting into the course, getting from one hole to another, people, security and obstacles everywhere.

Playing in the final round on Sunday, I almost felt like I was outside the ropes, constantly battling to get close to my player.

There were TV crews, a legion of scorers, observers, officials, policemen and other security personnel. With many narrow walkways off the tees you had to be fast out of the blocks to try to beat the charge for the narrow exits.

*Caddy Colin Byrne (left) and golfer Retief Goosen discuss strategy at the US Open in Shinnecock Hills, Georgia.
Photograph: David Duprey/AP.*

Retief is a quiet man, very soft spoken. He is a man of gentle movements, and his calmness is infectious. There are no sudden movements; no forceful conversations between us. So after every mad dash off the tee to beat the surrounding posse, I then had to throttle back to Goose pace when it came to giving him the information required.

I found myself shifting from charged to tranquil on every hole. With all the surrounding noise, it was getting hard to hear each other towards the end of the round, so we had to speak louder, without allowing any sense of alarm to creep in to our exchanges.

So, between the mad rush all around me and Retief's Zen-like tranquillity at the eye of the storm, it was a constant balancing of pace and energy for me. Despite Retief's single-mindedness and

clear focus, it turned out to be beneficial to play with his fellow countryman Ernie Els on Sunday.

He thought he would be, along with Phil Mickelson, the main challenger. As it became apparent that Ernie no longer had a chance to win by the back nine, he and his caddie Rickie Roberts gave us a lot of encouragement over the last few holes.

If you were the sensitive type the back nine at Shinnecock Hills last Sunday would not have been a good place for you. The mob were rooting quite vociferously for Phil Mickelson. They were audibly rooting against Retief. Comments like 'go on three putt, make it interesting' and 'all your's to lose now Retief' might have unsettled a more delicate competitor.

Retief manages to block it all out. In a game that has an abundance of etiquette left in it compared with many sports played at a top level, some spectators in the States would appear to want to drag it down to the lowest level.

There are two ways to approach such an event as a caddie. One is to get caught up in the emotion of the spectacle; the other is to stick your head down and get on with the job at hand.

Retief's calmness and serene manner were a very comforting influence on me as I was dealing with the relatively unknown pressures of major contention.

I opted for the head down strategy and avoided eye contact with anyone other than my boss. Even on the final hole with a two-shot lead, given the precarious nature of the course, the hardened pro and caddie are acutely aware of the perils of complacency.

I think it takes experience to be able to enjoy these moments. As I look back I am only now starting to enjoy what were the most intense moments of my caddying career so far.

As I grappled with the pin on the 18th hole trying to figure out exactly how to detach the flag for a keepsake – a tradition for major winning caddies – I realised that I was hopelessly unequipped to extract the flag, so the souvenir stayed put as I left the green. No matter now long you have been humping a bag around the fairways of the world, most days provide a new challenge. I'll know the fine art of flag-snagging next time.

# Protesting Brings its own Responsibilities

*Breda O'Brien*

My husband has the earliest memory in our household of an American presidential visit to Ireland. He was in primary school in Timahoe, Co. Kildare, when Richard Nixon visited. He remembers a wilderness of a graveyard being restored, and the grass being mown until it was as green and velvet as a golf course.

Up to that point, the only thing of interest to local children in the graveyard was a big, black dog with fiery eyes which was said to haunt it. Unlikely, given that only gentle Quakers lie there. In fact, the 300th anniversary of the graveyard is being celebrated this weekend by the Quaker community.

Aside from the supreme joy of a day off school, and of waving American flags that were of such high quality that they lasted for years afterwards, my husband remembers Nixon's big, tanned hands and imposing, almost scary presence.

Watergate burglars were two years in the future, and Irish people were more accepting of Republican presidents at the time of the visit than they ever have been since.

Ronald Reagan got a less ecstatic welcome. My memories of the protest marches are of a motley, disorganised crew. The only exception was the anarchists, who were all dressed alike in black and chains, and who marched in perfect time, chanting in unison 'Disarm the police. Arm the people.' Ah, more innocent days.

Of course, Reagan's recent death, and the obvious grief of Nancy Reagan, has softened public opinion somewhat. Now we focus on his skills as a communicator, of his ability to run with ideas that gripped the public imagination. 'Mr Gorbachev, tear down this wall.'

The idea that he was just an amiable dope who specialised in soundbites has also undergone revision. On this side of the Atlantic, there was some well-founded criticism of Reagan's foreign policy, but also some knee-jerk dislike of American Republicans.

Most people could not understand why Americans loved Reagan so much. It was fairly simple, really. He was a warm and accessible man. Unfortunately, he had some ideas and policies that had disastrous consequences around the world.

In contrast, another warm and accessible man,

Bill Clinton, received a hero's welcome when he visited Ireland. Yes, he deserved credit for the work which he put into the peace process in the North, but he had also sanctioned bombings in Khartoum and in Afghanistan, in clear contravention of international law.

Does anyone remember that the factory destroyed in Sudan was supposed to be manufacturing chemical weapons, but they were actually manufacturing pharmaceuticals?

Does anyone remember that Sudan practically begged to hand over information about Osama bin Laden, but that the Clinton administration was not interested?

The botched bombings in Afghanistan may well have been a spur for the attacks on September 11th, 2001.

And yes, there was Monica Lewinsky. Clinton may not be the first American president to transgress in this way, but what was striking was his absolute refusal to tell the truth until forced into it.

I haven't read his book, which has been mostly panned in the United States. I think I will wait until the mighty tome is remaindered. Much of the media attention has focused on what his philandering did to his relationship with Hillary. He apparently says now that his tawdry affair was a major moral mistake, that he did it because he could, which is the worst possible reason.

Fair enough, but it is a shame it took him so long to come to that realisation. When he should have been dealing with issues like the mounting support for Osama bin Laden, he was fighting impeachment, and his energies were diverted.

His two presidencies were full of missed opportunities, including on the domestic front, the opportunity to provide comprehensive healthcare when the economy was booming.

Lest you think that makes me a George W. Bush fan, let me disabuse you of the notion. I am glad not to be an American citizen, because I could vote for neither candidate in the upcoming election. However, can we justify the visceral dislike

that so many Irish people seem to have for Bush? We loved Clinton, who was venal, addicted to adoration and astonishingly immature.

Much is made of Bush's alleged intellectual deficiencies, but what use did Clinton make of his abundant brainpower? He was deeply indecisive. Yes, he intervened in Kosovo, but in a way which maximised damage to the country and minimised the danger to American troops. He ignored the genocide in Rwanda.

There are important and necessary criticisms to be made of Bush's policy in Iraq. They are provided nightly by news footage of continuing carnage. Yet the security preparations for his visit are almost farcical. Cromwell might have been impressed by our armoured personnel carriers, but al-Qaeda are unlikely to be daunted.

However, those of us who march against Bush's policy in Iraq, have a big question to answer. What alternative do we have to offer? Would we have allowed Saddam to go on his merry way, torturing and butchering people, secure in our moral superiority that at least we had prevented America acting like an imperial power?

Granted, the American invasion has shown that you cannot impose Western democracy on a culture which has experienced the anarchic insecurity created by a savage dictator, and which before that was riven and divided by religious and ethnic conflicts.

Yet again, what viable alternatives can pacifists and those who accept violent intervention as a last resort suggest? The world suffered because Clinton was unwilling to intervene when he should have, such as in Rwanda. It suffers under Bush because he is all too willing to intervene. Yet we applauded one man and excoriate the other.

We are moving towards a more repressive world in many ways. This column was written before the full impact of Bush's visit is clear, but my guess is that any protests will be smothered by the heavy security presence.

The right to protest peacefully is essential in any democracy, and we suppress it at our peril.

Nonetheless, the right to protest holds a responsibility, that of showing that we are not acting out of reflexive dislike, but a genuine desire to provide real alternatives to that against which we protest.

# Waterford Hint at Greater Things

*Tom Humphries, at Semple Stadium*

The older minds went riffing through the memories. Munster finals of other years. How did they compare? Where did this one stand in the canon of greatness? The verdict could never be definitive, but it was favourable. This was wonderful. This was as good as sport gets.

When it finished, Waterford people poured onto the Semple Stadium grass and danced and embraced. It's only two years since they won a Munster title, but this one was different. Beating Cork in the final for the first time since 1959. Turning in yet another substantial performance, enough to suggest that there might be two more such days in them. An All-Ireland.

This was a game which sung, a match which was decorated with moments of art and lines of pure poetry. The day was haunted by wind and threatened by rain, and still they slung scores over with the insouciance of men tossing water out of buckets.

It began with a flukey goal conceded by Stephen Brenner in the Waterford goal when the ball declined to hop up from Garvan McCarthy's snap shot.

Waterford were momentarily dazed and Cork added another pair of points quickly. Five points down, Waterford came out to play.

The scores. The lovely points from Dan Shanahan. A sublime goal from Eoin Kelly when he nips behind the Cork defence. John Mullane explosive as usual.

And Cork matching it. Joe Deane perfect. Brian Corcoran scoring a splendid point. Wonderful stuff.

And in the end Waterford prevailed. They had Mullane sent off early in the second half, just after he'd scored his second point, and at that point you thought that the merest sight of those red jerseys swarming would cause Waterford to buckle.

Instead they snuffed out Cork's half-forward line. Bossed most of the midfield exchanges. Eclipsed Brian Corcoran. Ben O'Connor kept going. Deane kept his head above water. It wasn't enough. Waterford wanted it more.

'Listen,' said their guru Justin McCarthy afterwards, 'they're good players. Every player was asked at half-time could they step up their performance. There's a lot of commitment in the team. There's a lot of character.

'I was glad we weren't ahead like we were last year. We sat on the lead last year, we were six points up and sat on it. It was very hard, Cork came back. We had the players to come back today though.'

They had. When Mullane went, others stepped up. Paul Flynn, who ended the day with 1-7 in brackets after his name, gave a classic Flynn performance, his audience one moment with their heads in their hands, the next rising to salute a moment of genius.

And Ken McGrath, whose move to defence has been so crucial, hurled beautifully, driving balls forward into the wind, finding the spaces and providing the inspiration. A joy to watch.

As the game got older so Waterford got better. It became clear after a while that the advantage in personnel wasn't working for Cork. Waterford were hungrier. Playing with an almost suicidal recklessness. Just wanting it.

Justin McCarthy recognised the pattern. 'We've played our best hurling in a lot of games in the second half, in the last 20 minutes. We set ourselves up for that. Lads have done work on their own, they've grown up a bit, they've taken more responsibility and more leadership. That's what you saw.'

*Eoin Kelly of Waterford sends the* sliotar *past Cork goalkeeper Donal Óg Cusack for a goal in the Munster Senior Hurling Final at Semple Stadium. Photograph: Dara Mac Dónaill.*

For Cork the setback is significant. Last summer at this stage they were four points the better team than Waterford. They had Setanta Ó hÁilpín beginning to unveil the full breadth of his talents and the mix of Donal O'Grady's disciplined, meticulous approach with the youngster's sheer unpredictability was intoxicating to watch.

Yesterday they were meticulous and good but the spark was missing. In the second half they got snuffed in areas where they needed to thrive.

'The sending off disrupted things a little bit,' said O'Grady, 'and I don't think we played smartly after that. We should have played possession like in the first half, but we went in for long balls. They hurled well, they tackled hard, but we never seemed to stroke the ball over the bar like they should have. We can blame ourselves in the end. Seven points in the second half with the breeze isn't good enough.'

When Cork contrast that dividend with what they enjoyed in the first half they will be concerned. 'Maybe mentally,' mused O'Grady, 'you drop. It wouldn't be the first time that 14 have beaten 15. It seems that mentally you drop. The team with 14 drive on. In a way when you have an extra man perhaps you feel this is easy enough. Look now, though. Anyone who isn't worried about going into the qualifiers wants their head examined. Look at the quality of the teams in there.'

Sure enough, within an hour Cork had been drawn against Tipperary in the glamour tie of the qualifiers. And Waterford. Scalps of Clare, Tipp and Cork hanging from their belt. Are they the real deal? 'If they end up as All-Ireland champions I suppose they are,' said O'Grady.

'The bottom line,' said Justin McCarthy at the end, 'is to get to an All-Ireland and win it. There's a rocky road left. Any team playing Waterford will

*A young girl enjoying the Ye Olde Falconry display team from the UK at the National Country Fair, held at Emo Court, Co. Laois. Photograph: James Flynn/ViewPoint.*

think they can beat them, but that's changing. Look, it's June. September is a long way off.'

Not as far off as it seemed at lunchtime yesterday though.

---

# 'There Were Those Who Said it Could Not be Done, But it Has Been Done'

*Tim O'Brien*

It could have been a scene from Riverdance. The lights were dimmed, the volume of the Celtic music rose, dry ice filled the stage and a Luas tram burst through a giant poster of

itself in the Sandyford dépôt yesterday, heralding the start of Luas passenger services. It had been delivered on budget and virtually on time, insisted the chairman of the Railway Procurement Agency, Mr Pádraic White.

The Minister for Transport, Mr Brennan, recalled the modest estimate of the cost more than 20 years ago. 'The Cabinet was told it would cost about £12 million [€15.2 million] to reopen the Harcourt Street line back in 1981. Now just wait for tomorrow morning's headlines. They will say that a project which started out at £12 million ended up at €800 million – and I am personally to blame for it,' he said.

Delivering an oration which touched on the historic nature of the day, Mr Brennan added: 'There were those who said it shouldn't be done, there were those who said it wouldn't be done, and there were those who said it couldn't be done, but

*The remains of 89-year-old Patrick Lynch, who for many years delivered fruit and vegetables by horse and cart to the stallholders of Dublin's Moore Street, are brought through the area by Lanigans undertakers before burial at Glasnevin cemetery. Photograph: Bryan O'Brien.*

it has been done.'

It was not just a day for Dublin to celebrate – it was a day for the whole country to be proud, he said. 'Luas may be located in Dublin, but everybody could use it when in the capital,' he pointed out.

Among the invited dignitaries, Dr Garret FitzGerald was dispelling a few myths of his own, insisting that he had never measured the width of the Nassau Street/Dawson Street junction at five o'clock in the morning. 'I never went down there at all. I didn't do that.'

And, at last, for those who never thought they would see it happen, the first passenger-carrying Luas rolled up to St Stephen's Green at 1.35 p.m. Reporters were looking at synchronised timers,

nodding when someone mentioned it was a minute early.

Such was the enthusiasm for the tram at the Green that its return journey to Sandyford, which began shortly after 2 p.m., became the Luas's first public passenger service – almost an hour before the first public rides were supposed to take place, from Sandyford.

On board the first passenger tram, a final myth was dispelled – that the Luas service was a Dublin investment, exclusively for Dubliners. Ms Eileen Maher had travelled from Enfield, Co. Meath, to be at St Stephen's Green for the trip. Mr Brian Kenny from Navan, was in Dublin on business. He said he loved it except for the absence of straps to hold on to when the tram started and stopped.

*Thousands of Dubliners queued for a ride on the Luas on the tram's first day of operation. Photograph: Bryan O'Brien.*

Sam Donegan (5) and his mother, Ms Anne Donegan, from Drumree, near Batterstown, Co. Meath, had also travelled just to use the system, and Ms Kathleen Spillane, from Mallow, had 'come just for the spin' and to be in the city for the day. Ms Mary Delahunty was enjoying a trip up from Longford, while Ms Mary Buckley, from Malahide, had her Luas brochure signed by the driver of the first tram, Mr Eddie Byrne.

At the Sandyford stop, as the initial 3 p.m. deadline for the first passenger trip approached, more locals were waiting. Among them was Mr John McKeever, who was looking for his children, Dylan and Ellie, who had gone on ahead with their granny, Noreen. 'Dylan is a fan. He couldn't sleep last night,' said Mr McKeever.

SATURDAY, 3 JULY 2004

# Best of Intentions

### Róisín Ingle

It's on my bedroom wall. A piece of cream linen, hanging like a scroll between two short pieces of wood. Just 92 black words, printed in a deceptively ordinary font, a simple design for life. The brother brought it back from India with him, along with enough bags of spices to open quite a decent take-away. He was going to use them to cook all these exotic meals for his new housemates.

Things didn't work out. Things went from close to cool between us. He's staying somewhere different now.

*Páidí Ó Sé (left), manager of Westmeath senior football team, shares a moment with Mick O'Dwyer, manager of Laois, after their teams drew in the Leinster Football Final in Croke Park. Photograph: Alan Betson.*

'A Precious Human Life.' That's what it says on the top of the scroll. And like all my brothers and sisters, he is precious to me. He doesn't think that now, though. I began to distance myself from him in an effort to avoid the confrontation I knew would come. But it happened anyway, the emotional distance making the meeting crueller than it might have been. I said too much. Didn't hold back. Put it all out there on the table, just the way he says he likes it.

But he didn't like it this time. She hates me, he told my mother. She really hates me. How to find a way back?

'Every day think as you wake up: Today I am fortunate to have woken up,' the scroll says. Sometimes I feel it. A box-fresh morning. The sun shining in where we haven't put up curtains yet, a snippet of good news on the radio and my dream job waiting at the end of a short cycle ride. It's not hard to feel fortunate when the off-side rule is

being explained patiently to you over a lazy Sunday salad. When you are moving little feta cheese defenders around a cucumber goal. On these days, anything is possible.

Other days are harder. Brooding over an argument. Disturbed about things said and unsaid. Feeling, as though it were my own, his heart breaking slightly from the hurt. But even then I know I am fortunate to have woken up. It's just on these days it's harder to remember.

'I am alive. I have a precious human life. I am not going to waste it.' What's wasteful, though? What's more wrong? The hours spent watching live streams from the Big Brother house, glued to that precious human zoo, or the guilt that sets in afterwards?

The guilt is more wasteful, I've decided, because at least what's going on in that house is real. Muscle man Jason's boredom and isolation. Michelle's all-consuming crush. Stuart's cowboy obsession. I'm not going to waste my life feeling guilty about my own big brother, either. Not if there is something more positive I can do. Maybe this is it.

'I am going to use all my energies to develop myself, to expand my heart out to others, to achieve enlightenment for the benefit of all beings.' This is different for everybody. I know what this means for me. I need to develop my creative side. Nurture it. Give it space.

I need to stop splashing around in the shallow end where there are no risks to be taken and, where, if I stumble, nobody will laugh at me for not being able to swim. I know diving into the deep end will help me expand my heart out to others. I don't know much about enlightenment, I don't think we can know until we achieve it. But we can nurture that which opens our hearts. I need to let my imagination run wild.

'I am going to have kind thoughts towards others. I am not going to get angry, or think badly about others.' Yeah, right. These words have a deeply aspirational feel. But even reading them once or twice a day, forcing myself to spend a few seconds taking them in, tends to melt something in me.

I have not been kind. I have been angry. I have thought badly about him. I may well do it again tomorrow. But reading the words aloud, saying with conviction, I am going to be kind, I am not going to be nasty, reminds me of my intention.

It seems unbelievable, unthinkable that I would forget that this is how I want to behave. Somehow I do, though. Every day. I read it to myself morning and night and at least for those brief moments in time, I remember.

'I am going to benefit others as much as I can.' This line concludes the advice from His Holiness

*Mary Kelly from Knocknacarra in Co. Galway at the Galway Races where she won the 'Best Dressed Person' competition. Photograph: Brenda Fitzsimons.*

The XIV Dalai Lama hanging on my bedroom wall. I met him in Belfast four years ago. I'd appreciate meeting the man in orange robes more now, I think.

'I am going to benefit others as much as I can.' All I can say is that I will try. I don't think this means asking my brother back to stay with me. I don't even think it means taking back what I said.

But I don't hate him. That knowledge may be of some small benefit. I hope with all my heart it is.

# Mr Gageby . . .

*Maeve Binchy*

There is a dangerous tendency of thinking your own time was the best, and there were no days like your days. Journalists fall into this trap more easily than anyone else. It's as if we want people to know what stirring times we lived through, what dramas our newsroom saw and what near-misses we had, and what amazing never-to-be-equalled camaraderie we all shared.

All over Ireland this week there will be people telling such tales of Douglas Gageby's time. And even as I write his name I feel forward. I never called him anything except Mr Gageby.

I met him when I was a 27-year-old schoolteacher in Dublin, sharing a dream with half the country that maybe I could write if someone would let me. Even when I nearly caught up with him in age and we were friends, when he asked me to call him Douglas I could never do it. He was too important.

At the job interview where he asked what I would do if I were to run the Woman's Page I suggested that we relegate Fashion to one day, Cookery to another, and then get on with what people would be interested in on the other four days. He asked mildly what I thought people

might be interested in, and I blinded him with my views.

'Of course, she's never worked a day in her life in a newspaper,' he said to Donal Foley, the news editor. 'She has to learn somewhere,' Donal said, and Mr Gageby nodded and said that was fair enough. So who wouldn't love someone who took such a mad risk?

My memory of those days was that he seemed to be for ever in his office. Day and night. That wasn't possible because we knew he had a great family life, he often talked about his children, and he always talked about his wife, Dorothy.

He was invited everywhere, but he was never a great one for going to receptions or dinners, except the Military History Society of Ireland which he was very keen on. He was handsome, he was confident at work, he was happy in his home life, he was courageous and he was dragging the paper into modern times. No wonder so many of us were mad about him.

He had, of course, a short fuse. There is nobody who doesn't have a Mr Gageby experience of some kind. Like when he would bellow his annoyance at something that appeared in Yesterday's paper.

There was never such a thing as Today's paper, there was the one we had written Yesterday which, according to him, was full of faults and mistakes and unbelievable oversights, or Tomorrow's, which was going to be spectacular and we would stick everyone else to the ground with our stories, insights and backgrounds.

I have seen Mr Gageby incandescent with rage about a sports writer who said that a match was a nip-and-tuck affair and gave no further detail, and a financial journalist who said the a.g.m. of some company was predictable, but hadn't explained what had been predicted.

He has been white-faced over someone who missed the one big row that week in the Senate, or called the ceremony that happens in England the Trooping OF the Colour when there should be no

*Douglas Gageby at home in Rathgar in front of one of his favourite things, a tree. Photograph: Dara Mac Dónaill.*

OF in it, apparently. And somebody invariably got it wrong, and somebody else invariably let it past.

I have been at the receiving end when the Woman's Page had a series of apologies in it.

We regret that when we said 11½ pounds of split peas, we actually meant 1 to 1½ pounds of split peas.

We regret that when we said this dress in Richard Alan's cost £20 we actually meant it cost £200.

We regret we have given the wrong number of the Gay Switchboard, the wrong score in the All-Ireland.

His eyes were narrow. I wondered how I had ever thought he was handsome. 'Your page is a laughing stock,' he said. 'With the possible exception of the *Straits Times* in Malaysia I have never seen a worse Features page.' My face was scarlet for 48 hours. I contemplated emigrating. Next week it was forgotten and we could breathe again.

But, by God, how he stood up for us, all of us. He never gossiped about one to another, and he fought our enemies and people who said we were less than great. He said that we reported what we saw. Even when his back was against the wall over what we had reported or misreported. We knew we would not be sold down the river. And I know he had hard times in Stephen's Green clubs when some of us were a bit light-hearted about the British royal family

And though I lived my whole life slightly in awe of him, it was not of his doing. He was warm and friendly and interested in the lives of all his workforce.

When I took all my courage in hand and invited him to lunch with us, he said he would come if we had one course, and that he really liked sardines with lemon juice. He may, of course, have been protecting himself and Dorothy against botulism, since they knew only too well some of my limitations through the cookery page and my misunderstandings of presenting food. If you were going to lunch with someone who had used a picture of open-heart surgery to illustrate veal casseroles perhaps you, too, might have asked for sardines.

But we lunched happily summer after summer, alternately in their house and ours. And it was wonderful to be in the presence of a couple who loved each other and never felt they had to hide this from anyone else. I would have liked them to live for ever as part of all of our lives.

But they didn't, and I hope their family will always know how many of us got a great and exciting start in our writing lives under his editorship. And how proud we were to be part of the time when he took our newspaper out of the shadows and into the light. Every time I think of Mr Gageby I straighten myself up a little and hope to try and do him some kind of credit somewhere along the line.

*AIB chief executive Michael Buckley (left) with the bank's chairman, Dermot Gleeson, at a press conference in AIB headquarters, Dublin, in response to the Irish Financial Services Regulatory Authority's report which outlined management failings at the bank when it overcharged its foreign exchange customers. Photograph: Alan Betson.*

# One Funeral and Three Weddings

*Frank McNally*

The weather story is a staple of journalism, especially on quiet news days. And when you're a lowly freelance, you get to write it a lot. So I can say with confidence that the summer of 1995 was the hottest in Ireland since records began. June, July and August averaged two degrees Celsius above normal almost everywhere. But August was exceptionally warm and dry, with a high of 31 degrees recorded in Kilkenny on August 2nd.

The American humorist Dave Barry visited the land of his ancestors that year and, when I met him at home in Miami a couple of years ago, he was still scarred by the ferocity of the Irish summer. They're used to heat in Florida. But Dave and his wife came here expecting rain and mist, and packed accordingly. Instead, they couldn't sleep at night because the hotels didn't have air-conditioning.

'We scoured the hardware stores looking for a fan,' he recalled. 'But the fans were all sold out.'

It was hot even in late April, when my father died. There was nothing sudden about this. His decline started two years before when, one day after Christmas, he had a mild heart attack. I remember him putting on his suit to go to hospital, as older people do, with the look of a man who didn't know if he'd ever come home again. He did, eventually, and in his last two years, I made a point of trying to penetrate the pipe smoke and silence that

*Bridget O'Donoghue from Cork enjoys meeting Shane MacGowan who was signing CDs in FM Records in Cork city. Photograph: Arthur Ellis/Provision.*

generally surrounded him. But not with much success.

Once I asked him what his father, who died before I was born, did during his years in America in the early 1900s. I was duly informed that Granddad had been a 'deputy sheriff' in Montana, a fascinating fact communicated to me as if it were the equivalent of him being a drains inspector in Longford (no offence to Longford). Further detail was not to be had.

By the spring of 1995 he was back in hospital, this time to stay, and mostly beyond talking. We took turns to spend nights with him. Twice a week I'd get the train up to Dundalk, armed with a book and a small bottle of whiskey to shorten the long hospital nights. In the mornings I'd walk to the station, past the Harp brewery, feeling relieved – and guilty because of it – to be out in the fresh air again.

A moving thing happened near the end. By coincidence, a neighbour and one-time friend of my father's – we'll call him Joe – was also in hospital, two wards away. Joe and he had not spoken to each other for 33 years, because of a row about land. Basically, when my father bought a 30-acre farm in 1962, Joe and a few others – who were hoping it would go unsold and be acquired by the Land Commission for redistribution – objected. The result was a campaign of small-scale agrarian terrorism – fires, sabotage, intimidation – that began the night my mother brought me home from maternity hospital and continued until the mid-1970s. After that it petered out into hostile silence, until the protagonists started to die.

My father always insisted that Joe, although the chief activist, was a good man led astray. But still the silence continued until late April 1995, when a delicate peace process unfolded. One day, after a number of confidence-building measures, Joe walked into my father's ward – he was the only one of them fit to stand by then – and shook his hand. Thirty-three years was a lot to catch up on, so they discussed the unusually warm weather

*Health Minister Micheál Martin eyeballs health worker trade unionists who heckled his press conference in Government Buildings, Dublin to launch the National Primary Care Steering Group Progress Report. Photograph: Cathal McNaughton/PA.*

instead, and said they'd pray for each other. Joe checked out of hospital, but died in the autumn.

In an echo of a certain romantic comedy of the era, our family had three weddings scheduled for that summer, including mine, and a fourth in 1996. In our case the funeral came first, but there wasn't much time for mourning. When my sister Patricia married in July, I – suddenly the senior male – had to give her away. I was due to give myself away in September, then another sister, Pauline. It was a summer clearance sale in the McNally family: everyone had to go.

Work was uncertain. The boom was just taking off, but freelance journalists were at the bottom end of a trickle-down economy. Shifts in the Irish Times newsroom were scarce, and jobs were only a rumour. Worse still, the Irish Press was on its last legs, and we all dreaded the expected flood of asylum-seekers from Burgh Quay.

It seemed a bad year to get married.

Most of my shifts were what is known in the trade as 'Night-town'. This is the graveyard beat, which then lasted up to 3.30 a.m. and had a reputation for driving journalists insane. After midnight, you'd be propping up your eyelids in between ringarounds of provincial Garda stations where night sergeants would inform you that, no, there was nothing stirring. Anyone worried about crime levels should ring provincial Garda stations at night and ask if anything's happening. It's very reassuring.

I don't know if it was the weather, or delayed mourning, or what, but some time in June a wave of gloom crept over me. The weather was definitely part of it. For weeks I would wake up at dawn with a knot in my stomach thinking, like the woman in *White Mischief*: 'Oh God, not another f★★★ing beautiful day!'

Some of it was work. Except for the weather story, everything I wrote about seemed to be on the theme of mortality, from the heat-related fish kills, to a grisly triple murder case in Cork.

I spent a week on the latter story, traipsing around Mayfield on the city's northern edge, where gardaí were digging for bodies. One day I made the mistake of walking up a lane near the scene marked 'private', where I was met by a hostile farmer who clearly didn't like trespassers but, equally clearly, was enjoying the area's notoriety. Ordering me off the property, he quipped: 'I've enough land to bury you in.' The walk back down the lane seemed a lot longer than the walk up.

There's no good time to be depressed. But it's a particularly bad time when you're a freelance journalist trying to appear enthusiastic, and you're also about to get married. Luckily, being male, I was superfluous to the organisation of the wedding, in which my main role was to turn up on the day and stand where I was told. That and arrange the honeymoon. So while Teresa busied herself with the logistics, I took a few days off in early August and went to Lourdes.

Actually, Lourdes was a bit of an accident. Before Ryanair, empty seats on Aer Lingus pilgrim charters were a cheap way to get to the south of France, where I hoped that a few days in the company of Bertrand Russell's *History of Western Philosophy* would sort me out. I thought I could pay for the trip with a travel feature on the pilgrimage business. It wasn't much of a plan, but it was all I had.

Despite hosting some of the tackiest souvenir shops on earth, Lourdes – where my parents had been several times – is not without its charms. I steered well clear of the baths, sticking to the cafés and immersing myself gently in French beer instead.

But I think I was half hoping for a cure, and I half found it. Although I liked my father, I wasn't close to him. He was a farmer and a Fianna Fáil politician, whereas I didn't have the vocation for either. And his death was so well foreshadowed, I'd hesitate to describe my feelings afterwards as grief. But no matter how little a surprise the event is, it's still a deep shock to realise that the person you've spent your life wanting to impress is gone forever.

Sometime around the start of September, the weather broke and the gloom lifted. Two days before the wedding, Hurricane Iris (although downgraded to a severe storm) swept Ireland, bringing heavy rain to most parts. The effect was clearly electrifying because, a full 24 hours prior to the wedding, I got around to booking the honeymoon, or at least a flight to Rome.

It started badly when I inadvertently booked us in one of the world's worst hotels, near Termini railway station; but then we headed south to Naples and Sorrento and things picked up. We stumbled around the ruins of Pompeii, stunned by the setting and the knowledge that we were walking on 2,000-year-old streets. From there we took a boat to the Isle of Capri. And as we crossed the straits at dusk, a lightning storm lit up Mount Vesuvius behind us. Teresa said it was very romantic.

**TUESDAY, 13 JULY 2004**

# Time Wasted Getting to the Bottom of Lies

*Mark Hennessy*

The Morris Tribunal has delivered a devastating litany of criticisms of the Garda Síochána, accusing two Donegal-based gardaí of corruption, senior officers of gross negligence and exposing major flaws in Garda Headquarter's control of the 12,000-strong force.

Dealing with the explosive finds that were fabricated in 1993 and 1994 by Supt Kevin Lennon and Det. Garda McMahon, the judge said some of the actions were 'unpardonable'.

In unprecedented criticisms of serving officers,

Mr Justice Morris went on: 'The entire story told by Det. Garda McMahon and by Supt Lennon was a cover-up. A huge amount of tribunal time was wasted in attempting to get to the bottom of the lies told by them.'

Urging Garda HQ to manage the force more actively, he said it was 'all too easy' for Dublin-based officers 'to be hoodwinked and misled' by local officers, while the Department of Justice, Equality and Law Reform 'is now utterly isolated' from Garda Headquarters.

He said: 'The flow of information is in one direction. It goes from Garda Headquarters to the Department of Justice. The Minister is obliged to take everything on trust.'

Mr Justice Morris added: 'The tribunal has reluctantly been forced to come to the conclusion

*Democratic Party US presidential candidate John Kerry at a campaign rally in Pittsburgh, Pennsylvania. Photograph: Jason Cohn/Reuters.*

that there was corruption among a small number of individuals within the Donegal division but it has also been compelled to find that this situation could not have flourished and gone unchecked had the leadership of the Donegal division not behaved negligently and slothfully.'

Certain senior officers 'fell below the standards that the public might reasonably expect of them', he said. 'It was as a result of a combination of corruption and negligence that the extraordinary events which are detailed in this report came to pass.

'Corruption can occur in many guises: here it was the abuse of police investigation for personal self-aggrandisement through fraud. That can happen again. Equally other forms of corruption, such as looking the other way, bribery, the taking of short cuts in investigations, the construction of cases based upon lies and many other examples can occur at any time.

'What is most serious about the situation in Donegal is the lack of leadership shown by officers at senior level whereby obvious questions were not asked. In the result, a growing situation of deceit was allowed to blossom to the fullest extent when the application of discipline and the energetic pursuit of proper standards would have snuffed out that growth at an early stage.

'The most shocking aspect of the Donegal investigation has been the extent to which ill-discipline came to pervade the gardaí through the abdication by senior officers of their duty to maintain the men and women under their command in good order and in the pursuit of standards based upon truth.

'The tribunal regards it as unacceptable that members of An Garda Síochána cannot be obliged to immediately give an account of their duties to a superior officer upon being asked.

'Thirdly, the tribunal regards with disquiet the promotion to senior ranks or persons who were unwilling or unable to give to their vocation the energy and aptitude that it demands.'

He said the tribunal's lengthy opening statement had met with an 'unsatisfactory' response, with most replies from the public dealing with other alleged issues of Garda misconduct.

'With the exception of a few replies, virtually no realistic response was received from members of An Garda Síochána in the Donegal division, past or present, even though letters were sent to each of them.

'The lack of co-operation from gardaí continued as the tribunal began its work, as could be judged by one officer, Garda Martin Leonard who said, in effect, that "you don't want to hang your own".

'It was clear that this ethic was active among many witnesses in order to prevent the tribunal making headway. This caused a terrible waste of valuable and expensive time,' said Mr Justice Morris.

Charging that gardaí 'deliberately withheld' evidence, he said they had sheltered behind 'Garda-speak' in order to avoid answering.

'By the term Garda-speak is meant the practice which the judiciary have witnessed in the courts for many years whereby gardaí in the witness box will parry and fence with counsel in a well-recognised choreography to avoid answering counsel's question.'

Unless tribunal barristers asked 'precisely the right question', Garda witnesses were not prepared to reveal information. 'If counsel is not so inspired, that information will remain undisclosed. Asking such people for assistance in terms of a general narrative on a particular issue evokes no useful response.'

However, the judge went on: 'The habit of lying was not by any means confined to the gardaí. Civilian witnesses resorted to the practice to advance the interest they represented.'

The investigation by Assistant Commissioner Mr Kevin Carty in 1999, provoked by allegations surrounding the death of Richie Barron, quickly heard of the allegations surrounding the 1993 and 1994 arms finds.

Mr Justice Morris said he found the lack of co-operation extended by gardaí to Mr Carty extraordinary, though he was given 'candid and helpful' assistance by two former Ministers for Justice, Mr John O'Donoghue and Mrs Nora Owen.

Furthermore, Mr Carty received 'reasonable co-operation' by the Department of Justice, Equality and Law Reform, the Attorney-General's office, and the Director of Public Prosecutions' office, which stood in 'marked contrast' to the attempts at evasion by gardaí when they appeared before the tribunal

Satisfied that the Carty investigation team had carried out 'a professional job and pursued their investigation thoroughly', Mr Justice Morris rejected Supt Lennon's allegations that the team had been motivated by 'malice and prejudice' because of Supt Lennon's earlier criticisms about the original Barron murder inquiry.

**TUESDAY, 20 JULY 2004**

# Stupidity on a Truly Heroic Scale

*Fintan O'Toole*

It's only when you look at the details that you understand the heroic scale of the idiocy, the magnificent, awe-inspiring, sublime stupidity of it all. The top-of-the-head, back-of-the-envelope nature of the Government's decentralisation programme does, admittedly, have the immediate appearance of a grand folly. But you have to work it out in concrete terms before you can appreciate its full grandeur.

Let's take just one example. Last month the Medical Bureau of Road Safety published a report on drug-driving. The bureau tested 2,000 samples taken from drivers by the Garda, half of them over the limit for alcohol. They found that an astonishing 68 per cent of people with low levels of alcohol were actually positive for drugs. Sixteen per cent of

all tested drivers were high on something other than drink. Clearly, we have a problem.

So who's in charge of deciding and implementing the public response to this problem? Last week, Noel Ahern, the Minister of State who runs the National Drugs Strategy, was on *Morning Ireland*. The issue of drug-driving was raised and he was asked the simple question, 'Is as much being done as could be done?' His reply: 'I'm Minister dealing with the Drugs Strategy. We're the Department who co-ordinate the activities of the other Departments. Driving wouldn't be specifically under my responsibility. I'm just trying to say, sadly, I'm not in control of everything. That's covered under the Road Traffic Act and the implementation of it but what we're doing blah blah local inputs blah blah alternative lifestyles blah blah sports centres, youth centres.' The one thing that was clear amid a barrage of verbiage was that the self-declared 'Department who co-ordinate the activities of the other Departments' in relation to drug use is passing the buck on this one.

It occurred to me then to wonder what Departments would be involved in this one little area of policy where lives are at stake. The Medical Bureau of Road Safety, which drew up this report, is listed as being 'under the aegis of the Department of Transport'. Straightforward. But its board is appointed by the Minister for the Environment and its main work is training and supplying the Garda, which is under Justice.

It is based at University College, Dublin, which comes under the Department of Education. A co-ordinated response to the urgent concerns it has raised would involve those departments, the National Drugs Strategy, which is run by the Department of Community, Rural and Gaeltacht Affairs, the Department of Health, the National Safety Council, which comes under the Department of Transport, but is part-funded by the Department of the Environment, and, since Noel Ahern tells us sports facilities are crucial to combating drugs, the Department of Arts, Sport and Tourism.

*Brian Cowen and Bertie Ahern – a successful EU presidency. Photograph: Maxwells.*

Obviously, at the moment, this fragmentation of responsibility means that no one is in charge of responding to the problem of drug-driving, including the Minister who claims to co-ordinate everyone else. Equally obvious is that in this, as in so many other areas, the real job for public service reform is to break down these institutional barriers and create some joined-up thinking. Instead, a vast amount of time, money and effort is being put into making the whole mess infinitely worse.

Let's map, for a moment, what someone trying to deal with drug-driving will be faced with if and when the Government's decentralisation programme is fully implemented. Noel Ahern, or his successor at Community and Rural and Gaeltacht, is sitting in Knock, Co. Mayo, trying to co-ordinate the State's response. His staff is in Furbo, Co. Galway. The National Safety Council is in Loughrea. The Medical Bureau of Road Safety is still in Dublin, as is the State Laboratory which is involved in testing.

The Department of the Environment is in Wexford, with staff in New Ross, Waterford and Kilkenny. The Department of Education is in Athlone. The Department of Justice is partly in Tipperary. Garda headquarters is in Thurles. The Department of Arts, Sport and Tourism is in Killarney. The Department of Health is at some unknown location yet to be decided. All of these organisations have, meanwhile, lost much of the expertise they have built up in this area because the people who had it are now dealing with fisheries or sewerage.

Come to think of it, it may be no bad thing that there will be no serious response to drug-driving, since whoever is going to be consulting with all these Departments will be on the road so much that he or she will need a ready supply of amphetamines to keep going and of LSD to make an apparently coherent picture out of all of this confusion.

It takes a kind of genius to look at the insanely fragmented system we currently have and to decide that what's wrong with it is that it's too centralised. We already have a system of governance that's about as co-ordinated as a jellyfish on a tricycle, and we're going to shake it all about like a St Vitus hokey-cokey. If the whole thing were an anarchist plot to destroy the State, it would be breathtakingly brilliant. The only hope is that those who are trying to do it won't be able to co-ordinate the strategy.

**FRIDAY, 23 JULY 2004**

# A Family United in Amnesia Leaves the Judge Feeling Puzzled

*Paul Cullen*

We've all waited six long years for Mr Pádraig Flynn to tell his story, but it wouldn't have done the tribunal any harm to leave things for another day by asking Mr Flynn to 'reflect' on his evidence. At times yesterday the former Fianna Fáil minister's lack of recollection about the handling of the £50,000 he got from developer Mr Tom Gilmartin stretched credulity to breaking point.

Here it was, the biggest donation he got in his political career, 'a monstrous, enormous sum' in the words of tribunal lawyers, and equivalent to a year's ministerial salary. So what did he do with it? According to Mr Flynn, he simply passed the cheque on to his wife, Dorothy, and asked no more questions.

Some £50,000 disappears off his financial radar, and he doesn't feel the need to inquire what

*Getting ready for 100 foot tall Tates Avenue bonfire in south Belfast to usher in the Twelfth of July when members of the Orange Order mark the victory of Protestant King William of Orange over the Roman Catholic James II at the Battle of the Boyne in 1690. Photograph: Alan Lewis/Photographpress.*

happened to it. He didn't discuss it 'as such' with his wife and he didn't notice its non-appearance in his current account. No surprise then that Judge Alan Mahon, who is less inclined to express exasperation than his predecessor, Mr Justice Feargus Flood, found it all 'puzzling'.

With Mr Flynn, his wife, Dorothy, and the manager of their branch at AIB Castlebar in the late

1980s all telling the tribunal they know nothing about the non-resident accounts that were set up in the Flynns' name, we are left with yet another tribunal puzzle. Add to this Ms Beverley Flynn and her 'selective amnesia' about the details of the money she invested for her parents, and you have a heart-warming tableau of family unity.

Not that Mr Flynn's limited powers of recollection are confined to the Gilmartin money. Some £155,000 was lodged in the three non-resident accounts in the Flynns' name that the former EU commissioner cannot recollect, we heard yesterday. Of this, almost £80,000 cannot be accounted for.

Having told the tribunal four years ago the money was 'an accumulation of political donations,' he then instructed his lawyers to say this was wrong and he didn't really know the source of any of the money.

Mr Flynn also had difficulty explaining why he accepted the developer's £50,000 in the first place.

After all, four months before the payment, he knew most of the allegations Mr Gilmartin was making, including those about Mr Liam Lawlor, a fellow member of Fianna Fáil. By his own account, he took them so seriously that he called gardaí in to investigate.

Yet none of this caused him to pause about accepting Mr Gilmartin's windfall. He didn't feel the need, in the words of a tribunal lawyer, Ms Patricia Dillon SC, to 'hold on a minute and take care' because, as he put it, he 'trusted' Mr Gilmartin.

Further, and in conformity with all similar evidence at this tribunal, he never offered a receipt or acknowledgment. And why? Because he was never asked for one.

As with other witnesses in similar situations, Ms Dillon made most progress following the money trail. There was little of Mr Flynn's trademark rambunctiousness on display yesterday morning as the

*Pádraig Flynn arriving to give evidence to the Mahon Tribunal. Photograph: Graham Hughes/Photographcall Ireland.*

tribunal lawyer pursued the strange twists and turns of the Gilmartin money in embarrassing detail.

However, while this £50,000 formed a large component of the funds that were ultimately used to buy a farm in Co. Mayo and to cover other personal expenses, the figures supported Mr Flynn's right to at least claim that little of this money was actually used for these purposes.

The fact is that no one can prove conclusively that Mr Gilmartin's cheque was the money that ended up growing trees on Mrs Flynn's farm and reaping handsome EU grants. Once money from different sources was mixed up, it was impossible to tell.

Mr Flynn was also on surer ground when quizzed about his ministerial work and his support for Mr Gilmartin's project at Bachelor's Walk. Here, the political autopilot kicked in again, and a decent level of recall was restored.

He was his usual expansive self when expounding on the art of political campaigning in his Mayo constituency. His description of election fundraising bore a remarkable similarity to Ray Burke's in an earlier phase of the tribunal.

His evidence continues today.

# The Zen of Sven

*Shane Hegarty*

Sven-Goran Eriksson has had enough. He is sick of the accusations, the speculation, the tawdry gossip. He is upset that the English Football Association announced that he had a fling with one of their PAs without consulting him first. On Thursday, it was finally time to break his silence, to speak out, to strike back hard. 'I wish to state unequivocally that I have at no time either categorically confirmed or denied any relationship with Ms Faria Alam,' he said.

Stand back. He's going to blow.

It was very Eriksson. He didn't say he had had an affair, but then again he didn't say he hadn't. He

*Valerie Courtney from Portmagee bunjee jumping at Sneem in Co. Kerry. Photograph: Don MacMonagle.*

was insisting that he wasn't commenting on his private life, but he was really. It said much, but clarified little. It was the latest lesson in the zen of Sven.

Once again the English public is forced to figure him out for themselves, to let speculation fill the gaps. Increasingly, the Swede who arrived with a reputation for self-control is letting his libido get him into trouble. Once upon a time Eriksson was hailed as the cerebral, icy football tactician who would rescue English football. Now he is ridiculed as a loose-loined lothario with a weak grip on both his personal life and his football team.

It further chips away at his frigid exterior. When Eriksson took the job as national manager he was easily caricatured. In a world of muddy tracksuits and bared teeth, this Scandinavian polyglot in Armani was an iceman, a thinker. He wears

*Sven-Goran Eriksson by Peter Hanan.*

rimless glasses. He knows a lot about wine. He released a CD of classical music before the 2002 World Cup. He learned the languages of each of the countries he worked in. He does yoga. That he has read Tibetan poetry is dragged out by the press as confirmation of his intellectualism, mentioned as if he reads it in its original form while in the crab position.

The *Mirror* editor Piers Morgan described him as 'Hoddle with brains, Keegan without emotion. This was a hybrid robotic figure that would lead us to glory.' To the percentage of English who still believe that football is only on loan to the rest of the world, the appointment of a foreigner did not go down so well. Jeff Powell in the *Daily Mail* wrote: 'We sell our birthright down the fjord to a nation of seven million skiers and hammer

throwers who spend half their year living in total darkness.'

Eriksson didn't throw the hammer, but he was a half-decent ski-jumper in his childhood. He was born – the son of a truck driver and a nurse – in the small logging town of Torsby in 1948. On the walls of the local football club, there is a faded black-and-white picture of Eriksson holding his only playing honour – a tin of coffee won in 1966. An undistinguished playing career was cut short by injury when he was just 27, but he became a successful coach in Sweden before moving on to Portuguese side Benfica and then on to Italy. While there, the press took to describing him as a 'successful loser'. When coaching Roma, he organised a victory party before the 1986 championship finale, only for the team to throw it all away by losing to the bottom-placed team. In 1999, his Lazio team lost the league at the death.

Still, in 2000 he brought that team its first championship in 26 years and attracted the attention of England. When he left Lazio, it was not popular.

Fans gathered at the club gates, yelling, 'Just go to your Englishmen. Go to hell and take your girlfriend with you.' That girlfriend was Nancy Dell'Olio. She is often described as a 'society lawyer', although her expertise was actually in the heady arena of securities exchange control. When they first met, Eriksson was married with two children. She was also married – to one of Lazio's biggest investors.

The story goes that the wronged husband loved the club so much that, in 1999, he allowed Eriksson take his wife rather than disturb the running of the club.

She once described herself as Eriksson's 'geisha', although she insists that the remark was misunderstood. Yet, there has always been something of oil and water about their pairing. He is the sober northerner; she is the flamboyant southerner. When they visited 10 Downing Street, she wore a red catsuit slashed to the navel, as if she had decided to pick up a dress along the way but the only shop open was in Soho.

She has said that he ignores the ridicule from the press. 'It's in his culture not to get upset. He does, of course, but he doesn't show it.' Of their arguments, she said: 'Sven and I have incredible wars of silences. It's incredible. Scary.' A war of silence with Eriksson, one would have thought, would be like holding a staring contest with a wall.

However, a Swedish journalist who interviewed him at the end of 1999 described a man at odds with the caricature. He drove at 160kph

*Commissioned officers from the 79th Cadet Class celebrate their graduation at the Military College in The Curragh, Co. Kildare. Photograph: Brenda Fitzsimons.*

without a seatbelt, smoked Cuban cigars and gulped Scotch. During a dinner, the journalist wrote of how Dell'Olio 'hinted that she was trying to encourage her Viking to loosen his grip on that famous self-control and to set his passions free'. Bad advice.

In 2002, just before the World Cup, it was revealed that Eriksson had been having an affair with TV presenter Ulrika Jonsson. The press loved it. Piers Morgan best explains the story's allure. 'The two most famous Swedes on the planet, at it!' There was a brief skirmish on the press battlefields between Dell'Olio and Jonsson before the Italian kept her man.

Meanwhile, there was a growing suggestion that Eriksson's commitment issues stretch beyond his personal life. He had almost come to England in 1997 to take charge at Blackburn Rovers, but reneged on the agreement and went to Lazio instead. And, more recently, he has been caught playing footsie with other teams. As England prepared for Euro 2004, Eriksson had separate meetings with Chelsea's owner, Roman Abramovich, and its chief executive Peter Kenyon. Meanwhile, there are those within the game who maintain that Eriksson was lined up to take over from Alex Ferguson before the Manchester United manager changed his mind about retiring. In response, the FA moved in and secured his services until 2008.

His record as England manager, though, has been unconvincing. He had a brief honeymoon period when England qualified for the 2002 World Cup thanks to a last-minute goal against a mediocre team, but since England threw it away in the quarter-final against a Brazilian team down to 10 men, a pattern has emerged. In important games England scorch into a lead. They then go into the dressing room for the half-time team talk and re-emerge as if someone's slipped a sedative into their tea. They retreat. They panic. They concede a goal. Eriksson slaps his knees and throws back his head in frustration. They go home.

These days, he goes home alone. Dell'Olio and he have split. The FA feels that he misled them over the affair with Alam. He always insists that his private life has nothing to do with how he does his job, but that has never dissuaded the British press from pursuing the time-honoured sport of manager-baiting, and his doubters may have found the excuse they need to oust him. Only the millions that it will cost the FA to terminate their relationship might prevent a messy divorce.

Perhaps Eriksson can find consolation in some of the homespun psychology included in his book *On Football*. Let's see: 'Work up your plus mind, eliminate your minus mind.' Not bad. 'Think outwards, not inwards.' Er, maybe. 'We are the sum of what we have thought during our life.' Now it's just getting silly – something that seems really smart but on further examination isn't so clever at all.

SATURDAY, 31 JULY 2004

# The Gift Shop Owner

*Irish Lives: Orna Mulcahy*

Antoinette rears up like a cobra from behind the till when she sees the three Americans coming through the door of Celtic Charms. Off goes Gerry Ryan so that Enya can be heard in the background and just a couple more drops of lavender oil on the burner to get rid of the damp smell. Then, checking her aura – it's so important to give off positive vibes – she sidles over toward the soap display where the ladies are toying with some shamrock-shaped bars that have gone a bit crumbly around the edges.

'Anything I can help you with, just let me know,' she says with what she likes to think of as her welcoming smile, though in fact it makes her look like a Bengal tiger about to pounce. With the stockroom full of knitted sheep, bodhráns, lucky stones from Blarney and a hell of a lot of Belleek, Antoinette can't afford to let this lot get away, even if they've only stepped in to get out of the rain.

Yes, she knows the type – nice, gentle, well-off people from somewhere in the Midwest, with lots of friends back home needing presents and possibly a niece getting married who just loves Irish crystal.

Good, they're now fingering the patchwork tweed which has been woefully slow this year, due to global warming or their appalling cut. 'These are terribly popular,' she says brightly, hauling one off its hanger and helping one of the larger ladies into it. Immediately the poor woman's eyes start to water from the hairy tweed, but the thing is a work of art and it does get very cold in Minnesota, doesn't it?

'What a marvellous fit, and those heather colours really suit you. What about a mohair scarf? You know the secret with mohair is to put it in the freezer, then it won't get up your nose!'

Amazingly, they buy three scarves each, so they're obviously fair game for some Aran. 'The wonderful thing about Arans', she tells the ladies, now hanging on her every word, 'is that each style of stitch tells a story, stories that were handed down through the generations.' She's not entirely sure what the stories are but 'gone ... gone ... the sea has taken them all' pretty much covers it, doesn't it?

*The Gift Shop Owner by Wendy Shea.*

'Oh goodness me, how terrible,' say the ladies, moving away from the heaps of cream wool and engrossing themselves in the linen napkins that Antoinette knows for a fact are made in China though they're cunningly trimmed with sham-rocky lace.

'Carrickmacross lace,' she says, 'lovely work. Started by the nuns over a century ago and still going today.' They take the lot, and throw in some silk scarves printed with bits of the *Book of Kells* for good measure. There's nothing like Americans for spending, but God they're annoying looking for their VAT-back forms, and maybe those lace napkins were just too cheap, she thinks, hauling out a fresh batch from the back and adjusting her price gun upward.

---

**MONDAY, 2 AUGUST 2004**

# Lighthouse Mission Accomplished

*Lorna Siggins*

A west Cork-based photographer has achieved his ambition of capturing all of Ireland's lighthouses on film. Aerial shots taken by John Eagle of the Maidens Lighthouse off the Co. Antrim coast last week marked the conclusion of a project lasting over a decade. Weather and budgetary factors determined the length of time it took him to capture all 94 lights and beacons around the 2,700-mile coastline, mostly from the air.

Mr Eagle had completed most of his project early this year, but Rathlin Island's three lighthouses off the north-east coast, Inishtrahull off Donegal, the Mew and the Maidens off Black Head, north Antrim, and Haulbowline, on Carlingford Lough, Co. Louth, had eluded him. He relied for his transport on Irish Helicopters, the company that holds the service contract with the Commissioners of Irish Lights.

Last week, weather conditions and helicopter delivery schedules synchronised and Mr Eagle was able to shoot Haulbowline, Mew Island and two lights at the Maidens. All 94 lights have now been reproduced on postcard, which he sells to lighthouse enthusiasts all over the world.

Mr Eagle is author of a book on Irish lighthouses and his work has appeared in international publications. His role models are French marine photographers Philip Plisson and Jean Guichard. Operating on a minimal budget, he has paid credit to the Commissioners of Irish Lights and to two Irish Helicopters pilots, Capt. Mick Conneely and Capt. Mick Hennessy.

Local boat-owners have also helped out where shots were best taken at sea level, such as Mr Gerry Donnelly of Shannon Estuary Ports who helped him take the Beeves Rock, the late Dr Tom McCarrick, owner of a catamaran, *Image*, in Sligo who transported him to Blackrock lighthouse and John Johnston, a sea-angling charter skipper on Achill, Co. Mayo.

A commission by the former ESB fish farming subsidiary, Salmara, paid for Mr Eagle's first work in the series.

Meanwhile, a series of events marking the 25th anniversary of the Fastnet yacht race in which 15 people lost their lives is due to be held on Cape Clear island and at sea on 15 August. The events will include a remembrance at sea, led by the Naval Service patrol ship, *LE Emer*, and involving the RNLI Baltimore lifeboat. The Baltimore lifeboat and the former Naval Service patrol ship, *LE Deirdre*, played a significant role in the rescue operation during the storm which hit the biennial yacht race and sank five vessels.

Some 40 sailors who participated in the 1979 race will travel to Cape Clear for a memorial unveiling on 15 August and launch of a history of the event by Dr Eamon Lankford. This will be preceded by a lecture on 14 August by Commodore John Kavanagh, who was in command of the *LE Deirdre* during the emergency.

*Maidens Lighthouse. Photograph: John Eagle.*

**FRIDAY, 6 AUGUST 2004**

# The Best Thing on the East Coast

*Seán MacConnell*

It may be simply a case of needing to get out of the city. Perhaps it's anticipation of that repetitive moan – 'I'm bored' – from young troops as they gaze at a computer screen during the umpteenth replaying of a game involving some form of bashing the enemy.

Do yourself a favour this summer and take yourself off to Luggala, Co. Wicklow, and take a stroll down to Lough Dan under Knocknacloghoge. If it's good enough for the Guinness family it should be good enough for you – and even those young terriers in need of open country.

Lough Dan lies in a valley between Djouce mountain to the east and Luggala to the west and it is truly one of the delights of not only Wicklow but the entire east coast.

If you are coming from Dublin city, travel over the mountains, heading for Sally Gap, taking in the views around Kippure mountain, one of the six mountains between Tallaght and the gap. At Sally Gap, which is 1,600 ft above sea level, turn left leaving the road to Glendalough and Wicklow Gap and head down into the valley for Roundwood. About three miles from the gap, the road begins to rise and to your right you will see down into the valley with the Guinness estate at its northern end, close to the bank of Lough Tay, the lake at the upper end of the valley.

Park your car in some of the forest roadways off to your left and seek entry into the estate with its well-kept gate and warning signs not to bring dogs of any kind on to the lands. Avoid, unless you want hassle, an adjoining roadway which also runs down into the valley where signs warn that you could be prosecuted for trespass. Fortunately, the Guinness family have the confidence of centuries of ownership to share our heritage with us without threat of any kind. Their privacy is respected by all.

Swing down into the valley past their gate lodge and make your way down to the valley floor. Check the skyline of Luggala mountain in front of you for peregrine falcons who breed on the steep cliffs there and seem to be involved in perpetual warfare with the ravens who compete for food with them. I don't think I have ever walked down into that valley without a sighting of the peregrine falcons that have been successfully breeding there for more than 30 years.

Watch too for deer. They are to be seen all over the valley which is a feeding and breeding ground for them. The white flash of colour around their tails should help you spot them. The deer in Luggala are Sika hybrids, whose Japanese ancestors escaped from Powerscourt estate in the 1890s and

interbred and eventually obliterated the native red deer which used to roam the Wicklow hills.

Your route down will take you past a farmhouse on your left where two years ago film crews were working around the clock making the film *Animal Farm*. Keep an eye open for local farmers who work the sheep with their dogs. Some of the best sheepdogs in Ireland are to be found working this valley.

Cross the wooden bridge on the valley floor and climb the well-maintained stile that gives access to the rough roadway leading down to the lake. There are always deer on the pasture land on your left along the river and, if you go quietly, there are rabbits in most of the fields. There are also the ruins of a village dating back two centuries.

One of the trees on your left, near the one gate you must open and close en route, has been the home to a swarm of wild Irish bees for nearly a decade. If the day is warm their homestead is easy

*Seán MacConnell. Photograph: Bryan O'Brien.*

to spot. The roadway leads down to the place where the river flows into Lough Dan, a few hundred yards away from the most perfect example of stepping stones to be found anywhere – short of reviewing the 1963 film *Robin Hood*.

These stepping stones are just yards away from a lovely old house which used to be a hunting lodge but is no longer used. It is an idyllic setting for a picnic. This is also a place of options. Depending on your age, agility or company, you can decide to stay with the lake, following its northern shore through a sea of furze to where another river meanders along the valley floor.

Watch out for dragonfly that live along the river and lakeshore and keep an eye to the flank of Knocknacloghoge for badger and fox or the beautiful little Merlin, the lady's hawk, which sometimes hunts there. There are fish in the lake too but they are small, trout mostly, and I have been told there are char, the prehistoric glacial fish left over from the Ice Age.

For the energetic, Knocknacloghoge beckons. There is a fairly decent path up its south-eastern flank through the ferns, not too far from the back of the hunting lodge. This path will take you to the top, at just over 2,000 ft, and a wonderful view over the lake below you and south as far as Lugnaquilla.

Drop over the top of the mountain but be very careful going down the far side where a river runs between Knocknacloghoge and Luggala mountain. Pick up this river when making your way downstream but again, be very careful because it drops quickly and there are dangerous drops to catch the unwary.

However, the waterfalls and pools on this river are tremendous and are worth seeking out. It is safer to walk on the left bank as you head downstream. This river walk brings you back to the wooden bridge crossed on the way in to Lough Dan. All that's left is the haul back up to the car well over 1,000 feet above! For those taking in all elements of the walk, completion time is usually within $4\frac{1}{2}$ hours.

A few tips with safety in mind: Make sure and wear strong boots or walking shoes and take wet gear with you. There is no such thing as bad weather, only bad clothing. Take a mobile phone if you are inexperienced. Take food if you are going to climb and bring a map, compass and whistle and please remember that the temperature drops as you climb by as much as three degrees for every thousand feet, according to my climbing tutor, Kieran 'The Navigator' O'Brien.

Finally, respect the mountains and those who live in them by closing all gates and leaving no rubbish.

**FRIDAY, 6 AUGUST 2004**

# Saying Goodbye to a Great Neighbour

*Newton Emerson*

The funeral has taken place in west Belfast of former IRA chief of staff, Joe Camel, who died last week after a long battle against everyone.

In a grave graveside oration, Sinn Féin president for life Gerry Adams paid tribute to the veteran republican. 'Without Joe there could not have been a peace process,' he said, 'for without Joe there would not have been a war process.'

Thousands attended the burial in Milltown cemetery, described by one grieving bystander as 'Joe's last republican plot'. Many had travelled from the Irish Republic, lending the event a truly international flavour. Among the leading mourners were Sinn Féin MP, Martin McGuinness, representing the IRA army council, Sinn Féin TD Martin Ferris, representing the IRA navy council, and Sinn Féin MEP, Mary Lou McDuck, representing Dublin council. 'I'll never forget the first time I met Joe Camel,' Ms McDuck told waiting reporters. 'He turned to me and said "Who's this pretty little thing then?" Joe had a revolutionary approach to the role of women in the struggle.'

*Eamon Whelan hits the water diving from the 5 m platform during practice at the National Aquatic Centre in Co. Dublin. Photograph: Alan Betson.*

Joe Camel was born in Belfast in 1920, just months before partition created the separate state of west Belfast. This traumatic event radicalised him from an extremely young age. 'That was just typical of young Camel,' recalls one neighbour. 'He was always getting the hump over something.'

In 1935 Camel founded the Andersonstown 1st Battalion A-Company IRA Brigade. 'He worked his way up the ranks just as quickly as he could invent them,' the brigade's only other member informed the RUC regularly. This daredevil early phase of Camel's career came to an abrupt end in 1942 when he was sentenced to death for the murder of a Catholic policeman.

Camel only escaped the hangman's noose after an appeal for clemency from Pope Pius XII, who is fondly remembered for his courageous wartime stand against the execution of non-Jewish people. Camel's accomplice in the killing was not so fortunate, although he was exactly as fortunate as the victim.

On his release from prison Camel rejoined the IRA, taking part in the inherently partitionist Border campaign of the 1950s and the inherently pointless armchair campaign of the 1960s, during which he became chief of staff.

In 1969 Camel played a key part in the split between the Official Irish Republican Army and the breakaway Northern Ireland Republican Army. Returning to active service he spent much of the next four years moving between safe houses while planning operations. 'During that lonely time I often thought of my family,' he later said, 'although obviously I didn't think twice about anyone else's family.' In 1973 Camel was imprisoned again for attempting to buy weapons from Col. Gadafy. He subsequently described the Libyan gun-running debacle as the biggest mistake of his life. 'I should have asked Charlie Haughey for the gear like everybody else,' he said.

Throughout the rest of the 1970s Camel oversaw the Northern Ireland Republican Army campaign from his cell and was responsible for some of its most celebrated military operations, including the Ballymena school bus bomb, the Lisburn church picnic massacre and the Enniskillen orphanage shootings.

'Joe was an unashamed physical force republican but he saw this as his last resort, not his first resort,' Gerry Adams told mourners. 'You may not realise, for example, that Joe stood for election until he was blue in the face before finally killing a policeman at the age of 22.'

In 1979 Camel's moral authority was curtailed when Pope John Paul II appealed to the IRA for clemency. Mindful of his own pardon, Camel felt he now had little option but to kill the Pope.

It is around this time that Gerry Adams suddenly replaced him and, eventually, everyone like him. Republicans took their first tentative steps towards peace soon after Camel's retirement and less than 13 years later he was persuaded to support the new agenda.

His final contribution was an appearance at the 1998 special ardfheis where he spoke movingly in favour of the Good Friday agreement. 'I was never wrong!' he screamed before being wheeled off the platform.

Joe Camel is survived by his wife and one million Protestants.

**FRIDAY, 20 AUGUST 2004**

# Digging of Dublin Port Tunnel is Completed

*Frank McNally*

Two years after the digging began in a blaze of publicity, the media glare returned to a large hole in north Dublin yesterday, and this time there were definite signs of a tunnel at the end of the light.

Commuters and pedestrians will have to wait another year and a half for their promised deliverance from trucks, but the digging phase of the project is over.

Having covered the 4.5 kilometre distance at an average of nine metres a day – only slightly slower than Dublin's rush-hour traffic – the Port Tunnel boring machine completed its journey when it pushed the last few inches of rock into the Whitehall 'reception pit', in front of the Minister for Transport and invited guests.

It was a dramatic breakthrough, by any standards. In a Japanese tradition, representatives of the Nishimatsu construction team poured sake and salt on the displaced earth, to sanctify the work. Moments later, in an Irish tradition, men in green and yellow GAA jerseys began climbing out the front of the tunnelling machine and shouting 'Up Donegal'.

These were the 'miners' – much-travelled underground specialists, including veterans of the Channel Tunnel – who marked the completion of another project by planting their county flag on top of the pile of debris.

The miners won a round of applause from onlookers, which is more than could be said for the Minister. But Mr Brennan still looked a happy man as he celebrated 'a bit of history'. The port tunnel was 'probably the country's largest ever feat of engineering', he said, and with the exception of increased land costs, it was coming in 'largely on budget'.

He was also quick to hint that the project would not be getting any bigger, although his formal verdict on the raising of the tunnel's height for super-trucks has yet to be announced.

Promising to 'sign off' on the decision early next month, he spoke of 'very compelling' arguments that any change in the height would have safety implications. But he would decide the issue in the context of another issue – a limit on the legal height of trucks in Ireland – and the Dublin truck management plan. Other countries had lower size-limits than Ireland, he added, and there had to be a 'trade-off' between the needs of commerce and environmental concerns.

Not everyone was as happy as Mr Brennan with yesterday's work. The Marino Development Action Group, whose members live over or close to the path of the new tunnel, was not on the list of invited guests for the event in Whitehall.

'It's typical of them to ignore us,' said spokesman Mr Fintan Cassidy, who also accused Dublin City Council and the tunnel contractors of 'dragging their heels' on agreed repairs to houses undermined by the work.

The council had acknowledged damage – from cracks in paving to warped door-frames – in 169 houses, he said. But only 15 had been repaired to date, including his. A former city councillor – he was co-opted to replace TD Mr Finian McGrath prior to the local elections – Mr Cassidy said that he had 'made a bit of noise' and forced the council to act.

*The Donegal Tigers boring team celebrate breaking through the second tube of the Dublin Port Tunnel. Photograph: Matt Kavanagh.*

'But it's not as easy for older people. There's one elderly lady whose roof slates needed repairing, for example. They told her they couldn't do anything about it because they didn't have a ladder.'

Work on the tunnel now moves on to the electrical and mechanical fitting stage, with a phased opening to traffic scheduled to begin in late 2005.

But the Donegal miners who cheered as they emerged from the ground yesterday were celebrating unemployment. After some mopping up, they will now get two weeks' notice and start looking for another tunnelling job – probably overseas.

Mr Eddie O'Brien (28), from Magheroarty, has already worked in England, France and Asia. He says his county's tradition for digging started 'years ago, with hydro-dams in the north of Scotland' and has become a habit. Tunnelling is hard work – 72-hour weeks in high temperatures,

noise and dust. But the Donegal crew will probably be getting together for the next job, wherever it is. It pays 'big money', he says candidly. 'That's why we follow it, all over the place.'

**TUESDAY, 24 AUGUST 2004**

# Not a Perfect Goodbye, but Sonia Bows Out with Grace

*Keith Duggan*

I t was far from the perfect goodbye but Sonia O'Sullivan's last night at the Olympics will be remembered as an oddly beautiful night in Irish sport.

Some time after ten o'clock on a balmy evening in Athens, our greatest track athlete accepted the dying of the light with a grace worthy of any Olympics.

We hoped, unreasonably, that it might be different. It did not matter that Sonia was a 34-year-old mother, lining up against women who were mere children back when she cast the longest shadow in middle distance running. It was Sonia and it was an Olympic 5,000 metres final and so we hoped that she could somehow tap into the glittering past and give us one more night that we had no right to expect.

Standing on the edge of the track against the new generation from Africa and China, O'Sullivan looked at the start as she has done on so many of these intense Olympic evenings. Vulnerable. Taut. Alone. And last night, she was. Although she reigned briefly at the front during a crazily slow first lap, it took just three minutes to realise that this was a race beyond her.

The easy option would have been to bow out. Edith Masai of Kenya, two years older than O'Sullivan and just as proud, chose that route. Sonia, though, was always going to leave on her own terms. For 10 laps she ran around the stadium in perfect isolation, tailed off from the rest of the field. A cluster of Irish flags waved harder each time she passed by.

'The Irish supporters and the Olympic games is what got me around that track tonight,' she said afterwards. 'It is hard to say but that was probably my last Olympic track race. And things don't always work out the way you want them to.'

As she toiled, the languid stride summoning ghostly remembrances of great nights in Gothenberg, in Stuttgart, in Sydney, the race was reduced to a sprint between Meseret Defar of Ethiopia and Isabella Ochichi of Kenya. They stepped around the Irish woman as they lapped her

*Sonia O'Sullivan finishing her unsuccessful Olympic 5,000 metres final race in Athens. Photograph: Patrick Bolger/INPHO.*

*Belfast housewife and cancer sufferer Iris Jeffrey, 58, and husband Robert celebrate winning a record £20.1 sterling (€29 million) in the UK Lotto. Photograph: Haydn West/PA.*

with just two laps to race. Quickly, other runners went past also so that when the final bell tolled, funnily, it was for all but O'Sullivan.

The medal winners were hugging as O'Sullivan heard the bell salute her and she started on her last lap. By now, the crowd understood they were witnessing something rare. In previous summers, Sonia trailing in last meant tears and torment.

Last night, she managed a smile and blew a kiss towards the Irish. She crossed the line in 16.20. It was a compelling sight, O'Sullivan sauntering down the home straight that was once her territory, her place to shine, and the crowd greeted her arrival as if she was a champion.

But, of course, she was that and more. If Ireland has learned anything from these Olympics, it is that she was a once-in-a-lifetime gift. At her best, Sonia O'Sullivan owned the track. On her last night, that much did not change.

**WEDNESDAY, 25 AUGUST 2004**

# Bland Maca Must Go

*Vincent Browne*

Mary McAleese has dismantled the office of President established by her immediate predecessor. Seven more years of the céad míle fáiltes, bodhráns at the Áras and interminable tedium is more than we can endure. Anyone is preferable: Dana, Tom McGurk, the Rose of Tralee, Slab Murphy, Twink, Seán Doherty, John Waters. She has to go.

Mary Robinson gave life to an anonymously ceremonial office. The Constitution had sought to ring-fence the presidency from public engagement and controversy. Dexterously, she gave life to the role. She did it by campaigning for the office as a left-wing, liberal feminist. It gave her a mandate. She used the office to highlight injustice. Her frequent use of the phrase 'there are no inevitable victims' became a theme. She signalled her support for the divorce referendum and other causes, without crossing the constitutional ring-fence.

As the historian Diarmuid Ferriter writes in a forthcoming book: 'The fact that she was edgy – and indeed sustained that edginess for seven years – is noteworthy … she pricked consciences at home and abroad; about emigration, human rights and the treatment of minorities, about genocide and famine in Africa, about the hypocrisy of speaking out of both sides of our mouths to the republican movement and the victims of violence.'

That is gone now. Far from 'consolidating' that edginess Mary Robinson brought to the presidency, Mary McAleese has restored the blandness that previously enveloped the role. She has been a Fianna Fáil President, operating within the consensus, non-confrontational, unchallenging, except in the safest of ways. All smiles, hugs, responsibility and ponderousness.

Yes, there was that kerfuffle over Communion in Christ Church and the speech about binge drinking. But that's been it. Just look at the last seven speeches posted on the Áras website.

She spoke at the European Parliament on November 19th last. She said: 'This Parliament gives power to the hugely diverse voices of the men, women and young people of Europe.' ('Young people'?) She said the Parliament 'demonstrates the central place of democratic politics in the Union'. OK, you wouldn't expect her to express a coded misgiving about democracy in the EU as Robbo would have done, but to claim the opposite?

There was the usual gibberish about how the EU rescued Europe from centuries of conflict (so predictable and, incidentally, absolute nonsense). Something or other was 'awesome'. She thought 'credit should be given where credit was due'. She wanted a reference to God in the new EU Constitution. She observed 'ours is an increasingly

interdependent world'. There were pieties about AIDS and famine in Africa and, at the end, an Irish seanfhocal: 'Ní neart go cur le chéile'.

It would give you the heeby geebies. Do we really want someone who would inflict this balderdash, even on EU parliamentarians, to be our first citizen for another seven years?

Not a hint of reservation about EU trade policy, no mention of 'fortress Europe', no hesitancy about the primacy of the market which the EU represents? Robbo wouldn't have copped out with an unrevised script from the Department of Foreign Affairs.

Maca spoke at Dublin City Hall on Holocaust Memorial Day on January 25th last. An opportunity to say – or, given the constitutional niceties, to hint – that there is a lot of bogus hand-ringing about the genocide of the Jews nowadays and at the same time a studied denial of new genocides in Yugoslavia and Africa. Ireland joined others in denying the evidence of our own eyes in Bosnia and Rwanda and, worse still, in depriving the Bosnian Muslims of the means to defend themselves. Robbo would have had a dig at that. Maca, nothing.

There was an affectionate tribute to Maurice Hayes on February 16th. Another tribute to award winners on February 23rd and praise 'to each and every person …'

On March 17th happy St Patrick's Day greetings to 'Ireland's sons and daughters'. 'Around the world, on this day, we come together to celebrate the music and song, the wit and humour, the friendship and fellowship that is our heritage and pride.' Please, please, not another seven years.

Off to Argentina a day or two later to do her bit for the Celtic Tiger. Robbo would have had a cut at the impoverishment of Argentina at the behest of the IMF. Maca was plugging Irish trade; not a word about the IMF. On to Chile a few days later, more plugging of the Celtic Tiger, at enormous length (3,041 words). Robbo would have made some reference to the Pinochet years. Maca, not a word.

I wrote earlier in this column that she had restored the blandness that previously enveloped the presidency. That was unfair. Unfair to Paddy Hillery, to Cearbhall Ó Dálaigh, to Erskine Childers, Éamon de Valera, Seán T. O'Kelly and Douglas Hyde.

They were never as bland and insipid as this. They didn't turn the Áras into a centre of anaesthesiology. She has to go.

**FRIDAY, 27 AUGUST 2004**

# I Have a Little Shadow — How Bono Stole My Life

*Neil McCormick*

As a teenage dreamer attending Mount Temple School in Dublin in the Seventies, I had my whole future worked out in careful detail.

I would form a rock band, make a series of epoch-shifting albums, play technologically mind-blowing concerts in the biggest stadiums on the planet until I was universally acknowledged as the most famous man of my times and I would indulge in all manner of secondary fantasies along the way: make films, break hearts, befriend my idols ... oh, and promote world peace, feed the poor and save the planet while I was at it.

There was, as it turned out, only one thing I hadn't counted on. A boy sitting on the other side of the classroom had a few plans of his own.

I went to school with Paul Hewson, a fellow gawky teenage rock fan who answered to the frankly rather ridiculous nickname Bono Vox. You may have heard of him. Bono is a big star these days but, the truth is, he was always a bit of a star, even in the limited environs of the school corridor.

Everyone knew Bono, with his pugnacious physicality, restless energy, mischievous humour and all-inclusive grin. I think of him in Mount Temple as a gregarious charmer, loping about the place like a stray dog, sniffing out interesting

conversations and activities, making sure he was part of whatever was going on.

His ascent to real stardom began on Saturday, 25 August 1976, when he attended a meeting in the kitchen of a house in Artane convened by a fellow pupil, Larry Mullen, who wanted to form a band. The reason I am so sure of the date is because my younger brother Ivan was there, and made the legendary entry in his diary: 'Watched TV. Joined a pop group with friends. Had a rehearsal. Great.' Sadly, it is not a matter of record exactly what he watched on TV. Such is the fickle nature of teenage diaries.

This was the first gathering of a band who would go on to conquer the world, once they had dispensed with my brother's services (he lasted three rehearsals). A band called ... well, Feedback actually. There would be a few name changes before they became U2. They were briefly The Hype and even more briefly The Larry Mullen Band. Indeed, for a while they considered calling themselves The Blazers, a name sensibly discounted on the prosaic basis that Mount Temple did not have a school uniform.

I vividly recall Feedback's first gig, on four tables held together by sticky tape in the school gymnasium. Bono stood centre stage at his microphone, guitar slung around his neck, looking defiantly over the boisterous crowd of kids. Guitarist Dave Evans and bassist Adam Clayton stood either side of him. Drummer Larry clicked his sticks together and the group launched into a coarse, speeded-up version of pretty boy rock star Peter Frampton's 'Show Me the Way', kicking off with a roaring D chord that sent a shockwave through the room.

With the wisdom of hindsight, I know this début must have been a fairly dubious affair. There was nothing remotely cool about their selection of songs, for a start. They played, of all things, the Bay City Rollers' pop anthem 'Bye Bye Baby' and a Beach Boys medley. They had no soundcheck, no experience, nothing to go on but hope and desire.

But when Bono stomped across the shaky stage, grabbing his microphone stand, yelling 'I want you ... show me the way!', the little girls from the junior classes started screaming. You could say I was impressed.

It wasn't long before I had a band of my own, formed with my brother Ivan and another teenage malcontent, Frank Kearns. We went by the name Frankie Corpse and the Undertakers. Well, it was 1977. We played a lot of gigs with the nascent U2, in the school disco (returning next morning to dutifully clean up the mess we had made) and in places like Howth Community Centre (with Larry sitting in when our own drummer, the aptly named Keith Karkus, was detained by police for unspecified punk rock atrocities) and McGonagles.

I loved U2 then, and I love them now. I watched them coalesce from a frankly rather terrible covers band (I will never forget the spectacle of them playing a version of a popular TV theme tune in the school common room, with Bono punctuating the instrumental blues riff by leaping into the air at appropriate moments to shout 'Batman!') into a white hot rock group, with sweat dripping off the walls of Dublin clubs, the Edge's echo-driven guitar splitting and separating into a chiming wall of harmonics, while Bono urged us on with a passion bordering on belligerence.

Those were my Beatles-in-the-Cavern moments. A lot of people in Ireland feel that U2 belong to them. And they do. But I was there from the very beginning, before anyone had any idea what it might amount to.

Including me. Sure, I thought U2 were good, but I thought my own bands were better! As the singer in a succession of outfits with names like The Modulators, Yeah! Yeah! and Shook Up!, I went through a lot of haircuts and fashion makeovers, always with my eye focussed on the main prize. And I came close. Well, close to getting signed by a record company. WEA offered Shook Up! a deal after our first show in London. They told us we could be bigger than The Police

*Neil McCormick (right) with his doppelgänger.*

or Duran Duran. Then they dropped us unceremoniously on the grounds that the MD thought the singer's hair was too short. My bandmates were supportive, but I didn't go back to a hairdresser for more than five years.

While my friends in U2 ascended to the stars, I found myself mired in the underbelly of the music business. By the time they were playing Wembley stadium, and I was still worried about whether enough people would turn up to our gig at Wembley Coach and Horses, the penny finally dropped. It was time for me to give up. Of course, this was several years after the music business had given up on me.

I became that journalistic cliché: failed rock star turned rock critic. One day I was sitting in my shabby, unheated excuse for an office above a bookies in London, watching rain drizzle down a dirty window, when Bono phoned from Miami to

*Éadaoin Ní Challaráin competing in the women's K-1 class slalom heat on at the Athens Olympic Games.*
*Photograph: Shaun Botterill/Getty.*

tell me about smoking cigars with presidents and singing duets with Frank Sinatra. I was in no mood to listen.

'The problem with knowing you is that you've done everything I ever wanted to do,' I complained. 'I feel like you've lived my life.' 'I'm your doppelgänger,' Bono replied. 'If you want your life back, you'll have to kill me.'

And in that throwaway remark was the germ of a book I would one day write about living in the shadow of superstardom. 'You're not the only one of my friends who complains about how hard it is knowing me,' Bono has admitted.

People think it must be great being pals with a superstar. And there are some benefits. You get access to the VIP section, where bouncers discreetly usher you beyond the red cordon to a magical place where tables are laden with champagne and whiskey, supermodels laugh at your jokes, film stars recite poetry in your ear, and someone else always picks up the bill. The downside is that every time you have flown First Class it's just that little bit harder to go back to Economy.

And there is always something to remind you that you are only in this exclusive world as a guest, not an inhabitant. Like the time Bono, David Bowie, Brian Eno and I had our picture taken together at a concert, only for it to appear in the newspaper the next day carefully cropped around Bono's shoulder to cut me out.

Or the time we went to the Pope's house in the Alban Hills. Now, that is a big house. The Biblical expression 'in my father's house there are many mansions' barely does it justice. You could fit entire streets in single rooms. Our small entourage was led from one vast chamber to another until we arrived at the Pontiff's quarters. But when we approached the door, a glorified bouncer dressed in the medieval costume of the Vatican Swiss Guard insisted I wait outside.

This was the story of my life with Bono. I never had quite the right pass or sufficient kudos to gain access to the final sanctum. 'Just don't tell them I'm not a Catholic,' Bono whispered to me as he was led inside by the Swiss Guard.

Oh, I've had some high times in Bono's company, moments when I glimpsed the dark appeal of being part of the entourage, like Elvis's mafia, enjoying glamour by association. I could tell you about the time I rode in a minibus over San Francisco's Golden Gate Bridge with Bono, The Edge and Noel and Liam Gallagher from Oasis. U2's 'One' came on the radio and everyone started singing, the biggest rock superstars in the world delivering an impromptu rendition of a song of brotherly love. 'We're one,' they sang, 'but we're not the same, we've got to carry each other, carry each other ...'

And I sang too. But, whatever it says in the song's lyrics, we are not one. While my own musical career crashed and burned, Bono's star swelled to such a magnitude that somewhere in the darkest recesses of my psyche, I felt as if I were being eclipsed.

Bono became inescapable. Walk into a shop and there he was, blasting over the in-store stereo. Turn on the TV and there he was, shaking hands with presidents and prime ministers. When your friend has achieved everything you ever wanted, how does that reflect on your own life? The small triumphs of ordinary existence can disappear in the blinding spotlight of superstardom.

The worst thing for me was that Bono became a kind of archetype who invaded my dreams nightly, a subconscious reminder of my own sense of failure. I would be standing on a stage in front of tens of thousands of people, with my band

behind me, only to slowly realise the band was U2 and I didn't know the words to any of the songs. Frozen with embarrassment, I would be gently pushed aside by Bono as he assumed his place at centre stage.

I complained about this to him one day. 'I don't want you in my dreams!' I complained. 'They're private!' 'I'll try to remember that next time I'm wandering about at night looking for somebody's head to get into,' laughed Bono.

So I wrote a book about all of this, which, as it happens, Bono loves. 'I was Neil McCormick's fan in school,' he wrote in the foreward. 'He was much cooler than me, a much better writer and I thought he'd make a much better rock star. I was wrong on one count.'

Bastard.

# A Question of Trust

*Tony Clayton Lea*

It has been said that the defining characteristic of being English 'is to be in a state of confusion about what it means to be English'. On entering Lacock village there is little doubt that this place is – archetypally perhaps, but nevertheless authentically – forever England.

Lacock (pronounced lay-cock) lies at the southern edge of the Cotswolds in the south west of England. This part of the country has attracted settlers since the Iron Age; its earliest probable inhabitants were the Saxons, who resided close by the Bide Brook, which flows through the middle of the village. It is from here that the area gets its name; the Saxons called the Bide Brook 'lacuc', meaning little stream.

Meriting a mention in the *Domesday Book* as belonging to Edward of Salisbury, the son of one of William the Conqueror's knights, early Lacock was bounded on its south side by Melksham Forest, part of the collection of royal hunting forests scattered throughout the country. In Church Street – one of four streets that form the square of the village – there is a restaurant/tea room/guesthouse called King John's Hunting Lodge, which its owner will inform you was once a resting place for the king after his frequent hunting trips.

A local historian, however, shudders at what he perceives to be a usage of the name of a royal figure to 'sell' the business. 'I rather doubt it,' he says, moving swiftly along past The Carpenter's Arms pub, a sixteenth-century free house whose claims to authenticity appear more rooted in truth and documented history.

And therein lies both the appeal and the conundrum of Lacock: the vast majority of buildings on its four streets – Church, East, High and West – have been owned by the National Trust since 1944, when the Talbot family bequeathed it. Yet, despite its museum-like first impression, Lacock is still a living, breathing entity.

Unlike some other National Trust properties, the village is not a still life painting. Neither are its villagers petrified nor its buildings smothered in aspic.

'It's got a lot more life in it than other National Trust villages, particularly in southern England,' says the National Trust's Graham Heard, property manager for Lacock. The reason for this, according to Heard (and it's clearly the reason that lies behind the special nature of the village), is that the National Trust has integrated the policy of letting houses only to locals – people who have close relatives in the area or in the village, people who were born or raised in Lacock, or who have gone to its school, which is one of Lacock's few privately owned buildings.

It is a policy that has strengthened the community spirit in Lacock and provided a virtually unbreakable social chain from one generation to another. The majority of the pretty villages in southern England, explains Heard, tend to be very expensive places to live. This can make them quite difficult to remain in, particularly if you happen to be from the locality. Therefore, new people frequently move in and the community spirit is regularly disrupted. This is not necessarily a bad thing in cities, where the flow has to remain constant in order for it to engender the type of buzz that mass populations thrive on (and indeed, that provides a city's potentially nullifying lack of personal contact). For a small, localised community, however, continual streams of 'blow-ins' break through the social fabric.

But is the presence of the National Trust valued? Rental fees are not up for discussion, but the impression one receives from the tenant villagers is that they have no reason to complain on this front. Some people, says Heard, have 'a bit of a grumble' about it. In general, however, the tenants seem pleased that their houses and properties are looked after.

The National Trust employs a strict method of repairing and decorating the exteriors of the properties on the four Lacock streets (the tenants look after the interiors). Essentially, it's a Forth Road Bridge operation – the National Trust works on one street per year and when it completes the fourth street it starts all over again.

'Decorating essentially means we do all the pre-painting repairs that people need,' says Heard, 'so if you have a rotting window frame we replace it before we paint it. We do all the exterior decoration, as well as plumbing, wiring, structure and roof areas, too.' Business leases operate slightly differently, as they have more liabilities, public and otherwise, and as such might require structural, decorative or utilitarian areas to be looked at straight away.

There is no such thing as a yellow line on the road in Lacock, and if you look at the rooftops and the frontages of the centre houses you might notice something very unusual: there are no television aerials.

This is another example of the National Trust's benign presence, a decision on its part to install a communal cable TV system (via an aerial situated

*St Cyriac's Church in Wiltshire. Photograph: britainview.com*

out of sight on a hill half a mile outside the centre) in order to present the village in a better light. How does it deal with the regular influx of visitors? For there is no doubt it is something of a tourist magnet. Aside from the central village area, Lacock also boasts the thirteenth-century Lacock Abbey, a fifteenth-century church and the Fox Talbot Museum, a memorial to the achievements of William Henry Fox Talbot, the inventor of the negative-positive photographic process.

There are few cars in the village centre, and the only ones to be seen are those owned by residents. Visitors and their vehicles used to be something of a problem, but from the early 1990s the National Trust, in association with the local county council, created a mini bypass around the village outskirts that directed visitor traffic into a free out-of-village car park (there's also free parking for less able-bodied visitors in a more central car park). Visitors can also locate orientation plans

and leaflets in the parks, which detail where shops and other places of interest are. It's quite apparent that at all times the National Trust as a landlord tries to strike the right balance between respecting the privacy of residents and the requirements of visitors.

So what makes Lacock tick? It's incorrectly perceived as something of a museum piece, a Sunday afternoon spot for the silver-haired twinset-and-pearl-necklace brigade. Its beauty, however, is derived from its sense of timelessness and its engagement with life as it is lived.

'It's a very lively place, with a lot of community spirit about it,' says Graham Heard. 'If you look at the village hall there's something on every night. You've got families growing up here, a community that talks to each other. You've got the added impact and benefit of tourism, without which there wouldn't be the pubs and businesses, or indeed, a business infrastructure.'

*Michelle Collins, age 5, from Castleknock in Co. Dublin looking at a Morpho Peleides butterfly native to Costa Rica during her visit to the Dublin Butterfly House and Insect World at Magillstown in Swords. Photograph: Brenda Fitzsimons.*

This infrastructure also includes a democratic acceptance of the village being used for movies (some of the *Harry Potter* series, *Emma*) and television (*Pride and Prejudice*, *Moll Flanders*, *The Mayor of Casterbridge*). The financial revenue from this localised business is equally shared between the National Trust and Lacock parish council, while individual tenants also get paid disturbance money.

'You've a lively mix of good, interactive community,' says Heard, 'and during the day you've got visitors that sustain the local businesses, which give opportunities for many people. Lacock has maintained quite a lot of facilities that villages of its size have lost over the past 20 to 30 years because they don't have people living there or have tourists coming in, keeping it going.'

Which is essentially what the National Trust wants to continue doing – protecting and oversee-ing the balance between Lacock as a place where people live and work and to preserve the village for the benefit of those who want to take a look around it. If you haven't been there, you're missing something very special indeed.

**SATURDAY, 28 AUGUST 2004**

# O'Connor Jumps to Gold

*Grania Willis, in Athens*

It looked as though Team Ireland would draw a complete blank at Athens 2004, but Cian O'Connor came out and took individual gold in the show jumping final last night.

Ireland's first Olympic medal of the 28th Olympiad and, not only the first ever Olympic equestrian medal, but the best colour of all.

'It's unbelievable,' a delirious O'Connor said as his closest rivals jumped off for the silver. 'The horse was class, but it was a real team effort from the whole Irish camp.'

Lying equal fourth after the first round, the 24-year-old was first to go of six on four faults. But he rode into the tension-filled arena and coolly asked one of the fence stewards to check the back rail on the first part of the double of water ditches before he started. As he cantered round towards the first, the British announcer stated that O'Connor was 23. By the time he'd jumped a magnificent clear, the announcer was claiming O'Connor was 25, but his supporters had aged far more than two years in the intervening 67 seconds.

Former world champion Rodrigo Pessoa had already gone clear, but his eight faults from the first round meant he couldn't overtake O'Connor. But there were plenty more waiting in the wings to try to do exactly that, including Ireland's Jessica Kurten, whose first round clear had left her level pegging at the head of the field with British hope Nick Skelton.

But one by one the opposition fell by the way-side, victims to Olaf Petersen's massive track. American Chris Kappler came off best, adding just four to tie on an eight-fault total with Pessoa, but O'Connor was still just out of the medal zone.

New Zealand's Daniel Meech, whose first round clear had just gone over the time by .22 of a second for a single time fault, was third last to jump but his medal hopes crashed and burned as Diagonal lowered three fences. Meech's misfortune was O'Connor's good fortune, however, as he moved up into the bronze, but there was still more drama to be played out and, most devastating of all, it was Kurten that the gods decided would be their next plaything.

Her superb first round clear had given Irish supporters their first sniff of a medal at these Olympics and, if luck held, it would be gold. But it wasn't to be Kurten's turn. Castle Forbes Maike, the mare bought by Lady Georgina Forbes before Christmas with the Olympics as her goal, flattened all three parts of the combination to boost O'Connor up into silver.

Two more rails hit the dirt before Kurten and Maike crossed the finish line and a distraught Kurten plummeted way out of the medals. 'It's a long way from finished,' the Co. Antrim born rider had said after her first-round clear, 'and we could still end up in 20th.' Ironically, 20th was exactly where she wound up at the close of play.

So only Skelton could deny O'Connor the greatest moment in Irish equestrianism since Dermott Lennon won individual gold at the world equestrian games in 2002. Riding in his fourth Olympics, Skelton had returned from a life-threatening injury to fight for his place on the Athens start list.

*Cian O'Connor on Waterford Crystal punches the air in celebration after they jumped the clear round that won them a Gold Medal at the Olympic Games in Athens. Photograph: Reinhard Krause/Reuters.*

Skelton broke his neck in September 2000 and watched the opening ceremony of the Sydney Games from his hospital bed. Originally told that another fall would probably be fatal, Skelton was given the all-clear to ride again in January 2002 and set his sights on gold in Athens. But the fates didn't favour the Briton either. When the big triple bar went down, O'Connor was going to have to jump-off for gold, but two more rails fell and the gold had gone to O'Connor and Ireland.

The Meath-based rider, whose grandfather Karl Mullen was on the Ireland Grand Slam winning rugby team of 1948, didn't even know he'd won, however. 'I thought I might win a bronze,' he said, 'so I stayed and watched all the four-faulters, then I went back up to get on the horse in case the other two had a fence down and I had to jump-off. I heard a steward shouting that there would be a jump-off for the silver and that's the first time I knew that I'd won.'

O'Connor's championship record had been mixed until yesterday, even though he has had great success on the Nations Cup circuit. A fall in the world games in Jerez two years ago robbed him of a chance at the medals, but he was part of the squad at last year's Europeans in Germany, where the Irish failed in the defence of their crown but a fifth-place finish guaranteed Ireland a team place in Athens.

But even his Olympic campaign didn't go according to plan at first. Clear the first day with a single time fault, Waterford Crystal then racked up an uncharacteristic 12 and eight in the Nations Cup. O'Connor was at a loss to explain the horse's dramatic loss of form. 'He had five down in the Nations Cup and he hasn't had five down all year,' O'Connor said yesterday.

The horse was examined by team vet Marcus Swail and found to be suffering from muscle soreness on the left side of his neck, but chiropractic treatment and massage sorted out the problem. 'It was like chalk and cheese today, he was a completely different horse,' O'Connor said.

'It was a real team effort,' he said last night,

giving credit to team trainer Eddie Macken, his personal trainer Gerry Mullins and vet Marcus Swail for his work on the horse. 'I told him if he jumped a clear he'd win a medal,' Macken said afterwards. 'It was worth all the fighting,' he said, referring to the controversy surrounding his own appointment as team trainer, subsequent sacking and eventual reinstatement.

It was a truly golden performance and O'Connor wasn't the only Irish person with a lump in his throat as 'The Soldier's Song' rang out across the arena while the Tricolour was raised on the flagpole for the first time in the Athens Games and for the first time at an Olympic equestrian venue.

---

**SATURDAY, 4 SEPTEMBER 2004**

# School Siege Ends in Bloody Chaos

*Dan McLaughlin*

More than 200 people died and more than 600 were injured yesterday when Russian troops stormed a besieged school after suspected Chechen rebels exploded bombs and began shooting hostages.

The tense, two-day standoff in the republic of North Ossetia erupted into bloody chaos, when militants detonated explosives as they fled and battled soldiers and gun-wielding locals intent on avenging the capture and the killing of dozens of children.

Distraught parents followed special forces troops on to the school campus, after huge blasts and heavy machine gun fire erupted inside the building. Many returned at a run with burnt and bloodied children in their arms, while other shocked pupils dashed semi-naked from the smouldering building.

*A volunteer carries a small child to safety after Russian special forces stormed Beslan school in North Ossetia where armed Chechen hostage takers were holding children, teachers and some parents — believed at the time to be some 300 but transpiring to number around 1,500. Photograph: S. Dal/Reuters.*

'It was stiflingly hot in there, and they kept us packed in the middle of the sports hall, with bombs all around us,' said one young girl, who was among as many as 1,200 children, parents and teachers taken hostage on Wednesday, the first day of term. 'They wouldn't even let us open the windows. We nearly suffocated,' she told Russian television, as dozens of unconscious children were carried past her on stretchers. More than 200 children were recovering in hospital last night, many with serious injuries.

A young boy said the gunmen — who had threatened to shoot 50 children for every one of their number killed — told the hostages to drink their own urine, after rejecting repeated offers of food and water from negotiators.

Another young pupil said at least one woman had blown herself up in the school, as up to 30 militants fired on approaching soldiers and tried to escape a building that they had booby-trapped in fear of attack by hundreds of troops gathered outside its grounds.

'The number of those killed in the terrorist act in Beslan could be far more than 150,' said Mr Aslambek Aslakhanov, an adviser to President Vladimir Putin. Mr Aslakhanov was reported to be on his way to the school for talks before the siege ended in carnage.

Witnesses said the roof of the sports hall was destroyed by a series of explosions, and its collapse probably killed dozens of the hostages. The bodies of at least 100 people were seen lying in the ruins.

'I want to underline that we did not plan any military actions. We were planning to continue negotiations to secure the release of the hostages,' said Mr Valery Andreyev, the head of security services in the North Ossetia region.

'At about 1 p.m. two large explosions occurred, and some of the hostages started running out of the school. They opened fire on the fleeing children and adults, and to save the lives of the hostages we returned fire on the bandits.

'Civilians with guns also opened fire, preventing the effective operation of the special forces. They did everything possible to save the lives of the hostages, and thanks to them many were indeed saved,' Mr Andreyev said.

Officials said the explosions were probably caused by homemade bombs accidentally falling from the ceiling of the sports hall.

Initial reports suggested the security forces had blown a hole in the wall of the school to allow hostages to escape, using as cover a bus that approached the building to collect the bodies of some of the 16 people killed when the siege began.

The gunmen had demanded an end to war in Chechnya and the withdrawal of Russian troops, and the release from jail of several comrades in neighbouring Ingushetia, where they killed dozens of soldiers and policemen in an audacious raid in June.

President Putin had vowed to use force only as a last resort, against rebels he says are funded by al-Qaeda. Officials claimed that nine or 10 of the militants killed were Arabs and were led by a close ally of the warlord Shamil Basayev, Russia's most wanted man.

Security forces said three militants had been captured alive, and that a further four were still on the run last night. Several of them were thought to have escaped the school wearing civilian clothes and tried to slip away as chaos engulfed it.

Russian television showed a gang of men surrounding one suspected guerrilla and beating him to the ground, where he appeared to lie unconscious as soldiers fired into the air above him to disperse the furious mob.

World leaders expressed their horror at the siege and its conclusion, which sent shock waves through Russia after a week in which Chechen rebels were also blamed for blowing up two airliners and dispatching a female suicide bomber to Moscow. At least 100 people died in those attacks.

'This is yet another grim reminder of the lengths to which terrorists will go to threaten the civilised world,' said US President George Bush.

**TUESDAY, 7 SEPTEMBER 2004**

# On One Desk a Child's Pink Shoe is Placed With a Book, a Pen and a Rose Laid on Top

*Chris Stephen, in Beslan*

Different things bring out tears for visitors to the battered blackened ruin that is Beslan High School No 1.

For some it is a sight of all those pairs of shoes, too small and too pretty for adults, lined up amid broken glass on window sills of the gym. For others it is the sight of the neat stack of little wooden chairs outside the front door, ready and waiting for the new intake of pupils who will now never need them.

Others break down in tears at the sight of the bouquets of flowers which make a bright counterpoint to the blackened rain-soaked floor of the gym. The gym where so many hundreds died is much smaller than it looks on TV, barely large enough for the basketball court whose bent metal hoops stand at either end. Hanging from them are the torn wires that held the mines that were strung across the gym, one of which reportedly went off by accident, triggering the carnage.

This is where reality leaves you.

It is impossible to imagine sane men cramming so many children into this hall, then stringing mines about their heads, primed to explode. You see it, you stand amid the burned clothing and rubble and pieces of white bone and you know it happened here.

But you still cannot believe it.

Nor can the people of Beslan. They come, singly or more often in groups, their dark clothing blending in with the smoke-blackened walls, to wander through the building.

The women cry and the men look solemn and few words are spoken. The disturbing thing is that this school, so smashed and broken, is also immediately recognisable with a layout that we all recognise.

There are the familiar corridors with windows now smashed on one side and classrooms with blackboards and teachers' desks on the other. Doubtless these corridors saw children lingering, perhaps sent out of class as a punishment, perhaps surreptitiously sneaking a few puffs on a cigarette as secondary school children do around the world.

The floor underfoot is thick with rubble and dust now churned into a muddy paste by the rain

*Fedosya Beroyeva, grandmother of 10-year-old twins Soslan, right, and Aslan, killed in the Beslan school hostage tragedy, cries holding their portraits as their mother Zalina, left, looks at Aslan's body during the twins' funeral. Photograph: Sergey Ponomarev/AP.*

*A mother caresses the forehead of her child, killed in the aftermath of the Beslan school siege and laid out in a row of other dead children. Over 320 people died in the tragedy. Photograph: Sergey Ponomarev/AP.*

water pouring through the great holes in the roof. In the classrooms desks, chairs and great piles of books sit where the hostage takers put them, barricading the windows. The floors of some classrooms are inexplicably covered in hundreds of pages from children's exercise books.

Everywhere there is smashed and broken glass and here and there are holes in the blue wall paper from bullet and shrapnel strikes. Pretty children's drawings remain cellotaped to the walls and on a desk is a child's replica of a Kalashnikov machine gun.

And in each classroom and in many other parts of the school little impromptu shrines have begun to appear. On one desk a child's pink sports shoe is placed with a pair of glasses, a book, and a pen with a red rose laid on top. By the school entrance someone has placed a football next to an unopened bottle of champagne, presumably to commemorate a graduation that there will never be. The smell of burning lingers in the corridors, mixed with the stench of excrement.

The school theatre is a jarring mix of the normal and the bizarre. A neat red curtain hangs by the stage where the head teacher had been due to address the children and welcome the new boys and girls for the first day of their school year. But the theatre's wooden floor is smashed, with splintered wooden planks showing where it took direct hits from rocket-propelled grenades. Two Russian soldiers died here fighting a group of rebels making a desperate last stand. The soldiers and police have gone and the school building is left open to anyone wanting to visit it.

Around the school the whole town seems to be crying. The families of the dead children hold wakes called *parmita* in the hours before a body is taken away for burial. But most people know many of the dead which means that the hundreds of *parmita*s have to be co-ordinated so that waves of mourners can move from one to the next. The strain of this is enormous. 'I have been to four *parmita*s today,' said Fatima, landlady of the room where I am staying. 'My eyes are hurting from all the tears.'

The sound of wailing is everywhere. You meet it first at the small rundown airport, a 20-minute drive from town. As the daily flight from Moscow disgorges groups of relatives who are met by mourners on the tarmac, you hear the wailing coming from apartments and houses in the streets. As I write this the sound of crying comes from an apartment building across the street where three families have each lost children. The streets of this little town are full of groups of mourners criss-crossing each other.

The concentrated misery is on the edge of town where a field has been set aside as a mass cemetery. A total of 170 people, mostly children, were buried yesterday in rows of freshly-dug graves. A group of sharp-suited officials, some local, some flown in from Moscow, stood with umbrellas watching the scene on a patch of grass. In front of them groups of mourners struggled across the broken muddy field trying not to drop the little coffins held on their shoulders. Groups of women followed each coffin, crying and holding each other up, with some losing their high heeled shoes in the thick mud.

When the last of yesterday's funerals finished the mourners trudged away through the pouring rain, resembling a defeated army. They helped each other into a fleet of tiny Lada cars which laboured away across the field and onto the main highway for the short drive back to town.

A group of unsmiling workmen then appeared, and pulled themselves into the cabs of three big yellow excavators. The engines were started with great belches of grey smoke and the machines got to work, excavating dozens of fresh graves for today's round of mass burials.

**6 SEPTEMBER 2004**

# Maimed Soldier Prepared to Go Back and Lose Other Leg

*Across America: Lara Marlowe*

Sgt Luke Wilson of the First Cavalry Division has not received his purple heart yet. The US army is organising a ceremony in the wounded soldier's home state of Oregon, and Wilson hopes the medal will be awarded by President Bush himself.

He'd be delighted if it won a few more votes for Bush. 'Any way I can help him I will. The Bush family have done so much for the military,' says Wilson.

Try to understand this: since Bush invaded Iraq, 1,013 US soldiers have been killed there, and another 6,987 wounded. Like Wilson, most of the wounded, heralded as 'warriors and heroes' on the banner welcoming them to the Walter Reed Army Medical Center in Washington, have lost limbs. And they love Bush. Perhaps they don't want to believe it was all for nothing. A steady diet of Fox News and distrust of Senator John Kerry only partly explain why they intend to vote for Bush in November.

When he was still in high school, Wilson's father, an Oregon state police officer, and his mother, a government employee, offered to buy him a truck and pay his way through college if he'd forget about the army.

'I'm very patriotic. I love jumping out of airplanes. I love going out on a mission, taking the weapons back to the barracks and going to the bars

*US army Sergeant Luke Wilson, who lost his left leg in Iraq and wishes he could return to fight, even if it meant losing his other leg. Photograph: Lara Marlowe.*

with the guys,' he explains now. His parents reluctantly gave permission for Wilson to join up at 17.

A medical doctor who disagrees with Bush and his Iraq war had agreed to take me into Walter Reed, so I could see for myself the human cost of the conflict. But he lost his nerve, fearing for his government job, and I had to talk my way through the security gate alone.

The doctor's timidity contrasted with the certainties proclaimed by Wilson, five months after he was maimed in Baghdad. I met the wheelchair-bound 24-year-old in the hospital canteen. No Public Affairs Officer was there to eavesdrop, but Wilson sounded like a recruitment advertisement.

Had he known he would lose his left leg in Iraq, Wilson said, he would still join. 'If the government would let me, I'd go back and lose my right leg,' he claims. 'If I can be there guarding my buddies' backs, I'm doing something worthwhile.' Is he angry about his lost leg? 'I'm a little pissed off I'm not over there still,' Wilson continues. 'I

joined the army looking for combat and I was taken out after two days.'

Wilson's 30-vehicle convoy was crossing a bridge from the Green Zone in Baghdad on the night of 8 April, the eve of the anniversary of the fall of the regime, when insurgents began firing rocket-propelled grenades from abandoned buildings on both sides of the road. He relishes recounting the sudden explosions; the sky lit up with tracer fire; return fire by his machine-gunner; a silhouette on the corner of a rooftop; a white flash.

Then 'everything went totally white and just hot.' Wilson had been leaning on his left knee to fire his M4 assault rifle. 'The RPG went through my calf and lodged in the other side of the vehicle,' he recounts. 'I knew there was something wrong when my knee moved all the way forward … it was just dangling. The RPG cauterised the wound, but the artery was pouring blood. My guys panicked; I had to tell them how to make a tourniquet.'

After his leg was amputated in Baghdad, Wilson was moved to the US base at Balad for transfer to Landstuhl, Germany, then Walter Reed. As he lay strapped to a stretcher, the morphine barely denting his pain, insurgents mortared the base all night. 'I was more pissed off than scared,' he says now. 'Three or four rounds would impact. They'd wait five minutes and start again. The nurses were crawling around on the floor.'

Wilson says his 'positive attitude' has made him popular with US authorities. He was guest of the chief-of-staff at the army ball, and has toured the White House three times during his rehabilitation. For him, losing a leg is less tragic than the end of life with his 'band of brothers'. He is resigned to building a house in Oregon with his fiancée Tonya and going to college. He will receive 60 per cent of his base salary of $2,310 per month for the rest of his life.

'I already got a prosthesis,' Wilson boasts. 'It's in my room charging right now. The leg itself costs anywhere from $50,000 to $100,000. It's got hydraulics in it and the computer works in two different modes, one for walking and one that swings, so I can ride a bike. I'm going to get a swimming leg and a running leg.'

When Kerry visited the hospital, a secret service agent asked Wilson if he'd like to shake his hand. 'I said, "I got nothing to say to that piece of shit." They had to get me out of there – fast. I mean this guy earns all these medals in Vietnam, which was honourable, and then he goes and throws them at the White House.' He accuses Kerry of voting against body armour for the military.

Bush supporters denounce 'liberal bias' in the media. Wilson calls CNN – hardly outraged critics of the Bush administration – 'the communist news network'.

Virginia Sanchez, whose son Michael is at Walter Reed after losing a leg in Iraq last month, told me: 'We got too many reporters in war zones. It gives too much information that should be kept secret, that's getting out to the terrorists.'

Wilson's world-view is shaped by Fox News and never quite meshes with reality: Arabs perpetrated the hostage siege in southern Russia last week, he tells me. There was a Hizbullah base in northern Iraq; the US found traces of nerve agents on Iraqi artillery shells; Bush did his utmost to solve the Israeli-Palestinian conflict by 'offering the road map'. Wilson believes that Arabs from the entire region, not just Iraq, are fighting US troops. 'I'm not sure why they feel the need to do it,' he shrugs.

The results of the insurgency were all around us in the canteen: a soldier propped the stub of his left leg on a shelf while he consumed a cheeseburger with his wife; a soldier with a swollen, disfigured face and a black eye-patch sat at another table.

Virginia Sanchez (62) and her daughter Ramona (27) had brought *People* magazine and a 'best of Mozart' CD for Michael, who is waiting to learn whether doctors will amputate his second leg. A demolitions expert, Michael was maimed by booby-trapped debris in Samarra.

Virginia is a cook in a home for foster children. Ramona runs a beauty salon. The women feel no

bitterness towards the US administration, but are shocked by the 'ingratitude' of Iraqis. They don't understand why Iraqis do not want US troops in their country. 'If I was one of the people that wanted freedom, I'd want us there,' says Virginia.

There is just a hint of confusion. Ramona felt angry towards anti-war protesters in 2003. 'At first we were so supportive,' she says. 'I don't know anymore. There's so much we can't know, that the military won't tell us.'

If the Sanchez family are a barometer, John Kerry doesn't stand a chance in November. Virginia voted for Bill Clinton and Al Gore in the last two elections. This time she's voting for Bush. Ramona did not vote in 2000. She doesn't trust Kerry. 'I think he's just saying things to get people to vote for him,' she says. 'He's not really for the people.' On the other hand, Bush 'stands for his beliefs,' Ramona says. 'He's very Christian and that's important to me.'

**TUESDAY, 7 SEPTEMBER 2004**

# FF Looks to Spiritual Therapy to Relieve Stress and Strain

*Frank McNally, in Inchydoney*

They have a treatment for every condition at Inchydoney Lodge and Spa, and political conditions are no exception.

There's the 'Marine Body Scrub' to remove dead skin cells and impurities, for example: perfect for a Taoiseach preparing a Cabinet purge.

And there's 'deep-tissue massage' (buttocks included): tailor-made to relieve the tension that builds up when you have a marginal seat – in the Dáil or at the Cabinet table.

But when Fianna Fáil TDs and senators arrived for two days of therapy yesterday, it was a spiritual session they all booked in for, delivered by master conscience manipulator Father Seán Healy.

*President Mary McAleese at Áras an Uachtaráin announcing she was nominating herself for a second seven-year term in office. Photograph: Alan Betson.*

Father Healy's massage technique is controversial in Government circles – he has sometimes rubbed the PDs up the wrong way. Yet his approach of inflicting short-term pain in the interests of long-term growth found willing victims here in Fianna Fáil.

The pain was not so short-term either. Scheduled to speak for an hour on his vision of a fairer society, the CORI man came in at 30 minutes over the Government estimate. But when the Fianna Fáilers emerged from the session, they had an inner glow, and not just because Father Healy had finally stopped talking.

It was his audience's many questions that took up the time, the speaker said, and there had been 'a lot of resonance' for his message.

Not everybody heard the message, however. His theme of social exclusion was dramatically highlighted by – among others – the Minister for Defence, who opted out of most of the session, in favour of a quiet drink with friends.

The media were excluded too.

But afterwards the happy face of the Government Chief Whip, Mary Hanafin, welcomed us to the press conference. 'Thank you for joining us in this beautiful place,' she said, leaving us to wonder if she meant Inchydoney Island, or the spiritual place that Fianna Fáil was in after a session with Father Healy.

The island was certainly beautiful in yesterday's balmy conditions. A Gulf-Stream-warmed sea tempted Mary O'Rourke and Dermot Ahern in for a swim. The Taoiseach strolled on the beach with a barefoot Ms Hanafin.

Even the anti-Government picket was more like a gentle exfoliation session: a few protesters held placards saying 'Hands off Clonakilty Post Office', but – this being west Cork – they were too polite to chant anything.

The only negativity in the area was caused by the spa's 'Brumisation' therapy ('deep-breathing seawater mist for increasing your negative ions'). Not that there was much time for that. After the CORI talk, TDs and senators broke up into workshops around the hotel. They discussed 'Disaffected Youth' in the solarium; childcare ('The Early Years') in the residents' lounge; and so on. Despite the many distractions, there was the appearance of a party at work.

But then the whole point of the therapy is to avoid a repeat of the treatment received in the June elections, when the party received a kick in the deep-tissue massage area from which it is still recovering.

# Treat Yourself

### Single File: Priscilla Robinson

Tracey Emin, the English artist, once said you could get a good nanny for €600 a week, which sounds like great value until you remember that you need one for the baby as well.

She has a point. I often wonder at people with children, because I know how hard it is to look after myself, let alone anyone else.

Self-care is laborious. There are so many things you have to do just to stay acceptable. Such as remembering to buy food. Food and living on your own don't seem to go together. Not in the sense of abundance. I did once have three loaves of bread on the go, but two were on the verge of

*The Labour Party TD Michael D. Higgins after party colleagues in the Dáil and Seanad decided not to nominate him to oppose Mrs McAleese. Photograph: Eric Luke.*

going mouldy and the other was hard.

When you live alone nobody will come in, slam the fridge door and say: 'There's no food.' Well, nobody except me. But then I have to respond as well. I have to promise to go shopping for one. Sometimes I find seemingly simple tasks such as this one almost impossible.

Procrastination is a vital weapon in the fight against shopping. I muddle over a list. In the end it usually reads 'food', but sometimes the list is more specific and says 'food and a treat'.

I muddle over my shopping destination. I live in the city centre and don't drive, so I remind myself that Superquinn and Lidl are out of reach. On special shopping days I take myself to Marks & Spencer. I give myself a break from Tesco, Dunnes Stores and Spar.

But I am scared of Marks & Spencer. As I go down the escalator I can hear the voice of my inner mother shouting. 'Should you really be shopping here when you only have €10 in your purse?' it says. 'What are you going to do if rich people stand behind you at the checkout and pile up the lovely food you can't afford?'

I have worked it out. There should be a bouncer at the bottom of the escalator, a very polite and gentle Marks & Spencer bouncer, saying: 'Come along now, open your purse. Madam, can you tell me what you are hoping to buy here with that amount?' 'I know,' I'd reply. 'If you like I won't take a basket. I'll just fridge-window shop.'

Eventually, I would sigh and almost smile, and he would beckon to a minder, who would then escort me back onto the street. The minder would shake my hand and wave me kindly on my way.

Or at least they should have a sign: 'Enter at your peril ye broke, bad budgeters and ye non-credit-card-owning minority. Ye will see much that ye would dearly like to buy, and little ye will be able to, excepting perchance some tasteless low-fat wonder foods and some Percy Pigs. For ye will be living beyond your means.'

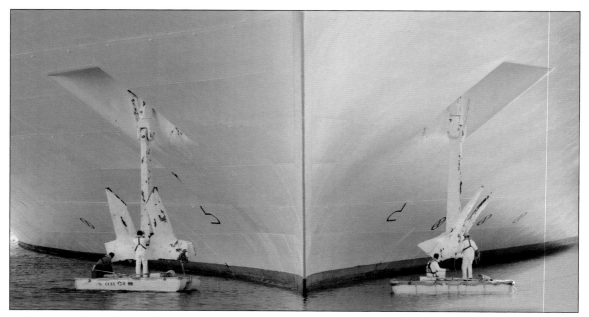

*Sailors paint the anchors of the* **Grand Princess**, *a P&O cruise liner, the largest ship in terms of tonnage (108,806 tons) to enter Dublin Port. The vessel can carry 3,000 passengers and has a crew of over 1,000. Photograph: Alan Betson.*

The pain of being broke comes home just too clearly in Marks & Spencer. I don't think they get a lot of shoplifters in there: people just break down and run out, screaming at the wonder of it all.

My not coping seems to rub off on others in Marks & Spencer. I ask a tall, thin, depressed-looking assistant three questions, but he can answer none of them. I break his spirit. I shout at the hearing-impaired woman on the till. Her badge says she is hearing impaired, but the print is very small, and today I seem to be paying-attention impaired.

Why doesn't it just say 'PLEASE SPEAK CLEARLY, DO NOT SHOUT' in capital letters? We are tired, us shoppers. We are living beyond our means in every sense.

I was thinking they should have a basket of badges up at each till, to help you communicate with your seller. I would choose one that says 'Kindly redirect to cheaper shop' or, maybe, 'Life impaired'.

Sometimes in Marks & Spencer I walk around stunned. It uses up shopping time. Sometimes I choose nothing. I queue up anyway. I thank them for their time.

There is so much beauty here.

**FRIDAY, 10 SEPTEMBER 2004**

# Delving Into the Havoc of the Past

*Deaglán de Bréadún*

Outspoken but softly spoken, that's Ronan Bennett. His life is conducted at full volume: he's a man who welcomes controversy and likes to tackle issues head on. Although I met him briefly eight years ago, it is still a surprise that he speaks so quietly and insistently, more the chatty priest in the confessional than the platform speaker declaiming at a political rally.

Now in his late 40s, Bennett has been to places few of us will ever get to and learned things most

would not want to find out. In 1974, aged 18, he was wrongfully convicted and sentenced to life for taking part in an IRA operation that led to the murder of an RUC officer. That was quashed, and he was released after a year in jail. But three years later he was arrested in England under the Prevention of Terrorism Act, held for a month, then released and arrested again a year later. His trial for conspiracy, to commit crimes unknown against persons unknown in places unknown, developed into a cause célèbre. A jury acquitted him on all counts.

His reputation vindicated and liberty restored, he dropped out of the headlines to pursue a course in history at King's College London, leading to a doctorate called Enforcing the Law in Revolutionary England: Yorkshire, 1640-1660.

He came back into the spotlight as a novelist and screenwriter. *The Second Prison* (1991) was a psychological study of a man released from jail in Northern Ireland who cannot get the experience out of his head and tries to discover the truth about the circumstances that led to his sentence for murder. The next book, a political thriller called *Overthrown By Strangers*, was set in South America. In 1998 Bennett moved into the heavyweight division with *The Catastrophist*, a love story set in the chaos and bloodshed of Congo in the early 1960s, which was shortlisted for the prestigious Whitbread Novel Award.

Now his latest novel, *Havoc, In Its Third Year*, has been longlisted for the Man Booker Prize, one of two books by Irish authors (the other is Colm Tóibín's *The Master*, a highly praised reconstruction of the life of the American writer Henry James). Bennett is amused that, in a 22-book longlist, someone rated his chances at 25 to 1. At those odds it's a bet worth having.

*Havoc, In Its Third Year* is set in an unnamed town in northern England in the 1630s, when puritanism was on the rise and any sign of human weakness was liable to be severely punished. The central character and reluctant hero is John Brigge, coroner and one of the governors of the town, as well as a closet Catholic at a time when 'popery' could be a pathway to the gallows.

Although it is neither academic nor studious, Bennett draws heavily from his research on the period. It took him five years to write, and he says he was forever having to lay aside some highly enjoyable historical study to get back to the demanding business of fiction.

Although the locale is in England, the fierce passions and atmosphere of virulently opinionated intolerance are reminiscent of Northern Ireland in the grip of the Troubles, specifically Portadown at the height of the Drumcree fever.

Bennett responds that different readers will draw their own parallels. He was inspired by the intolerance of what he calls the Bush-Blair project, as well as Tony Blair's own crusade against crime, in partnership with the British home secretary, David Blunkett. It's his first and probably last historical novel, but he finds it illuminating to explore the present through the past. The nearest place to the fictional town of the novel is Halifax, although there are some important divergences.

Brigge, a flawed and ambivalent character worthy of Graham Greene, is both a harsh and stern administrator of the law and a tender and loving husband and father. Bennett sees no contradiction. Brigge's position was not for the squeamish, but that was the temper of the times.

Bennett points out that, even in more recent days in Northern Ireland, well-known figures have been capable of bitter and unyielding sternness towards their political or religious opponents and loving kindness to their dear ones. He argues that to have portrayed Brigge as a card-carrying liberal or a twenty-first-century humanist would have been anachronistic.

Much of the action takes place in a legal or court setting. Bennett says he studied the period through its court records and concedes that his approach in the novel may have been influenced by his own experiences of the judicial system.

Although *Havoc, In Its Third Year* is primarily a novel, it also contains an implicit message. The puritan reformers try to build the godly city on the hill, but their authoritarian approach of sanctions and punishment doesn't work, can't be sustained, and the havoc of the title is the result. 'The world needs more compassion,' says Bennett.

He initially wrote the narrative in full-blooded seventeenth-century prose, but this didn't work; he shifted down a gear, so the novel still gives a flavour of the discourse of the period without becoming too specialised and confusing. There are some fascinating usages from the time – 'intellectuals' is used with its former meaning of 'faculties', as in 'His intellectuals became unclear and imperfect' – but he has also borrowed rhetorical touches from US President George W. Bush, who sees himself as leading 'a monumental struggle of good versus evil'.

Ronan Bennett was born in Oxford, in January 1956, but he grew up in Belfast, and his life has been shaped by the Northern Ireland conflict. When is he likely to tackle the subject again in fiction? He prefers to approach it obliquely, he says, but isn't shying away from it. 'I would never not write something because I feared there would be an adverse reaction.'

He expected adverse reaction to another literary endeavour, the screenplay he wrote with Alice Perman for *The Hamburg Cell*, a docu-drama about the September 11th hijackers recently shown by Channel 4. As part of his research, Bennett went to Hamburg to meet former acquaintances of some of the hijackers. He observed the places where they lived and the mosque they used for worship. He also studied the Koran, as well as the culture and politics of the Islamic world.

He feels it is not enough simply to disapprove of and condemn the 9/11 terrorist hijackings: to dismiss the perpetrators in blunt terms as evildoers and fanatics is counterproductive and an oversimplification. Ziad Jarrah, who piloted one of the planes, was by all accounts a fairly hedonistic and well-to-do Lebanese who had received a Catholic

*Ronan Bennett. Photograph: Dara Mac Dónaill.*

education but then got caught up in radical Muslim politics. Dreadful as it may seem to many, people who knew him had to admit they couldn't help liking the guy.

So how does this square with the terrible deeds of 9/11 where we have Jarrah, for example, steering an aircraft loaded with innocent people towards the White House? Bennett attributes this to the perception among young Muslims that their co-religionists have been subjected to a 'holocaust' in places such as Chechnya, Bosnia, the Palestinian territories, Kashmir, Indonesia and Iraq. The would-be hijackers used to sit around in Hamburg watching graphic videos of the cruelties being visited upon their Muslim brothers in Chechnya.

He says there was pre-production difficulty when the celebrated US channel Home Box Office (HBO) withdrew its support for the movie.

Bennett was in Los Angeles at the time and went to see the HBO people. They told him, 'We like the script and the director and so on, but the American public is not ready for this film. It shows Jarrah, for example, to be a likeable person.' He recalls that noted Irish writers used to portray republicans as lacking any human dimension.

Bennett is a strong supporter of the peace process and a great admirer of Sinn Féin leaders such as Gerry Adams and Martin McGuinness. But he expresses himself 'kind of disappointed' with David Trimble whom he accuses of failing to grasp the opportunities presented by the Belfast Agreement. 'The history of the last six years or so could have been very different if Trimble had been a bit braver.'

But he admits with a wry smile that Trimble and himself have 'a bit of a history'. When Bennett was commissioned to write *Rebel Heart*, a drama series about the War of Independence, Trimble, who was First Minister at the time, protested in a letter to the BBC that Bennett was 'a most unsuitable person' to write such a screenplay. Despite the setbacks to the peace process, Bennett believes there is no likelihood of a return to conflict. 'The war is over,' he says. 'It's been over for a long time, I think it was over before the ceasefire really.' He believes the republican leadership has handled its 'unruly membership' extremely well despite the political stalemate.

He does not know to what extent his early experiences with the legal system 25 or 30 years ago have an influence over his work, because they are so deeply embedded in his psyche at this stage. But one cannot avoid the feeling that, without them, Ronan Bennett's writing would have nothing like the force and meaning that has helped establish him on the literary scene.

His next novel will be about privacy and will draw to some extent on his own experiences of building a successful career as a writer despite attempts to highlight his political views and his travails in the courts by elements in the media who prefer their republicans to be either apostates or informers.

The key question in his next book will be, 'When are people allowed to let go of their past?' The corollary of that is, when does your past let go of you? This is the tension that has made Ronan Bennett the writer he is today.

**THURSDAY, 16 SEPTEMBER 2004**

# New Orleans Prepared for Worst of Ivan

*John Moran, in New Orleans*

On Decatur Street, the Corner Oyster bar and grill was also defiant in the face of Hurricane Ivan and had greatly reduced its prices.

The popular 'Hurricane' rum cocktail was going for just $2.25. A sign on its shuttering read: 'We don't run from hurricanes, we drink them.' Further on up the street, one of New Orleans's best known landmarks, the Café du Monde, was closed for business and its famous coffee and beignets were not to be had.

Bourbon Street is the epicentre of the French Quarter. It is normally heaving with hedonists, even more so than Temple Bar on a Saturday night. Revellers move up and down the street hopping from bar to bar from each of which live bands play jazz, blues and rock that blares out onto the street. From balconies on each side, party animals usually dare those below to flash some flesh, and those who do are rewarded with a shiny beaded necklace. Then there are the sex clubs, one of which advertises topless and bottomless performances, but even here the greeter outside was becoming lonely.

Further up Bourbon, a glum hotdog vendor gave me his hurricane forecast: 'I'm not worried. There'll be a lot of weather, but we shouldn't blood too much.'

In Tony Moran's Old Absynthe House — whose list of famous past customers include Oscar Wilde and Lafcadio Hearn — waitress Lisa bemoaned the departure of 10,000 visitors who had cut short their convention.

'And the convention was about safety,' she exclaimed. 'But you know, there's worse to come, there's another one coming behind Ivan.' At the end of the bar an old-timer chuckled, 'It's the end of the world.'

Some businessmen who continued working questioned the way the hurricane threat was handled. 'They're running around like chickens with their heads cut off,' said computer shop owner Michael Anderson. 'And the weathermen have this one big chance to hog the limelight. They're hyping the whole thing up.'

Lined up in front of the cathedral on Jackson Square, a dozen or so tarot card readers and

*Cork senior hurlers Jerry O'Connor (left) holding his daughter Katie and the Liam McCarthy Cup, with his brother Ben after Cork beat Kilkenny 0–17 to 0–9 to win the All Ireland Hurling Final 2004. Photograph: Morgan Treacy/INPHO.*

clairvoyants had so few customers they were accepting small donations for their insights. One called Michael was revealing my inner self to me when one of his colleagues dropped her bag loudly behind him and walked off. 'She's my girl-friend,' he said looking warily up at the sky, 'and she's very good on weather – so I think we better go now.'

Overall most people seem to take the view that it's best to prepare for the worst and hope for the best. But there's also a dark side. The shuttering isn't just to keep Ivan from wrecking businesses – it's also to prevent looting. There's a visible police presence around the city, keeping an eye on abandoned houses and businesses.

With the hurricane's 'cone of uncertainty' still moving erratically about, nobody can say for sure how hard it will hit when it makes landfall.

Meanwhile back in the Corner Oyster bar and grill at noon yesterday, shortly before the curfew, a handful of tourists engage in graveyard humour at the bar. Everyone is drinking Hurricane cocktails, and the bar owner, Brad Darr, is under some pressure. 'There's a goddam hurricane on its way and you want a coffee – aw c'mon now, honey.'

Brad then turns off the music and announces: 'If you're here after two o'clock, you're gonna have to stay overnight.'

Now that sounds like a plan, whatever way the wind blows.

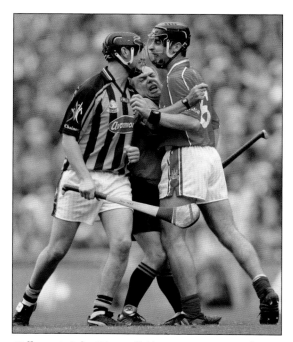

*Kilkenny's John Hoyne (left) squares up to Cork's Ronan Curran (right) as referee Aodán Mac Suibhne does his best to keep them apart. Photograph: Alan Betson.*

**MONDAY, 20 SEPTEMBER 2004**

# Monty Puts Final Nail in US Coffin

## *Philip Reid, at Oakland Hills*

In sport or in life, the Americans don't like to lose. Quite simply, they don't like to be second best to anybody. Yesterday, they had no choice as, in the 35th edition of the Ryder Cup at Oakland Hills Country Club, Europe retained the trophy in a more stylish and emphatic manner than any team in history.

If the US players were looking for inspiration en route to the course for the final day's singles, they didn't find any. Private lots around the course that all week were charging up to $60 for parking had reduced rates to $10 and metaphorically reflected the mood of their own fans. In boxing parlance, it seemed that the towel had been thrown in.

And, to be sure, that sense of inevitability was to be borne out as Europe – who had dominated the first two days of foursomes and four-balls, carrying an 11-5 advantage into the singles – controlled the singles too. The stranglehold was unrelenting, sucking the spirit out of their rivals with a display of precise iron play and peerless putting on greens that grew slicker and slicker as the day grew older.

There was to be no slip-up, no faltering from a majestic European team who claimed a fourth victory from the last five contests. In taking the singles by $7\frac{1}{2} - 4\frac{1}{2}$, Europe claimed the match by a record-breaking total of $18\frac{1}{2} - 9\frac{1}{2}$.

This win was different from all others, remarkable for the manner in which the team totally outclassed an American team that included four players from the world's top-10. But, while the US had its superstars, even though they failed to live up to the expectations (Tiger Woods and Phil Mickelson between them took just three points from a possible nine), Europe had strength in depth which was evident from the stark fact that every one of the 12 players contributed to the final total.

Fittingly, and as if fate had its say, Colin Montgomerie had the distinction of actually winning the Ryder Cup for Europe. For a man who suffered so much personal turmoil earlier this year, and who had to rely on a captain's wild card to take his place in Detroit, his one hole win over David Toms – where the Scot holed from four feet – was the stuff of golfing fantasy. Monty's win brought Europe to the magical $14\frac{1}{2}$ points mark, guaranteeing victory.

Early on, the Americans' aim to go out with all guns blazing looked to be effective as a sea of red figures dominated the leaderboards dotted around the course.

Slowly, but surely, the Europeans fought back, and Sergio Garcia – who was to finish with four and a half points from five – overcame a two-hole deficit after eight to finally beat Mickelson by 3 and 2. It was his first ever singles win in the Ryder

*Pádraig Harrington (left) helps Colin Montgomerie line up a putt during their winning Ryder Cup match against Tiger Woods and Phil Mickelson. Photograph: Rebecca Naden.*

Cup, and the timing couldn't have been better. It set the trend for those behind and the back-up came thick and fast.

Darren Clarke, two down with three to play against Davis Love, won the 16th and 17th – where he chipped in from off the back of the green – before settling for a halved match, missing a four-footer on the last to win the match. But the half point edged Europe closer to their mark – 'it's always difficult when you're playing against friends. I was smoking his cigars that he brought me up here earlier this week,' said Clarke – and then Lee Westwood closed out his match against Kenny Perry, leaving it to Montgomerie in the match behind to guarantee victory.

After that, it became a rout.

Thomas Levet beat Freddie Funk by one hole; Ian Poulter beat Chris Riley by 3 and 2; Paul McGinley beat Stewart Cink by 3 and 2. And, fittingly, the final putt of the 35th Ryder Cup was sank by Pádraig Harrington, who closed out a one hole win over Jay Haas with a 20 footer for par on the 18th.

Given that Montgomerie and Harrington on Friday morning had set the trend for Europe by taking on and beating Woods and Mickelson in the first four-balls of the contest all of three days earlier, it was appropriate that the two should finish off their singles in the same style in front of the huge galleries gathered by the 18th green.

Two years ago, McGinley was the hero of the hour; this time, he raced around the 15th green

*European Ryder Cup golf team members celebrate Colin Montgomerie's winning putt at Oakland Hills Country Club in Michigan. Photograph: Andrew Reddington.*

handing out golf balls as if to seals at feeding time to the large army of Irish supporters who had followed him and finally serenaded him with 'Molly Malone'.

'Marvellous, fantastic for European golf,' said McGinley. 'When word came to me that Monty had won it, I was delighted. I was talking to him at breakfast and it was almost his destiny to do it this time. No-one is more deserving of holing a winning putt in the Ryder Cup than Monty. His contribution to the Ryder Cup down the years and again this week has been phenomenal.'

The only wins secured by Americans were by Tiger Woods – 'the only thing we've lacked is that we haven't made any putts. The Europeans have made so many more putts than us, basically just flat-out outplayed us,' he said – who beat Paul Casey by 3 and 2; Jim Furyk who outplayed David Howell; Chad Campbell, who beat Luke Donald; and Chris DiMarco, who beat Miguel Angel

Jimenez. But it was all too little, too late. It was Europe's Ryder Cup, by the biggest margin they've ever beaten the US. The previous record was $16\frac{1}{2}$ to $11\frac{1}{2}$ at the Belfry in 1985.

While the players went out and outplayed their American opponents, much of the praise was heaped onto captain Bernhard Langer. 'Everyone's same goal was to win but we've achieved it much easier than I could have imagined. We beat one of the strongest ever US teams on home soil. It all worked better than clockwork, beyond my wildest dreams,' said Langer.

'This was a lot more exhausting than playing. I've worked for this all year, for 12 months, preparing and double checking and triple checking that everything was right and it all came out perfect.' For now, the European players can savour a job extremely well done; but it won't be long before eyes start looking forward to The K Club in 2006. By then, will Montgomerie by a player, or captain?

# Index